Betrayal

Betrayal

Agricultural Politics in the Fifties

*To Ray + Laura.
Two good friends , Be Well
Herb*

HERBERT SCHULZ

UNIVERSITY OF
CALGARY
PRESS

University of Calgary Press
2500 University Drive NW
Calgary, Alberta
Canada T2N 1N4
www.uofcpress.com

National Library of Canada Cataloguing in Publication

Schulz, Herbert, 1926–
Betrayal : agricultural politics in the fifties / Herbert Schulz.

(Legacies shared, ISSN: 1498–2358 ; 11)
Includes index.
ISBN: 1–55238–098–x

1. Schulz, Herbert, 1926–. 2. Agriculture and politics — Prairie Provinces — History — 20th century. 3. Family farms — Prairie Provinces — History. 4. Agriculture and state — Canada — History — 20th century. 5. Manitoba Federation of Agriculture. 6. Agriculture — Prairie Provinces — History — 20th century. 7. Farmers —Manitoba — Biography. I. Title. II. Series.

HD1486.C3S38 2004   338.1'09712'09045   C2004–902113–3

The University of Calgary Press acknowledges the the support of the Alberta Foundation for the Arts for this published work.

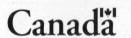

We acknowledge the financial support of the Government of Canada through the Book Publishing Industry Development Program (bpidip) for our publishing activities.

Canada Council   Conseil des Arts
for the Arts   du Canada

Printed and bound in Canada by Houghton Boston, Saskatoon, Saskatchewan

◯ This book is printed on acid-free paper.

Cover image by Karen Schulz
Cover design by Mieka West, The University of Calgary Press, Calgary, Alberta
Interior layout by Jeremy Drought, *Last Impression Publishing Service*, Calgary, Alberta

Contents

✦

Introduction

DURING THE PAST DECADE much has been written about the lowly estate to which western Canadian agriculture has descended. This is a story of how it got to be that way.

Half a century ago the Prairies echoed to the sounds of battle between two philosophies concerning the future economic and social face of Canadian agriculture. One argued that aggregate farm income should be increased, by enlarging markets or by government intervention, to sustain those who wanted to remain on the land. The other saw aggregate income limited by markets and governments reluctant to intervene, and therefore agriculture as an industry could be sustained only by allowing the number of farmers to shrink to fit the income available. The latter contention prevailed. A fork was taken in the road that led to the current destination, and the way back has not yet been found.

At the centre of the contention was the *family farm*. Those taking the former position were not Luddites seeking return to a primitive community *where the village smithy stood*, but they believed the rural community had a social as well as an economic value and it cost less to maintain it than to let it collapse. That required higher prices for farm products. Those advocating the latter view, swept up in the post-war euphoria and the almost miraculous evolution of agricultural machinery, technology, and science, were seduced into believing the economic problems of agriculture could be solved by more efficient production. The problem that evolved was, as in industry, farmers saw increased efficiency in size, which led to larger farms and fewer farmers.

Both sides made obeisance to the idea of the family farm, but differed on its nature and on the policies needed to sustain it. New farm spokespersons emerged to challenge the status quo and the prevailing view. They organized the direct-membership Farmer's Unions around a core of policies comprising primarily of **(a)** publicly administered but voluntary crop insurance for

1

protection against natural disasters, **(b)** producer-controlled commodity marketing boards giving farmers collective power in the marketplace, **(c)** cash advance payments on farm stored grain to alleviate the cash crunch when grain was harvested but could not be sold, and **(d)** a system of parity prices for farm goods to provide prices commensurate with the cost of production, but with limits to favour the smaller farmer and discourage gigantism.

Established farm leaders saw the emergent spokespersons as naive and their policies, especially the last two, as impossible to implement and dangerous if they were. These would interfere with the market, lead to surplus production, and ultimately leave farmers worse off than they were. They were so certain of their views, and so secure in their positions, that they were prepared to ignore, or defy, the expressed directives of their own members.

The inter-organization contention led to virtual civil war as farmers, like ancient gladiators, fought each other instead of the conditions that were destroying them. By the time this ended, the family farm was to a large extent nothing more than a romantic memory. Like Margaret Mitchell's antebellum Old South, it was gone with the wind.

The positions taken by the leaders of the established farm organizations were vigorously supported by university faculties of agriculture, politicians, governments, newspapers, and all others who believed the economic imperative must be allowed to take its natural course with no obstruction to market forces.

In March 1969, the Government of Manitoba published the *Report of the Commission on Targets for Economic Development*. Its authors looked into the future, predicted net income available to Manitoba farmers by 1980 would be $200 million, decided individual farm income should be $10,000, divided $10,000 into $200 million, and concluded that a decade hence the province's agricultural economy could sustain no more than 20,000 farmers. Since projections indicated a likelihood of 30,000 farmers by that time, they advised that "the decline should be faster than the natural rate of attrition, and farm people will have to seek new employment," and recommended that government undertake policies to effect that end.

In December of the same year, the Government of Canada published the *Report of the Federal Task Force on Agriculture: Canadian Agriculture in the Seventies*. It concluded that the central problem of agriculture was that the farmers had worked too hard and produced too much, and that "the surplus must be reduced by reducing production drastically." Like the authors of the Manitoba *Report*, they recommended that, "the only way to have family farms capable of a decent income is to have fewer of them."

Ingeborg Boyens in her recent book, *Another Seasons Promise: Hope and Despair in Canada's Farm Country*, quotes Mr. Don Dewar, then president of the Keystone Agricultural Producers, Manitoba's premier farm organization. He criticizes the conditions to which the "bigger is better" philosophy has led and states: "We can't follow the industrial model. It doesn't make sense to sell more but earn less." Ironically, it was the organization, under another name, of which he was then president, that either consciously promoted the *industrial model*, or allowed it to develop because they did not appreciate its consequences.

Farmers did as they were told by the leaders they trusted, and a generation passed before it was realized that if a family could not make a living on fifteen hundred acres of productive land, there was more wrong with farming than the weather. By then they were caught up, like a dog chasing its tail, in having to increase production to compensate for low prices, which declined because they were producing too much. This has led to impossible debt loads and the obscenity of farmers with half-million dollar investments having to seek off-farm income to pay operating costs. Meanwhile, farming is falling under the control of a neo-feudal off-farm aristocracy: Instead of the farmers owning the processing facilities as had been envisioned in the forties and fifties, the processors own the farm — and the farmer.

Today that is clear to most. To some it was clear long ago.

Joseph Phelps, a successful farmer, founding president of the Saskatchewan Farmer's Union and first chairman of the Inter-Provincial Farm Union Council, predicted in 1954: "The yeoman farmer who opened the West and built the community is being reduced to a serf. If vertical integration of agriculture continues, he will end up as a hired man on his own land working for subsidized, non-resident investors."

I observed it happening. I grew up on a farm and operated my own farm for twelve years, 1949–62. During that period I was also an organizer for the Manitoba Federation of Agriculture, an organizer for the Manitoba Farmer's Union, a member of the executive of the largest pool elevator association in Manitoba, a delegate for six years to the policy-making annual convention of Manitoba Pool Elevators (now Agricore-United), a member of the executive of the Manitoba Federation of Agriculture (now Keystone Agricultural Producers), a member of the national board of directors of the Canadian Federation of Agriculture, and a political activist.

This work is a blow-by-blow account of the politics and personalities of farm organizations from the perspective of one who was at the eye of the storm for a dozen years. It is an insider's memoir about some of the salient events of the crucial and turbulent decade of the fifties when decisions were taken which set the mould for the current structure and conditions of Canadian agriculture. This is how I remember it.

1

To the Land of Milk and Honey

Take hold then; let reflection rest,
And plunge into the world with zest.
GOETHE, *Faust*

WE IMMIGRATED TO CANADA because my father wanted wide horizons, a frontier environment — and a farm with fields a mile long.

The province of Bessarabia was part of Romania when I was born there, but part of the Russian Empire when my parents were born there in 1901, and part of the Turkish Empire until 1812. That was four years before my ancestors followed the stream of Germans who had accepted the invitation of Catherine the Great to bring their Teutonic energies and renowned farming practices to her growing domain. These adventurous, land-hungry people sank their roots into communities with German names that stretched like "Islands in the Steppe" in Al Reimer's graphic phrase,[1] far beyond the eastern limits of the ramshackle Habsburg Empire through the ancient Roman outpost of Romania, which still spoke a Romance rather than a Slavic language, across the southern Ukraine, and along the productive alluvial-soil northern slope of the Black Sea where the mythic Argonauts had found the Golden Fleece.

My own German/Lutheran forbears, six generations earlier, had settled in the newly founded German-named village of Friedenstal, in the Latin-named county of Cetatea-Alba, between the Pruth River to the west and the mighty Dneister to the east. It was a hundred miles north of the Black Sea in the Turkish-named province of Bessarabia, next to the province of Transylvania, home of the legendary Vlad the Impaler — the prototype for Dracula — a name long invoked to frighten nubile young maidens into remaining at home on inviting summer evenings.

Lutheran Church, Friedenstal, Bessarabia, Romania (c. 1940).

My father, Jacob Schulz, an only son, attended high school, was an excellent scholar, played piano and trumpet in the village band and soon became involved in the social, political, and economic life of the village. The maternal language of the village was German, but because of the polyglot population of southeastern Europe, he learned Romanian, Ukrainian, and Russian. In 1917 the Czarist regime collapsed and the Romanian Army crossed the Pruth and annexed Bessarabia. From nineteen to twenty-two Jacob did compulsory military service,[2] a drill sergeant in the cavalry, taking his own proud-necked, slim-legged, wind-fleet, jet-black Arabian stallion who attracted crowds in the village when ridden on the cobbled streets bordered by low stone walls and square gateposts surmounted by ornate lanterns of burnished bronze.[3]

At twenty-two, he married a shy, attractive woman of the same age from the same village, established his own homestead and devoted his energies to operating and enlarging their farming industry, grinding flour from their own wheat, and making wine of grapes from their own orchard. Fascinated by new technology, he built a tractor from parts, a grain-separating machine, and a feed-cutter which gave him a commercial enterprise doing custom work for neighbours, and which was operated by hired men requiring him only to make the rounds collecting the money. He was active in village institutions and the *Kirche* — the impressive, multi-tiered Evangelistic Lutheran Church patterned after the sixteenth century cathedral at Ulm in Bavaria, which for several centuries boasted the highest tower in Germany — through which the people of this frontier *Gemeinde* sustained their values.

He read prodigiously and listened to his wife's uncle — the village wise man who became his friend and mentor — explain that humans come into the world to bring something, not to take something out, and that a society is a living organism that can collectively change itself and improve the quality of life for its members. At twenty-six, he was the youngest man ever elected to the village council; at twenty-seven, he purchased one of the very few cars in the village and became the owner-operator of a 450-acre farm, one of the largest in the county, and life was his for the taking. At twenty-eight, he decided to go:

> Away from Europe; from her blasted hopes,
> Her fields of carnage, and polluted air.

Friedenstal was on the eastern edge of the Balkans, the unstable powder keg of Europe, where empires, nations, and races had contended against each other for two millennia. As a fifteen-year-old high school student, Jacob had watched in horror as invading Romanian soldiers dragged an accused spy from an outdoor oven where he had hidden and summarily executed him while on his knees pleading for his life, and he wondered if someday that might be his fate. He observed the proud *njemsti*[4] farmers at the village marketplace selecting poverty-stricken Ukrainian field hands by feeling their muscles as though at a slave market, and after a fourteen-hour day of brutal physical labour:

> Bowed by the weight of centuries, he leans
> Upon his hoe, and gazes at the ground[5]

sending them back to their hovels with a package of tobacco as their pay, and he wondered how soon they would exact revenge. Riding through the cornfields at night invited being robbed or killed by desperate men wanting a few *lei*[6] to buy food or material to patch their roofs, and he wondered how long it was possible to maintain social order under such conditions.

Jake Schulz, author's father, Sergeant in the Romanian Cavalry, at age 21, in 1922.

It was necessary to speak a different language — Russian, Polish, Ukrainian, Magyar, Bulgarian, Greek, Turkish — in almost every village one passed through and there was the constant turmoil of ethnic riots among people suspicious because they were unable to understand each other. Even attempting to court a girl in a neighbouring village was risky, and he wondered if there was some place with a common language in which people from every race and religion could communicate and where one was not maimed or killed for no offence other than having wandered beyond its perimeter.

The government bureaucracy was remote, authoritarian, and Byzantine,[7] right down to the local constable who, on his rounds, would casually comment that his flour bin was empty and would find some way to terrorize the person who failed to take the hint to fill it. He wondered if there was a place where one need not bribe an official to get service and where it was not the employee-administrator but the citizen-taxpayer who had the last word. In the army he observed famished cavalrymen eat a breakfast of corn kernels picked out of their horse's manure, and he witnessed conscripts, when their emaciated bodies did not respond fast enough, having the skin peeled off their face by a single downward blow with the flat of the hand of an officer, and young Sergeant Schulz suspected these soldiers would take advantage of any war to shoot their officers and go home. He heard the frightful stories of Stalin's collectivization program and the destruction of the kulaks,[8] and he knew the Soviets had been humiliated by the seizure of Bessarabia by Romania in 1917, and one day they would come to take it back.

"I smell gunpowder," he would say to neighbours and relatives, urging them to accompany him and his wife, but they were comfortable and saw no point of risking the substance for the shadow. And they were there when the Red Army came in 1940.[9]

We escaped that experience by a decade. In March 1930, while neighbours gathered in the yard and sang the melancholy refrain, "*Schoen ist the Jugengzeit; Sie kommt nicht mehr,*"[10] my parents and I, age three years and eight months, left Romania.

My father had been exasperated by the patchwork of vari-sized fields, laid out on the old Medieval pattern, scattered and requiring hours to move the wagon and horses from one small and irregular field to another, and increasingly inefficient with the coming of mechanization. His choices of a new home were the United States, Argentina or Canada. He chose the last because he had heard and read that it was underpopulated, had "elbow room" for those with a sense of adventure, and offered cheap and productive land on the frontier where one could have fields "a mile long."

We travelled by train to Bremen, on the liner *Montcalm* to Montreal, and by train to Winnipeg. While my mother and I stayed in a hotel, my father went looking for land. With the help of the Lutheran Church, he found a quarter section for sale in the municipality of Grandview, 240 miles northwest of Winnipeg. On May 10, 1930, we took possession. We had a fine, two-storey house with oak trim and banisters, which my parents filled with good furniture such as they had been accustomed to, and a piano of rosewood. They marvelled at the fields and enthusiastically prepared to mix their labour with the soil. Within days they were ploughing and seeding. They had arrived in the Promised Land.

The Great Depression did not come like a thunderclap: it oozed in, but was unstoppable, and in a year the roar of the twenties degenerated into the moan of the thirties.[11] By the following spring, the cows purchased for sixty dollars each were worth six dollars, and the Fordson tractor purchased for two hundred dollars was traded for twenty-five dollars worth of seed wheat. The fieldwork was done with four wind-blown horses bought from a bankrupt neighbour, and their transportation was a one-horse, two-wheeled cart with different-sized wheels because we could not afford two the same size. In early 1932 my father hauled a large Holstein steer to the town of Grandview for shipment to the stockyards in Winnipeg. On the road he met "Gypsy" Bill Smith, a cattle buyer, who offered him twelve dollars. He declined and shipped the steer, and with freight deducted he realized six dollars, less than a cent a pound. The government of Romania stopped the export of currency, so my parents never realized the proceeds from their estate and the little cash they brought with them was quickly dissipated. Unable to make payments on the farm, they sacrificed their deposit and abandoned the farm and fine house. In the spring of 1932 they moved four miles east into the municipality of Gilbert Plains to be tenant farmers.

They rented a half-section abandoned by another Depression-hit farmer, and which the mortgage company was desperate to lease out on a crop-share basis before it went to weeds.[12] It had an old, unpainted, two-storey, clapboard house that the wind blew through, and which needed to be periodically sealed and fumigated with mustard gas to kill the bedbugs while we slept in the hayloft. Within two years after coming to the Promised Land, the man who had been a gentleman farmer and a political power in Romania was reduced to earning grocery money by doing odd jobs for neighbours. But he would tell his wife when life looked bleak:

> *Wenn mann wirklich glaubt es geht nicht mehr,*
> *Dann kommt von irgendwo ein lichtlein her.*[13]

But the light was a long time coming. The economy had gone from cash to barter so, during the winters, in an unheated shed, he painstakingly built wagon boxes and closed-in sleigh vans which he traded to neighbours for horses and cows.[14] Chickens and hogs provided eggs and meat for consumption or trade, cream was separated from milk and put in cans or laboriously churned into butter, carefully moulded into one-pound packages, and wrapped in waxed paper. Saturday's, during the winter of 1934–35, my father drove the team of horses and sled seven miles to town, taking a load of hay, a can of cream, several dozen eggs, some butter, and oven-ready chickens. Money had virtually disappeared in rural areas so these were bartered for farm tools or material to build vans and wagon boxes to barter for more horses and cows.

In the early thirties, winters were abnormally cold, summers abnormally hot, crops almost uniformly poor, and farm prices abysmal. Saskatchewan historian John Archer has written:[15]

> "Agricultural products did not strike bottom until 1932 and 1933. Wheat prices fell to the lowest level in 300 years when No. 1 Northern traded at 39 3/8 cents per bushel, basis Fort William. In 1933, yearling steers at the Saskatchewan Feeder Show averaged $2.75 per hundredweight and $2.35 in 1934. Farmers selling thin cattle or low-grade grain could report receiving bills, rather than cheques, because the sale had not covered transportation and other charges."[16]

Farm work was hard and the prospects grim, but nothing deterred the couple from integrating into the land of their adoption. In 1936, having satisfied residency requirements, they proudly applied for their Canadian naturalization papers. And they relocated. They wanted *new* land. With the four hundred dollars from the sale of twenty-two head of fattened cattle that spring, they made a deposit on 320 acres of land — for two dollars per acre — eight miles directly south of the town of Grandview. The *farm* comprised boundary-to-boundary trees, with no cultivated land and barely enough open area to park a wagon. But the couple and Canada seemed made for each other: the big-shouldered, super-energetic man and the quiet, workaholic woman, in a new, virgin-soil country waiting to be developed. These were the progeny of countless generations of land-hungry people who knew well the song of the plough: "That built Chaldea and the Cities of the Plain."

Two home-built granaries drawn side-by-side became our living quarters for the next two years. A deposit was made on an old $150 Allis-Chalmers tractor that was coaxed into running well enough to pull a breaking plough, and the forest was slowly and laboriously converted into productive land. A sixty-dollar battered Model-A Ford car was acquired to bounce over the rutted trails. Summers were spent clearing land and winters cutting trees, which were squared with broad-axes and used to build a house and barn; the chinks between the logs filled with moss from dried-up meadows and the logs held together with wooden pegs.[17] Two four-horse teams were acquired, a herd of livestock, and a flock of poultry was built up. My parents were creatures of boundless energy in a boundless land where, it seemed to them, milk and honey need only be coaxed from the soil or stripped from the trees.

And we were lucky. Saskatchewan, parts of Alberta and southwestern Manitoba literally blew away in the legendary dust storms of the Depression, but we were in the Parklands area where many CPR and school sections remained completely forested, and there were bluffs of trees on virtually every farm, so the winds could not get a clear sweep. Occasionally the sunlight was made opaque orange by blowing dust from elsewhere, but our land did not blow. In 1935 wheat rusted and entire fields were burned, but barley and oats survived. Nineteen thirty-seven was the year of the drought, but crops not worth harvesting were gathered for livestock feed. Nineteen thirty-seven was also the year of equine encephalitis and we lost several horses, but enough survived; flies and mosquitoes drove the livestock frantic, but smudges of old straw and manure relieved them and allowed them to produce milk and meat; huge colonies of gophers played havoc with the crops but left enough so we were never hungry.[18] We were poor, but did not know it because so was everyone else.

Prices were still at record lows, but so was the cost of material — and of labour. An army of young men were seeking work. They were usually sent from the *soup kitchens*, or relief camps, the government paying them five dollars a month — plus a three-dollar issue of clothing — to work for a farmer, and paying the farmer five dollars a month to provide bed and board.[19] Most farmers turned their five dollars over to the men and perhaps supplemented it a little, but few received more than twenty dollars a month.[20] We usually had half a dozen hired hands — a dozen at harvest time — cleaning out hog and cow barns, cutting trees to clear land, picking stones and tree roots off the fields, stooking sheaves, stacking hay for livestock feed, cutting firewood to sell to townspeople, cutting logs to be squared for building or sawed into lumber, seeding or threshing grain.

My father took over an abandoned sawmill, sawing lumber for our own use and for neighbours. He bought a threshing machine to harvest our crop and that of neighbours. He acquired a powerful Model L Case tractor to drive the threshing machine and pull the large plough with which he broke up more new land and did custom work for neighbours. For us this meant a few more dollars of income, but for the men it meant dust-choking, backbreaking, ten-hour-a-day brutal work. Some lasted only a few days, but most worked for at least a season because, if nothing else, they had plenty of good food and a clean place to sleep.

My mother, usually with the help of a hired girl, milked up to fifteen cows, separated out the cream, made butter, fed the cattle and hogs when the men were in the field, got her children off to school (my brother was born in 1930 and my sister in 1937), and prepared three full meals a day — plus an afternoon lunch in the harvest season — for as many hired hands as we had at any particular time.[21] She planted a large garden and picked the vegetables to eat during the summer and preserve in large wooden barrels as sauerkraut and dill pickles for the winter,[22] played doctor to the children and hired hands, and kept the house tidy.[23]

Sundays were reserved to attend church (first rented from another congregation, but later built on land my parents donated to the Church) and for visiting, but there were the regular chores and pasture fences to be repaired, and machinery to service. And for my mother there were meals to be made for the hired men and for the minister and neighbours that sometimes came to visit after church. This was a world in which, indeed, "man works from sun to sun, but woman's work is never done."

There was a farmstead on almost every half-section, our neighbours were from half the countries of Europe, and community life was informal and congenial. Our door key was lost shortly after the house was built, so it was never locked. Entertainment was largely homemade. Adults gathered at some one's house in the evening to have Bible readings, organize charity drives for unfortunate neighbours, or play cards. Young people would sit in the corners and read, wrestle, play softball, or shovel the snow off the dug-out and play hockey on improvised skates, using a frozen horse turd and a bent tree-branch as puck and stick.

The community seemed to draw together in direct relation to the economic difficulties — the greater the problems the greater the community spirit. In 1934, local farm boys gathered in the evenings, bringing hammers and saws, and built the landmark four thousand square foot Tamarisk Hall which became famous province-wide, featuring local musical families which kept people dancing on Friday nights until it was time to go home and change into work clothes. The same farm boys formed a baseball team, practised after supper, and became good enough to tour Canada and the United States. The community looked forward to the annual Tamarisk picnic. Those with cars drove once a year to the Dauphin Fair, thirty miles away, which featured a Midway, steer roping and bronc riding, and the spectacular RCMP musical ride. A full-course meal at Mulligan's Cafe was twenty-five cents.

In 1936 a radio was purchased and listening to the evening news became *de rigeur*. We got CBC and several American stations,[24] but also several European stations by short-wave. One day my father said: "There is going to be a war and farmers make money only in wartime,"[25] and he set about acquiring, by purchase or lease, as much land as he could farm. The barn was enlarged and filled with milk cows, hogs, and young livestock for fattening.

After 1937, crops improved and so did prices. By the time they had been in Canada a decade, my parents were farming twice as much land as in Romania. They purchased good machinery, a new truck, a late-model car, and the log house was clad with cedar boards and finished on the inside with white plaster. In 1941 they became the envy of the community by purchasing, for seven thousand dollars, the prize of the municipality: 320 acres of land less than ten years old, not a weed or stone on it, a half mile wide — and a mile long. In 1942 it produced almost twenty thousand bushels of barley.

My father was progressive and innovative. The mould-board plough was replaced with the one-way disc which covered more ground and left the trash on top to restore fibre to the soil and control blowing. To allow for double tilling in the autumn to kill weeds and conserve moisture, the disc and binder were fastened together so the land was cultivated as soon as the crop was cut instead of having to wait until the sheaves were removed perhaps a month later. Yellow mustard, which could choke out an entire crop, was controlled by hiring local school kids during the summer holidays to walk through the fields pulling the plants out stalk by stalk.

Continuous cropping replaced the two-one rotation system (two crops and then summer fallow) as legumes (clover, alfalfa) were seeded every four or five years with a nurse crop: the legumes restored nitrogen, were cut early for cattle feed, fallowed for the balance of the year, and the cycle began again. When he bought a combine and could not buy a swather because of wartime rationing, he built one by welding together two old binder tables. He attached a straw cutter to the combine, leaving the straw on the field instead of burning it. The livestock herd was improved with pure-bred bulls and boars. The farm was operated with Prussian efficiency and my parents, having learned to live frugally, knew the value of a dollar when they finally had one.

My father was proud when he had to begin paying income taxes. "Be happy we are paying," he would say to my mother who felt they had worked too hard to pay a remote government from which she perceived no benefits, "It means we are making a profit."

Our relative prosperity did not go unnoticed. My father bought an old World War I army rifle at a local farm auction for six dollars, but we seldom used it because the barrel was badly worn. Several days after Germany attacked Poland, two RCMP officers came to our home and confiscated the rifle. We never saw it again, but fifteen years later an Anglo-Saxon neighbour told me the RCMP had come to him, told him they were suspicious of my father because he seemed to have money, and said: "This is Schulz's rifle. We are leaving it with you. Keep and eye on him. If he does anything you think he shouldn't, shoot him."[26]

Immediately after the war began, a man came to work for us. He was from Ste. Rose and knew about farming, especially taking care of horses and cattle. He was only nine years younger than my father and they soon became friendly. He worked almost as hard and long as my father, sometimes round-the-clock, and he never complained about the work, whether in searing heat or bitter cold. He was good to me, sometimes helping me with my chores, and he gave me my first taste of chewing tobacco (it put me off any kind of tobacco for life). He never raised his voice, was clean-featured, five-foot nine-inches, slim, and his muscles rippled under his shirt. He was with us for two years and then left to join the army.

Twenty years later my father met the man on a street in Winnipeg and was invited into a hotel for a beer. Later he told me the man had said to him: "Jake, I should not really tell you this, but you are a pretty good guy. I did not come to your farm for a job. I was planted on you by the RCMP. You were doing well while many others were not and they wanted to know where you were getting your money."

My father, who had developed considerable respect for this man with the quiet competence and unflinching attitude toward hard work, was stunned. He finally blurted: "Well, you found out where I got it. I worked your ass off."

In 1944 the most savage war in human history was coming to a bitter end. The crops were excellent, the bins and barns were full, and prices comparatively good. My father bought a thirty-two-volt Delco electrical plant, with batteries and a sixty-five-foot steel tower surmounted by a wind charger. It provided light for all the buildings a decade before Manitoba Hydro came to our farm, and greatly reduced our manual labour by powering the seed-cleaning mill, the cream separator,[27] and the pumps supplying water on-tap for the house — one of the few in the municipality with such services. As my parents stood by the kitchen table packaging food parcels for the few relatives in Europe who had escaped the cataclysm, they quietly — my mother sometimes tearfully — congratulated themselves for having escaped it all by coming to Canada. Thirty-five years later, when their daughter was chatelaine of Rideau Hall, I said to my father: "Isn't life wonderful? You came here as a sheepskin-clad immigrant and your daughter is First Lady of Canada!" He half smiled, looked into the distance as though his mind was filled with myriad images and quietly said: "No, it's not life that did this. It's the country. This could not have happened anywhere else."

The young men went off to war and the young women to factories, hospitals or auxiliary services, and the nature of farming, overnight, changed by a magnitude. Rubber-tired tractors and cars replaced horses, the two-man combine replaced the dozen-man threshing gang — in 1945 we farmed the same acreage as in 1939 but with two hired men instead of many — and the lack of manpower shifted many farms away from livestock into straight grain production. Rural society also changed. Horses needed to rest in the evening so the young people gathered at local schools to play softball and court, but the tractor needed no rest so the local gatherings ended and farm youngsters found entertainment on week-ends in local, or distant, towns.[28] The stage was set for larger farms, fewer farmers, and new community needs.

My father frequently reflected on the philosophizing of his wife's uncle in Romania: that a community is a living organism which responds to challenge and serves the collective interests of its people by remaking itself in the light of changing circumstances. It seemed to him that the time had come.

Larger farm machinery needed wider roads to be moved; cars replacing horses needed roads ditched to keep them dry in summer and raised to keep them clear of snow in winter; larger trucks carrying heavier loads needed better bridges. Local rural councillors, accustomed to the old ways, did not comprehend the new conditions. Most rural roads were of dirt: our home was three miles from school and nine miles from town and the roads were laced with impassable ruts most of the summer and covered with impassable snow banks most of the winter. Any forecast of rain meant leaving our car at the end of the gravelled portion of the road from town and walking the last four miles.

My father began writing to the local newspaper, and holding meetings, damning the condition of the roads and the indifference of the councillors who left them that way, and explaining what needed to be done. In October 1944, he was elected councillor for one of the four wards in the rural municipality of Grandview. Most of his Anglo-Saxon and Central European neighbours voted for him. Most Germans did not: They feared the consequences of a German immigrant being too conspicuous just when Canadian soldiers were preparing to cross the Rhine.

In the next four years he revolutionized the municipality. The spring he took office, heavy rains and run-off from Riding Mountains washed out nineteen bridges and numerous culverts in his ward. He had noticed the CNR had concrete culverts in their roadbeds and proposed to council that they buy forms to make these for their roads. When council refused, he asked permission to use his own ward budget for that purpose. When council refused he purchased a set of vari-sized metal forms with his own private money, found a gravel pit on the Valley River one mile north of Grandview, hired men to operate the equipment, and soon had a small industry manufacturing concrete tubes, three feet long and from twelve to sixty inches in diameter.

He installed them throughout his ward and then goaded council into investing in an elevator grader to raise the municipal roads — when it was in his ward he operated it himself when the men ate or rested so the machine would not sit idle. Two years later, after neighbouring municipalities came to buy his products and the municipality of Grandview won the award for having the best rural roads in Manitoba, council bought his concrete bridge-building operation for what he had invested.

His four years on council were a *tour de force*. He did not run for a second term. His attention had shifted elsewhere.

Fifteen years earlier, in 1934, an incident had affected him deeply. My mother became ill, so my father began driving her, on a wagon, to see the doctor in the town of Gilbert Plains, seven miles distant. On the way they began to realize the call at the doctor's office would cost them a dollar — and they did not have a dollar. So they turned the team and drove back home. It caused my father to reflect: he was thirty-three, had an above-average education, stood five-foot ten-inches, weighed two hundred pounds, was strong as a bull and willing to work, but he could not make a dollar. So did the fault lie with him or with the economy? He concluded it was the latter. The following year he joined the newly formed Canadian Commonwealth Federation. On January 1, 1947 the CCF Government of Saskatchewan introduced its Provincial Hospital Insurance Plan, allowing health services for all as a function of health, not wealth. It seemed, on a larger scale, like the plan operated by the village council in Friedenstal: membership was a right of citizenship, all contributed a fee, costs were pooled, and the service was available when needed: "This is wonderful," he said of the Saskatchewan Plan; "Sick people have trouble enough without having to worry about how to pay the bill with money not being earned while they are sick."

In October 1949, my father announced he would seek nomination as the CCF candidate in the provincial election.

❖ ❖ ❖

2

Learning Politics

Those who take no interest in politics
are condemned to be governed by others.
PLATO, *The Republic*

THE FINE THREAD OF POLITICS had run through our family since my father
joined the CCF in 1935. The Great Depression had destroyed the myth
that the corporate paladins, generously supported with tax money collected
by fawning politicians, would guide the economy. It was to revolutionize
attitudes.

In *Legends of the Fall*, the bittersweet saga of a western American family
in the early part of the twentieth century, James Harrison wrote of one of
his characters: "Of late he had been frightened of government ... the structure
was debasing people rather than enlivening them in their mutual concern.
The structure was no longer concerned with the purpose for which it was
designed, and a part of the cause ... was probably that all politicians and
bureaucrats wore suits."[1]

During the decade of the thirties, the *men in suits* failed miserably, and
throughout the industrialized world ordinary people turned elsewhere. The
dozen Germanic families in the Grandview/Gilbert Plains municipalities
within horse-and-buggy driving distance, sought each other's companionship
in their common misery. At the after church tête-à-têtes in some farmer's
home, usually focusing around the minister, who was the best educated in
the group, they speculated on the causes of, and solutions to, their economic
woes. Sunspots was one cause considered,[2] and Technocracy and Social
Credit were other solutions flirted with.[3]

The radio had made its appearance in several homes, including ours, so
they gathered to hear demagogues like Father Coughlin and Huey Long

19

("Every man's a king and I'm the kingfish."). On crackling short-wave they heard Mussolini, whom they did not understand but whose spirit they appreciated, and Hitler, whom they did understand but whose ranting, made more raucous by radio static, left them uneasy. Faced with similar circumstances in which, as with Bobbi McGee "freedom's just another word for nothing left to lose," the disinherited and disenchanted in Italy turned to fascism, in Germany to Nazism, in Britain and France to local adaptations of the "man on the white horse," or in the armoured car. In the United States the old money aristocracy suggested Marine General Smedley Butler stage a coup, but the ordinary people chose FDR, making him a *traitor to his class* to those whose only solution to poverty and unemployment was lower wages and longer breadlines. But his fireside chats informed the suspicions and inspired the aspirations of rural Canadians.[4]

In western Canada, particularly worst-hit Saskatchewan,[5] the ordinary people, having nowhere else to turn, turned to each other. They found their collective refuge in the Co-operative Movement, which gave them some economic leverage by sharing what little they had, and in the CCF which gave them hope.

More than a century earlier, the German philosopher Georg Hegel, in his apologia for the power of the Prussian state, had named the political state as the bearer of the historical dialectic and the creator of the economy. Half a century later Karl Marx had inverted Hegel's theory — claiming he was standing it right-side-up — by stating the political state is a superstructure developed to protect the economic advantages of the ruling class. On the basis of this theory it was only natural that those who had found economic salvation in the co-operatives as a bulwark against the ravages of the men in suits of the railways and the banks, should create a leftist-populist political structure through which to protect and preserve their economic gains. That was the Co-operative Commonwealth Federation.

S. M. Lipsett,[6] in his epochal study of the CCF in Saskatchewan, wrote that this was no sudden aberration. An urban Jewish boy from the University of New York, inculcated with stereotypical images of *cracker* farmers, he went to study why the most rural-agrarian jurisdiction in North America had ruptured the theory — formulated by his teacher and mentor, Robert S. Lynd

— that landowning, capitalist-minded farmers would be the last to adopt socialism. He found to his genuine surprise that, while the Saskatchewan farmer might fit the stereotype of living in a sod-roofed shanty surrounded at its base by a berm of livestock manure to mitigate the fearful winter cold, and his well-worn trousers held up by a rope belt, the kitchen table was covered with daily newspapers, monthly magazines, and copies of Henry George's *Progress and Poverty*.[7] He concluded the people of Saskatchewan had "thought their way into the CCF."[8]

Our table too, was graced by the local newspaper, the *Free Press Weekly*, and the *Country Guide*,[9] official organ of the United Grain Growers Grain Company. My father could not read English so I, beginning in grade three, was recruited to read selected articles to him. My mother's information about the world around her was obtained from the Winnipeg-based German-language *Der Nordwesten*, but she could look at pictures in English-language newspapers and was familiar with the photos of the Hollywood heartthrobs of the day (Clark Gable, Ida Lupino, Joan Crawford, Charles Chaplin, Greta Garbo, Mae West, Marlene Dietrich, Ann Baxter, Lionel Barrymore ...), and she was determined to contribute to the family income. When a contest appeared in a paper requiring the unscrambling of lines of letters to spell the names of movie stars, she urged me, at age nine, to respond. I unscrambled the five names and, with the required one dollar — I never learned how my mother acquired it — mailed them.

The reply was heartbreaking but encouraging: we had the right answer but so had others, so we received a tie-breaker in the form of ten names to unscramble. And as a consolation prize we received a one-year subscription to a magazine. The run-off contests continued until my mother ran out of one dollar bills. By then we had won eight years of subscriptions to the *National Home Monthly*. Then she insisted I read them to her. Thus I developed the lifelong habit of reading anything I saw with print on it.

In such an environment, any observant youngster who sat in dark corners and listened could not avoid learning by osmosis the problems and politics of the Depression: crop failures due to grasshoppers, dust storms, drought, excessive rainfall, rust, hail and early frost; the struggle to develop early maturing grains; efforts to breed livestock that gained more fat with less feed, and hogs with a shorter snout and heavier hams; market watching for the best time to sell; co-operatives; health plans; farm foreclosures; the Bennett Buggy;[10] the Canadian Wheat Board;[11] the Board of Grain Commissioners;[12] grain elevator charges; freight rates; economic privation; and development of social and national tensions in Europe, and war. When I arrived at school on September 1, 1939, my erstwhile chums looked at me as though I had personally ordered the German invasion of Poland. This led to a few fist fights, but nothing serious.

"Keep your mouth shut when you are out in public. Our neighbours have sons in the military and they will not appreciate comments about the war from a German immigrant. And if you can't keep silent and get beaten up, don't complain." It was the only advice my father gave me about behaviour, and it was enough.

In the thirties, life for a farm boy with no responsibilities was hard work but fascinating. There were moments of wonder that left one breathless: watching, half frightened, the black storm clouds with the white underbelly suggesting hail, roiling ominously forward on a sultry summer afternoon; looking up at the diamond-glitter of Orion in the velvet softness of the night; revelling in the colour of field and sky and "the autumn-painted trees along the river"; seeing the brilliant hues of a rainbow's end splashing on the rain-soaked earth almost within reach. In the morning of a new-made day, one could bathe in celestial fire as Apollo rode his chariot across the heavens of delicate pink and azure blue, or stand in the warm, humid, early summer haze, feeling like the first man on earth, in the Carboniferous Age, with a herd of dinosaurs lurking just beyond the veil of mist. I could ride my spavined Pegasus along dry creek beds under overarching trees, or spur him up steep clay banks to the crest of hills; or look back off the tractor to watch the ploughshare hypnotically slicing through and gently folding over the brown-black soil; or stand mouse-quiet under the spruce-grove cathedrals as "night crept in on little cat feet" while:

> Dark is the forest and deep, and overhead
> Hang stars like seeds of light.[13]

Life could also be dangerous. Farm accidents were commonplace in those days when most work was manual and required risk taking. My father's cheekbone was split by a tractor-driven grindstone that broke and struck his face; in 1938 he almost died of blood poisoning when he sliced off his big toe with a razor-sharp broadaxe when squaring the very last log for our house; he almost died again in 1943 when a hired man accidentally drove a tractor over him and crushed his rib cage and pelvis.

It was July 2, 1940. I was thirteen, had just graduated from grade eight at the head of my class, and was experiencing the ephemeral but powerful emotions of adolescence. Hard work had given me a body tough as whipcord and muscles like a man. It was a joy to be alive in this bucolic paradise....

The fire exploded in a great *whoosh* and enveloped me.

I was burning trees and brush stacked in piles in the process of clearing new land. The heat from the sun and the fires I had lit were blistering my skin and scorching my throat, but my father had ordered me to burn brush and I was too proud to admit it was too much for me. I was proud when I glanced back across the field and saw my handiwork in the score of fires I had lit, which were crackling and swirling while consuming the brush and trees with the smoke billowing and the heat waves rising into the atmosphere, reminding me of what I had read of Gehenna where ancient Hebrew townspeople had burned their garbage and which became the prototype for the Christian *hell*. A fire I had lit a few minutes earlier was not burning well, so I picked up the three-gallon, open-topped pail and walked back to the recalcitrant fire and stepped forward to toss some gasoline on the flames and stumbled.

The upward rush of flames took my breath away and turned me into a torch as they caught on my clothes soaked with the gasoline I had spilled on myself when I fell into the fire. I attempted to brush the fire off myself but my hands were burning, and I attempted to rip off my shirt but it was the new denim one with no buttons down the front, and I attempted to roll on the ground but the sharp tops of the brush cut off with an axe did not allow it, so I stood there, panic-stricken, and burned. Finally, with adrenalin pumping, and gagging from the smell of my own burning flesh and hair and the flames blowing in the wind, I ran the fifty yards to where my father had begun to plough up the virgin land and threw myself into the foot-deep furrow — which seemed like a grave — and watched as the smoke curled up through the soil I had covered myself with, and waited for the flames to smother.

By the time I stumbled the half-mile home the pain, temporarily delayed by the primal anaesthesia of shock, was sweeping over me in great, nauseating waves. My mother wept uncontrollably as she pulled off my clothes, accompanied by great swatches of skin from the deep burns, and wrapped me in a blanket like a winding sheet, and my father's tears made silent rivulets through the dust on his face as he placed me in the car and drove me the nine miles to town and carried me, half conscious, into the tiny, privately owned hospital. I lay soaked in my own body fluids, passing in and out of delirium, in the suffocating heat of the days and through the unbearable endlessness of angry nights:

> Wounds hurt more at night. Perhaps so no one hears you,
> When you cry out at night from pain that sears you.[14]

Two months later I overheard the doctor tell the nurse: "There's nothing we can do for that boy. He's dying."

When I told my father, he wrapped me in the bedsheet and put me in the car and drove me to the hospital in Dauphin, thirty miles away. They applied butter and beeswax and tannic acid and egg white and fish oil, and periodically burned off the ugly excrescences of proudflesh with silver nitrate. Several times they attempted skin grafts which would not hold because the massive wound was too badly infected and the agony was fierce, and eleven months later I overheard the doctor tell the nurse: "There's nothing we can do for that boy. He's dying."

Again my father refused to accept that prognosis. He carried me out and drove me to Ste. Rose, another thirty miles away. They sprinkled me with sulpha powder, widely used for military field dressings and just released for public use. Ten days later they peeled skin off one side of me, placed it on the now-cleansed wounds on the other side, and sewed it on with over two hundred stitches. Three months later I was discharged.

"*Iligetami non carborundum*," said our pipe-smoking Black-Sea-German neighbour, an encyclopaedia of quaint expressions.

"My Ukrainian is not good enough to understand that."

"That's Latin. It means 'don't let the bastards grind you down'!"

The quotation was elicited by the sight of my tortured, desiccated body, and was to become my mantra. My left pectoral looked like that of the woman who was attacked by *Jaws* in a later movie and I would be condemned to periodic skin grafts for the rest of my life. The musculature of my left arm was virtually destroyed and the fingers of my left hand numb and lifeless.

"Here, learn to type. You're no more good for hard work anyway."

My father had brought home a typewriter and placed it on the kitchen table with the peremptory command. It proved excellent therapy. A year later I could type. More importantly, I had recovered full use of my hand. And I fooled my father: My body was covered by unsightly scars but was slowly regaining strength. But that took several years. I had intended to quit school after grade eight, as most farm boys did at that time, but while convalescing I took grade nine by correspondence and then grades ten and eleven at nearby Tamarisk High School. That got me excited about education, but I wanted to be a farmer.

"Then you may as well be a good farmer," my father said. In September 1944, he insisted I take the diploma course in agriculture at the University of Manitoba. I protested: "You are the best farmer in the municipality. I can learn it from you."

"You can learn the practice from me but it is important to also know the theory. If nothing else, the university will teach you where to look for solutions when you have problems. And it will broaden your horizons and provide you with new friends."

I learned all that, and also a new type of social politics. The class of 112 included many veterans. Most were quiet and studious, driven by recollections of "riding the rods" and living in "Bennettvilles" before, and the horrors and waste of the war, and grateful for the opportunity to improve their lives. A few spent their time being inebriated, noisy, and fractious. Their response to their low grades was to circulate a petition demanding the resignation of the dean of Faculty of Agriculture. I was approached to sign:

"If you guys would spend more time studying in the evening instead of getting drunk, and more time in class paying attention instead of sleeping off a hangover, your grades would be better and you would have no quarrel with the dean."

There was some physical jostling and verbal threats: "You are the only hold-out and you better sign or else...."

One noon I went through the cafeteria chow line and was looking for a table when the ringleader of those seeking the dean's resignation and the bully of the class, a tall, gaunt, hawk-faced veteran in his mid-twenties, stabbed a cigarette butt into the mashed potatoes on my plate. My five-foot five-inch frame was stronger than it appeared — and I had a bad attitude. I kicked the offending classmate hard in the testicles, knocking him over the next table. The harassment stopped. I learned the basis for future political action: no one needs to go along with the crowd.

And I learned the politics of divided loyalties.

"You will never get into the army with those scars. Go home," the gaunt, harassed, middle-aged, bespectacled doctor told me.

I had responded to my draft call by walking from the Fort Garry campus to Fort Osborne Barracks. It was February 12, 1945, the day I became eighteen-and-a-half years old, and the day General Crerar launched the Canadian Army on its first direct attack across the Rhine at Nijmegen. Did I really want to do this? But what choice did I have? Well, could I not request postponement? But had not several of my classmates in similar circumstances already enlisted? But did I really want to go and kill relatives in Europe? Well, had they not started this terrible war? But they were probably just very ordinary people, caught in circumstances beyond their control, reluctantly trudging off to the barracks because they had not the courage to refuse — just like me!

But are there not times in life when one must play the cards one is dealt without whining? Is it whining to act autonomously and refuse to allow fate to have the last word? But this country has been good to my family and what will the neighbours think if I refuse to take the risks being taken by others with less interest in the outcome of the war? Well, to hell with them: I was the eldest son of a farmer and entitled to deferment!

Join the army and see the world: I rounded a curve on Corydon Avenue and suddenly came face to face with the huge poster displaying the caption and showing a handsome, smiling but resolute soldier. It was settled.

"I am Captain Leader," said the imposing figure in the razor-creased uniform at the front of the hall. "That may be a misnomer but it will have to do." He paused portentously: "Gentlemen — and this is the last time I will call you that — in the next few weeks we intend to remove the *gentle* and make you *men*. Let me begin by getting something straight. Some of you have come here believing you are going to travel, or learn a trade. In fact, you will go only where you are sent. And the only trade you will be taught here is how to kill...."

My guts turned cold. I glanced surreptitiously at others of the score of recruits in the Spartan room and saw on their faces the same shocked expression they must have seen on mine. But it was too late: I already had my urine tested (I was too nervous to urinate into the bottle so was told to turn on the water tap which induced my bladder to function), and taken an intelligence test (consisting of matching words to symbols and drawing the missing leg on a table) and signed too many documents.

"Do you wish to enlist for active service?"

"What does that mean?"

"It means you might be sent overseas."

"Okay. I've always wanted to travel." The lieutenant seemed amused and gave me a document to sign.

"Do you have a preference of branch of service?"

"Paratroops." I signed another document. I was hooked.

Three days later I removed my shirt and the startled doctor observed my scars and issued his decree.

So the war, in which young men died to serve old men's purposes, which cost some forty million lives, 42,042 of them Canadians, including the boy next door with whom I had so often walked to school, passed me by, leaving me no memento but a small bronze lapel button with a red maple leaf in the centre and the inscription "Applicant for Enlistment." After that I never thought about the fire which had left my body scarred and my left arm crippled without pondering on the outcome of life's little accidents. And I never drove down the esplanade on Memorial Boulevard in Winnipeg and passed the bronze cenotaph bearing the simple but poignant inscription "Know all ye who pass by that for your tomorrow we gave our today," without wondering if, under slightly different circumstances, I would have been among them.

After graduating in April 1946, I spent most of my time on the tractor, the rolling, roaring, belching beast, going round and round the field, sometimes around the clock, falling asleep while the unguided machine wandered crazily across the field, to be repeatedly rescued on the very precipice of disaster. I greatly enjoyed driving at night, with no headlights, following the furrow by the moonlight gleaming on the new-moist surface, watching the blue exhaust flame shoot up while the pipe turned red, exhilarated by the extra power the internal combustion engine drew from the cool, oxygen-enriched night air.

And in those long hours, alone but never lonely, I memorized poetry, read books blurred by the bounces, kept myself awake by doing mental puzzles such as how long it would take to walk to the moon, marvelled at the sophistication of the machinery made by man to ease his toil, and pondered on how much of this resulted from pure intellect and how much from accident or serendipity.

I marvelled while American generosity, memories of the train of tragic consequences flowing from the attempt to extract reparations from Germany after World War I, and the fear of communism, combined to produce the Marshall Plan, and the *miracle* which rebuilt Germany into an economic titan within a generation and demonstrated that the *Lebensraum* for which Hitler went to war was not essential to prosperity in an industrial world. I watched in wonder as, on the other side of the globe, Japan arose out of its blood and ashes to become a new economic giant courted by the world. I noted with ambivalence, moving between fury at its arrogance and gratitude for its umbrella of protection, as America became the new Rome, sending its legions to patrol the world by Jeep or U-2 in efforts to maintain the *Pax Americana*. Later it would impale itself on another of those — in Chamberlain's memorable post-Munich reference to the Sudetenland — faraway places with strange-sounding names and people about whom we knew nothing … Vietnam.

I wrestled with thoughts my mother considered heretical: did God create man or did man, the product of primal slime, in the supreme vanity of his aspiration to immortality, create God in his own image in which to subsume himself? The ancient Greeks, unfamiliar with the concept of the anthropomorphic Christian God, had developed a philosophy that appealed to my intellect: energy could be neither created nor destroyed, so a human died and was buried and the decomposing body fertilized the earth, which produced a plant, which was consumed by a cow, which produced milk, which nourished a human child, and so the spirit and energy, in various organic forms, remained in the *cycle of life*. Yet, beholding the wonders of the star-bright sky, intellect struggled with viscera, which held with Einstein that "the more we learn through knowledge, the more we find of mystery."

But there was no escape from intellectualizing. Control of agricultural processes, and industrialism, had triggered a quantum leap. Freed from the *dark ages* of superstition, man had begun to see himself as the end of all things. "The Enlightenment philosophers made God into an hypothesis, but as an hypothesis He was no longer God," wrote Santayana.[15] They had been followed by the rationalists who made God man, and the Marxists, who made man God, able, with the application of intellect and determination, to revolutionize his social and physical environment.

I joined the CCF. I had not intended to. In 1945, at age eighteen, I accompanied my father to a meeting at Dauphin. The languorous warmth of spring and the dispassionate drone of speakers allowed my mind to drift: how did we get here and whither do we go; why are things the way they are and how did they come to be; do conditions shape the man or does man create his environment? ...

I was jerked back to reality. The final speaker, "Old Socialist" Fred Tipping, his voice low and melancholy, was commenting on the obscene irony of the war that cost Canada over thirteen billion dollars, yet left it more prosperous than ever envisioned in the "green and pleasant" Jerusalem of William Blake. Tipping concluded by quoting "The Red Flag."[16] It was my first exposure to its message. It moved me. I purchased a membership card.[17]

My political education came primarily from my father, who had witnessed the extremes of wealth and poverty in Russia, Romania, and Canada, and had observed the corrupt autocratic capitalism of the Czars and the equally corrupt state capitalism under the guise of communism. To him socialism was not an esoteric political theory. He had, of course, not read Arthur Koestler,[18] but he had observed first-hand the failure of the Soviet system to harness human potential because it crushed human initiative. He had not read Milovan Djilas,[19] but he had observed the new bureaucratic class in the communist countries of eastern Europe establish itself on the wreckage of the old capitalist class. He had not heard of "The God that failed,"[20] but would have known that God was being blamed for what was the failure of man. He profoundly believed a new social and political philosophy was needed to share Nature's bounty.

My father was too much a realist to be a revolutionary and too socially conscious to accept Hegel's dictum that " What is, is right."[21] He could not be a communist because he had observed the Soviet system destroy the connection between productivity and self-interest. Conversely, neither could he support a capitalist political party: despite his own success, his sense of history would not allow him to believe in either the ethics or the survival capability of a politico-economic system he equated to that described by Thucydides as one in which "the strong take what they want and the weak suffer what they must." "The rich and politically powerful, surrounded by the poor and powerless, are clearly the most vulnerable in a society, or they would not need to surround themselves with armies," he would state, explaining that socialism was a delicate, danger-fraught path between two equally destructive extremes. It was Plato's "golden mean," the middle way, in which the fortunate secured their own future by assisting those around them to rise above economic subsistence and destructive envy. His dedication to the sanctity of individual rights against the power of the state later led him to find his philosophical inspiration in John Stuart Mill.[22] But his personal experience as a municipal councillor in both Romania and Canada, and with *gas and water socialism* as a mechanism for collectively providing for all what few could provide for themselves, and his deep disgust with what he saw as the unprincipled *opportunism* of the Liberal Party, kept him a lifelong social-democrat rather than a liberal.

So I joined the party but, like a bride accepting the duties of the marriage bed but holding something of herself in reserve, I maintained my distance. I saw politics as a potential ravishing of the human spirit and destructive to social relationships. I had not yet read Julien Benda but, as *he* did, I sensed that political parties represented "the organization of political hatreds."[23] My father saw it differently: "In the last analysis, everything is politics. If the political process did not exist it would need to be invented because it is the vehicle for peaceful change. Politics is war without weapons and political parties the equivalent of regiments into which people organize themselves to pursue objectives. You cannot change things alone. Power flows from the people."

"I understand what you are saying but I see partisan politics as separating the people of a community into groups suspicious of each other," I reasoned. But my father countered: "But the alternative to partisan politics, in which ideas can contend and men rage against each other while remaining agreed on the basic social order, is either chaos or totalitarianism."

Having read some history, I appreciated my father's statement but remained reluctant. When my father quoted Plato's injunction that, "those who do not involve themselves in politics will be governed by men less wise than they," I replied that many were wiser and I was content to leave the governing to them.

I had both a natural and learned deference to authority, imbibed from my mother's religious-medieval attitude that *"Herrschaft ist von Gott"* (authority is divinely ordained), and those elected to positions, be they politicians or executives of organizations, especially those elevated to the ethereal sphere of cabinet or company presidents, were superior beings not to be doubted, or even questioned, by ordinary mortals such as I. I had not yet read John Locke[24] or Thomas Jefferson[25] and vaguely believed authority emanated from power, not from the people. The first time I walked through the great, imposing doors of the Norman-towered edifice on the Rideau, I felt as though I was entering a temple and should remove my shoes.

My father's arguments appealed to me intellectually but I differentiated between *politics* as the organizing principle of a society, and *political partisanship*, which meant conformity — and I was not ready to conform. I

Fred Zaplitny, CCF Member of Parliament, 1945–49 and 1953–58.

wanted to remain distinct from the crowd, intuitively sensing the crowd could become a mob and the mob a beast. I remained more observer than participant.

I paid my dues but was reluctant to actively engage. Even when my father ran in the provincial election in 1949, I became only peripherally involved. But being a party member interested me in politics and political processes. Before television, political meetings were a form of entertainment. I attended meetings of all political parties. I became political, but not partisan.

Even peripheral participation gave opportunities to learn of the structure and function of political parties. I learned of the intricacies of policy-making to seek maximum inclusion of people with a wide spectrum of ideas, but minimum deviation from ideology. I absorbed the nature of political promotion, and when it crossed the undefined line from policy presentation into propaganda. And I learned the lessons of political intrigue.

In 1945 Fred Zaplitny, a screen-handsome — he looked like 1950s actor John Hodiak — soft-spoken schoolteacher savant of Ukrainian descent, totally fluent in both languages when being bilingual meant speaking English and another language, not necessarily French, shocked the establishment and transported the CCF into a state of euphoria by being elected the Member of Parliament for the federal riding of Dauphin, which included the Municipality of Grandview. In 1949 he lost the election to William Ward, a limp-wristed but friendly back-slapper who had held the riding for the Liberals during the decade prior to 1945.

As the 1953 federal election approached, it appeared that Hally Parker, a large, loud, excellent but unpopular local farmer desperately wanted the Liberal nomination. CCF Party apparatchiks believed he would be easy to defeat in the election, but the problem was how to get him nominated as candidate despite the determination of the sitting MP to remain the Liberal standard-bearer? A group of eighteen CCFers purchased Liberal membership cards, attended the Liberal nominating convention, and voted for Parker. He won the nomination by a few votes. Then he was methodically destroyed.

One afternoon a neighbour came to the field where I was working to inform me Parker was to speak at a meeting in Grandview at seven o'clock. Others and I had been attending meetings of all political parties, so I changed my shirt and, accompanied by several neighbours, drove the nine miles to town. We were told that, *No, Parker was to speak at Pleasant Valley, twelve miles south-west, at eight o'clock.* Followed by several other carloads of politically conscious persons, we drove there only to be informed that, *No, Parker was to speak at Venlaw, fifteen miles north of Gilbert Plains, at nine o'clock.* The appearance that the governing Liberals were attempting to avoid questions by changing the time and place of the meeting made us more eager to attend. We drove the thirty-seven miles, more cars joining the cavalcade as we passed back through Grandview and then through Gilbert Plains, on our way. We filled the hall.

The chairman was Nick Hryhorchuk, from Ethelbert, a quick-witted, articulate former MLA elected as a Progressive in 1922 and later as a Liberal. Parker made his presentation. We listened intently, with no heckling — my friends and I made a point of never heckling a speaker. Then came question time.

One person after another stood up to ask Parker questions. Hryhorchuk invariably answered them. Finally I rose: "Mr. Chairman. I note the questions are being directed to Mr. Parker, but they are being answered by you. Could we please have Mr. Parker's answers."

Hryhorchuk smiled benignly: "Well, I just happen to know something about these things."

"I'm sure you do, but Mr. Parker is the party candidate and we would like to know if he knows anything."

A furious Hally Parker, seated, jumped up so fast his feet left the floor. He let out a roar that shook the hall, grabbed his coat, and stormed out. He was not the ideal candidate.

Ward, furious at losing the nomination, ran as a Liberal Independent. The Liberal vote was split. Zaplitny won the election. The Liberals had been defeated by a clever stratagem.

I had been informed of the plot but declined the invitation to participate. I was uneasy about the ethics. I was an eager learner, an interested observer, and a sometime participant, but not spiritually committed.

But within a month, because of events in another arena, I became committed and politics became a blood sport.

3

Farming in the Fifties

I too, sing the song of all Creation
A brave sky, and a glad wind blowing by.
ANON

I met her as a blossom on a stem,
Before she ever breathed, and in that dream
The mind remembers from a deeper sleep.
THEODORE ROETHKE, *The Dream.* *

O N OCTOBER 12, 1949, I married Ellinor Alexander* and we took over the family farm. Of Scottish-English ancestry, she grew up on a farm ten miles from ours, walked three miles to elementary school, took grades nine and ten by correspondence, and grades eleven and twelve at the Grandview High School. She taught for a year on permit, worked for a year at the local Co-op store, attended Teacher's College, and taught for two years in a rural school east of Dauphin.[1] My parents feared being a teacher had ruined her for hard farm work, but when, a week after we married, they watched her feeding the livestock, she won their hearts.

Actually, she could do much more than that. She milked cows, fed hogs and fattening stock, raised poultry, drove our two daughters to school when they reached that age, and brought lunch to several fields for hired men and myself. She helped put bales in the hayloft, drove the truck hauling grain from the combine, sometimes drove to town several times a day to test grain kernels for moisture content, kept our home clean and tidy, and was always ready to go to a dance or to a meeting. When we became involved in organizational activity she was the realist, and my unfailing guide to what was possible — and right.

My parents retired to the house they had built in town. Grandview was a bustling centre of about eight hundred, with five grain elevators, four general stores, three restaurants, and an assortment of fuel, service, vehicle, and implement agencies. There were seven churches of various denominations, an impressive two-storey brick bank, a doctor-owned four-room hospital, a large high school, a newspaper, a drug store, a post office, a theatre that showed movies and staged plays, a stockyard for shipping livestock, and a platform over which farmers could load their own grain. There was a livery stable operated by the town character, a legion hall for meetings and dances, and a two-storey hotel with a knotted-rope fire escape but with — one of the few in Manitoba — hot and cold running water in each room; the gift of a lumber baron who had operated here early in the century.

We were given the home quarter-section with all the buildings as a wedding gift and leased the remaining seven quarter-sections on a crop-share basis.[2] We were young, strong and ambitious, cultivating our Elysian fields, growing grain, feeding hogs, building up a herd of livestock — and soon raising our two young daughters. We revelled in the land, the new-born calves, the warm spring rain, the straight rows of grain emerging from the earth, the roar of combines in the autumn, the blizzards that marooned us for a week at a time so the world could not touch us. Our world was wondrous and life was good. We had good machinery and land, a reasonable sense of business, and sixteen-hour days of work gave us a feeling of accomplishment. To us farming was more than a way of making a living or a way of life: farming was a romance.

Economics invaded our paradise. The fifties were not kind to farmers. Cow and hog prices fell to six and twelve cents per pound respectively. Grain prices based on comparative production costs were as low as in the thirties. The weather was not felicitous: one spring was so cold, emerging grain froze; on two successive years rains necessitated ploughing down much of the crop which was mostly weeds; another year it was so dry the granules of fertilizer were still undissolved in the autumn and some fields were not worth harvesting. One year we had a bumper crop, but so did everyone in western Canada, and the market was quickly saturated.

More than half of Canadian wheat was exported and 40 per cent of western farmer's income depended on the international market, which was inelastic. Government of Canada policy was to export only for hard currency, which most countries did not have, and those who had it did not need our grain, so it was piled in huge pyramids that rivalled Giza. Those who needed it starved, while those who had produced it could not sell the fruits of their labours and pay their operating bills and taxes.[3]

Farmers in western Canada were experiencing American author Robert Lacey's aphorism that "The history of North American agriculture is a history of false dawns."[4] Good crops were no salvation: suppliers of inputs (machinery, fertilizers, fuel, herbicides[5]), as if by clairvoyance, anticipated possible increases in farm income and adjusted their prices upward to siphon it off. And when farm product prices went down, input costs remained up.

Charles Schwartz found the cost of a twelve-foot self-propelled combine (Massey-Harris) f.o.b. Regina was equivalent to the farmer's receipts for 1,983 bushels of wheat in 1946, but 5,593 bushels by 1958.[6] Saskatchewan historian John H. Archer wrote: "The relationship between the costs of production and price received for the product is well illustrated when one compares cost of machinery and price of wheat. Thus, while cash income rose significantly in the early fifties, farm costs rose even more dramatically and farmers found themselves caught in a cost-price squeeze, [which] was accentuated, as a surplus of unsold wheat glutted domestic elevators and plugged farm bins."[7]

These events conspired to turn our attention elsewhere. Farming had come far from being a few acres of rocks and a shack with a hole in the roof for the smoke to escape and a goat tied to the back fence, when a man with a strong arm, an axe, and a mule could wrest a living from the wilderness – or even from living in grain bins and working with horses. We were on the cusp of a revolution in agricultural technology rivalling that of the eighteenth century. This was no longer simply a way of making a living with the primary risk being a season's work, but a capital-intensive and market-oriented industry, highly vulnerable not only to the elements but to decisions made thousands of miles away in which Canadian farmers had no voice and from which there was no appeal.

Survival in such an economy required not only individual, but also community, effort. Slowly I began to comprehend that politics, in one form or another, is the crucible in which society is periodically reshaped in the light of changing conditions, and that Aristotle was right that "man is a political animal," but perhaps less by *nature* than by necessity. However, when I did become involved in the politics of agriculture, it was not through a political party but through what could be seen as its antithesis, the Co-operative Movement.

Politics is the forum in which ideas are expressed, suppressed and/or modified, and is pervasive, insidious, and internalized. It exists where there is social and/or economic activity in which human beings organize to collectively provide themselves with goods and services or contend either to change things or to keep them as they are, be this at the federal, provincial, municipal, or school board levels, in the church, or in organizations. Among these are the co-operatives: business organizations, owned and operated by their members through which they pool their selling power to force up prices of goods they sell and pool their buying power to force down prices of goods they buy.

My first experience with a primitive form of co-operative — and politics — was the beef ring. Lacking facilities to keep meat fresh during the summer, a dozen farmers would form a *ring*. Each week, one member provided a fattened beast, which was slaughtered and cut up by the local butcher, and the following week it was another farmer's turn, so for twelve weeks each household had fresh meat. My job, beginning at age eleven, was to ride my horse to where the beast was butchered, pick up twelve bundles of meat weighing about twenty pounds each, sling the bags over my horse's back, and ride a dozen miles, with blood oozing out of the bags and down my legs and the horse's flank, followed by a billion flies, delivering the gruesome, sticky bundles to ring members. Politics entered, like the serpent into Eden, when one farmer was suspected of delivering a sick animal, and the ring members were divided on if, and how, he should be punished. The beef ring experience taught me early in life that there is a solution to every problem, that the sum of a community is larger than its parts and is strengthened when its individual members pool their efforts, and that someone always seeks an advantage. Later I was to recall all that many times. And I was to learn by experience what my father had told me: "In the last analysis, everything is politics."

My real initiation came by accident.

"I notice the co-ops are having a folk school in town in two weeks. Perhaps you should attend," my father said at supper one evening in 1947, a year after I graduated from the university.

"What's a folk school?"

"It's some kind of a school for learning about how co-ops work and for training community leadership."

"I have no more interest in becoming a community leader than I have in becoming a politician. And it will cost me good money."

"Attending a meeting does not make you a politician nor does attending a school make you a community leader. Whether or not you want to pursue these things further is something you can decide later. The point is that ignorance has

Helen Sisson (née Matheson), Director of MFAC Youth Education Program (1942–48), educator extraordinaire.

a greater price than education and you will never know less from listening nor become narrower by looking at the world through the eyes of others. *Horchen macht mann nicht dumm.*"[8]

So I attended the folk school, organized by the Manitoba Federation of Agriculture and Co-operation which had been established in 1939 to provide a lobbying spearhead for all Manitoba farm organizations, and as the educational arm of the Co-operative Movement. I met nineteen young men and women, whose parents were similarly involved in co-operatives, from all over the province. More significantly, I met the incomparable Helen Matheson (later Helen Sisson), the model-slim, mannequin-dressed, black-haired, flashing-eyed, kinetic, effervescent woman of thirty-something who was the youth education director for the MFAC and conducted the school. She taught by the Socratic method, forcing her charges to find answers to their own questions, and I would often say later, "she taught me everything I know." She was as much a spirit as a person and was to leave the imprint of her personality upon me, and hundreds of other young men and women who attended her schools. Also, she would leave me with both a gift — the ability to look upon the world with eyes of wonder, and a curse — the desire to remake it. I was hooked.

She fixed on me the Chinese curse, "May you live in interesting times." From then on I would carry *interesting times* with me.

I became an organizer and proselytizer for the MFAC.

I organized a number of *farm forums* — local farm discussion groups — for the MFAC, and began attending local meetings of co-operatives — Manitoba Pool Elevators where we sold grain, the Consumers Co-operative where we bought groceries and dry goods, the Dairy and Poultry Pool where we delivered cream and eggs, the Credit Union where we banked or borrowed money, Canadian Co-operative Implements Limited where we bought machinery. But my real interest lay in agricultural policy, and that would lead me, unwittingly, deviously, obliquely, insidiously, but with increasing acceleration, into the tenacious and unforgiving embrace of the tar baby of politics.

In the summer of 1950, my wife and I attended the annual provincial convention of the MFAC, purportedly the voice of organized agriculture and the farmers' advocate. Even as an enthusiast, I was disappointed. Most delegates were a generation my senior and their oft-expressed refrain was that, no matter how bad things are down on the farm "they are better than in the thirties." Having witnessed some of the miseries of the thirties, I was not interested in them except as an historical memory and an economic aberration. At a time when a baker made more profit on a loaf of bread than the farmer who had produced the wheat in it, and the label on a can of corn cost more than the farmer received for the corn in the can, I believed the agricultural industry was being raped. I wanted to discuss farm policy to change that, while most delegates seemed to see the conventions as a once-a-year opportunity to visit.

And I resented the cavalier comments of the guest speakers.

Farmers were the victims of economist Alfred Marshall's "theory of marginal utility," which held that a few sacks of surplus potatoes or a few bushels of wheat available for export set the price for the entire crop. Of course, classical economic theory, deriving from Adam Smith,[9] held that the individual, out of self-interest or greed, would compensate by tailoring his crop to the available market: if prices went down so would his production.

Author James Gray exposed the wretched fallacy of this theory as it applied to farming by quoting a displaced Depression-era farmer in the Winnipeg Relief Yards, explaining how it had affected him: "I was readin' about a law of supply and demand in the *Prairie Farmer*. Said if prices went down farmers would plant less wheat, and if prices went up they planted more. Any damn fool knows that if the farmer's got a mortgage he sure has to plant *more* wheat when prices are low."[10]

Everyone knew that – except the economics professors: "If you cannot make a living on a section of land, you should either sell your farm and go into another line of work or acquire another section of land and produce more,"[11] intoned the guest speaker at the annual MFAC convention, an economics professor in the department of agriculture at the University of Manitoba.

In answer to a question from a member of the audience about what farmers should do to improve their income, the professor had parroted the prevailing view of the emerging *intellectual elite* that "bigger is better." As one farming two sections of good land — a large farm at that time — and watching my bank account being depleted, this angered me:

> But Sir, if I must compete in a world market against the farmers of France and the United States who are subsidized by their national treasuries, and if such subsidies are driving down the world price, and if I am compelled to sell my product on the world market with no help from the Canadian Treasury, and if I am losing money on every bushel of grain I produce now, and if Marshall, with whom surely you are familiar, is correct in holding that the price for the entire crop is set by the last bushel sold, and if that means that the more I produce the lower my prices will go, how do I survive?

The professor, disconcerted, gazed toward the ceiling: "Well, if things are that bad and your farm operation is not viable, at least you have the pleasure of fresh air and sunshine."

It seemed that to the farmer's normal risks of too much rain, too little rain, late spring, early frost, grasshoppers, hail, head fungus, root rot, pests and weeds, there had to be added another – the ubiquitous economists. They seemed creatures of their culture and in times of trouble had neither diagnosis nor remedy, and they invariably attended farm conventions and set the tone for policy thinking. And as infuriating as the smug, supercilious flippancy of the learned professors was to me, many farmers paid rapturous attention to such vacuous sophistries.

"Indeed, sir, whose salary increases each year regardless of productivity, plus benefits from your employer, the taxpayers, would you please explain how that fresh air and sunshine can be converted into cash so your admirers can pay their bills?"

North American industry applied Smith's formulation to Marshall's theory. Whether monopoly, oligopoly or monopsony, they estimated the available market, limited production to that minus one unit, and let scrambling consumers anxious to buy remaining supply compete against each other to set the market price. Prices kept going up, consumers paid, and profits were enormous.

Axiomatically, because of the greater difficulty of organizing them, the larger the number of producers the weaker their market power. With some three hundred thousand full-time farmers in western Canada competing against each other, the harder they worked and the more they produced the lower prices went. Farmers sought compensation by enlarging acreage, increasing productivity, spending every dollar – earned or borrowed – for larger machinery and more fertilizer, and generating a production miracle.

And the farmers' miracle of productivity was destroying them.

The MFAC represented farmers to government, but its leadership seemed flaccid and its advocacy apologetic. I sympathized with these genial people, but could not agree with them. There were seventy-five delegates and there should have been twenty times that. Farmers were becoming the helots of Canada, and no one was protesting in such a way to catch the attention of public and the policy-makers. I was restive. I was impatient. I wanted something more.

So did my father.

4

The Making of the Manitoba Farmer's Union

In unity is strength.[1]

Who else overproduces and sells his product at public auction while buying his supplies from oligopolies that maintain prices by controlling production? Does General Motors auction off its products in competition with other vehicle manufacturers and produce more units to make up losses, or does it produce for a known market and maintain profits? Our young people are leaving. Rural communities are dying. Do our politicians and economists not realize moving these people into cities will cost more than keeping them on farms or rural towns with cheaper services?

We are told by government and farm leaders the only way to deal with our surpluses is to reduce prices because the consumers will not pay more for food and the taxpayers will not pay supports. Yet when car companies have acres of surplus cars do they reduce prices? No! They maintain price and lay off workers who then go on unemployment insurance or welfare. That is a public subsidy to the richest corporations in the world.

MY FATHER HAD A TALENT for encapsulating complex concepts. He had lost his bid for election to the Manitoba Legislature, and turned his attention elsewhere. He was elected to the Board of the Consumers Co-op and began selling John Deere machinery for which the co-op was agent. That introduced him to the stark reality of post-war agriculture. Those who survived the Depression and paid for their land during the war, as he had, were in a good position. Those just starting had no money, few prospects, and little hope. Their income would not cover their costs. Young people

Jake Schulz, President, Manitoba Farmer's Union (1951–54); President, Inter-Provincial Farm Union Council (1955–56). (c. 1952). Poster announcing public meeting as MFU swept Manitoba.

abandoned farms and went to new industrial job centres at Fort Saskatchewan, Elliot Lake and Kitimat. The countryside was being depopulated. Those who remained, or their wives, got jobs in towns to support the farm. Everything appeared backwards, as it did to Alice through the looking glass. It was intolerable. And no one was saying anything.

The Canadian Wheat Board had been established when farmers persuaded governments wheat was too important to be left to the tender mercies of the Grain Exchange speculators. It had shown what could be done by collective effort to mitigate destructive competition which most damaged those most vulnerable,[2] while providing the touch of Midas to the grain merchants whose wealth increased in direct relationship to the misery of farmers, and whose ostentation is still displayed by the spectacular mansions they built along Wellington Crescent and in the verdant loop of the Assiniboine River sheltered behind The Gates.

My father set himself the task of retaining that wealth in the hands of the primary producers. He concluded farmers needed a louder voice in economics and politics, such as an industrial-style union. Then he discovered there already was one, but it was inactive so he began signing up members. On February 2, 1951, at the annual convention at Portage la Prairie, he was elected president, with Ed McNabb of Minnedosa as vice-president, and given permission to write a new constitution. He took over the moribund shell of the Manitoba Farmer's Union and became, effectively, its founding president. The MFU, established two years earlier, had failed because its president, Joe Gunia of Gilbert Plains, was rumoured to be associated with communism. And this was the beginning of the McCarthyist era.

My first speech, at the founding convention of the new MFU, was in response to delegates from southern Manitoba arguing this stain would keep the organization reduced to a corporal's guard, and proposing that anyone elected a director, provincial, district, or local, take a *loyalty oath*. Like my father, I had little sympathy for communism in Canada, but I had a sufficient sense of history to know the Depression had bred different solutions to social and economic problems, and I had no patience with people who allowed themselves to be frightened by shadows:

> Mr. Chairman, and fellow delegates. My parents took an oath of loyalty to this country when they immigrated to escape communism. I took an oath of loyalty to this country when I responded to my draft call. If that is not enough, nothing is. Any Canadian wishing to betray this country would readily swear an oath of loyalty as a cover. Let us build our organization to improve conditions so people will not turn to exotic "isms" and let us not allow ourselves to be seduced into foolish diversions so the press can report we have nothing better to do than go on witch hunts.[3] For the record, I am not defending communism, but man's inherent right to follow different paths to the same goal.

My father proved a superb organizer. He wrote the constitution (limiting his term to four years), absorbed the remnants of the old MFU – including

Mary McIntosh, MFU Women's President, 1952–58 (c. 1958).

its dedicated secretary, Joseph Galonsky, wrote and presented briefs to governments, scoured the province for men and women in equal proportions for district and provincial boards. He structured the organization, insisting on a parallel women's section fully integrated into the organization — energetic Mary McIntosh of Neepawa was elected its first president — patiently persuaded directors and organizers of the importance of their mission while reconciling their spouses to the time away from home, scheduled tours of meetings for himself and others, guided the organization, spoke at hundreds of meetings in every town and hamlet in Manitoba, established an MFU monthly magazine,[4] and wrote a book.[5]

The MFU blitzed the province, responding to a felt need among farmers for a voice in policy-making for their industry. At the annual convention in December 1951, Secretary Joe Galonsky reported to the 470 delegates (twenty-seven in 1950): "In a year we set up 260 locals for a total of 17,000 members. We held 216 meetings from October 8 to December 8, 1951, as many as fifteen a day." In four years the MFU signed up about 30,000 members, some 50 per cent of the farmers of Manitoba. Some communities had a sign-up of 80 per cent.[6]

Together with dynamic, volcanic Joseph Phelps[7] — he and Schulz became known as the "Terrible Twins" — founding president of the Saskatchewan Farmer's Union, and tall, big-shouldered, soft-spoken, Henry Young,[8] president of the United Farmers of Alberta, they formed the Inter-Provincial Farm Union Council, with Phelps as president, and became a power to be reckoned with.

Left: Joseph L. Phelps, President, Saskatchewan Farmer's Union (1950–54); President, IFUC
(1952–54). Right: Joe Phelps in characteristic pose, with journalist Chris Higgenbotham.

And I became an organizer and proselytizer for the MFU.

I travelled throughout Manitoba and Ontario to establish MFU associations. My pay was five dollars a day and out-of-pocket expenses, which was all the MFU, with its five dollar membership fee, could afford. And it was not easy. Sometimes I drove a hundred miles to a scheduled meeting to find a lone attendee — the hall caretaker who came to collect his fee. The curse was curling, which inspired a couplet:

> Curling, curling, late and early, walking up and sweeping down.
> Deeply mourned the organizer, entering another empty town.

Farmers and rural townspeople had discovered an antidote to their economic woes, and governments happily subsidized the construction of curling plazas in which to indulge these careless raptures.

"All is bread and circuses." Just as in Juvenal's Rome.

MFU organizers were not always welcomed. Our modus operandi was to send an advance person through communities, renting halls, placing ads in local papers advertising meetings, and placarding the town. Then the speaker

They Built Two Farmer Empires

HARRY HALLIWELL
(Tribune Agricultural Editor)

Two of the most colorful personalities in the prairie farm movement are due to retire this year, but the betting is that they won't be satisfied to sit back and vegetate.

Jacob Schulz, president of the Manitoba Farmers' Union, and J. Phelps, president of the Saskatchewan Farmers Union, will be casualties of clauses in their organizations' constitutions at their June conventions, starting early December and late in November respectively.

From The Start

Each has been president of his organization from the beginning. The SFU constitution limits the president to five consecutive terms, the MFU constitution to four terms.

A move was made in Saskatchewan last year to alter the SFU constitution to permit Mr. Phelps to continue in office and a similar move may be forthcoming at this year's annual meeting, but both he and Mr. Schulz have affirmed their intention of retiring.

They are both reticent to talk about their future. This summer Phelps told The Tribune he intended to go back to his farm at Glenkie, Sask. Mr. Schulz says he will take things easy and be on

Now They'll Retire — But Won't Quit

call to help out the MFU any time he is needed.

People who know them find it hard to imagine either taking things easy.

This is particularly true of Mr. Phelps. Active in local organizations and politics for many years,

JACOB SCHULZ

he won his first seat in the Saskatchewan legislature in 1938, won again in 1944 and became minister of Natural Resources in Industrial Development in the first CCF administration.

Losing in Saltcoats constituency in 1948 he faded out of the provincial political picture, leaving behind him a trail crowded with friends and enemies, the result of his tremendous enthusiasm — some thought over-enthusiasm — for development and reorganization of the province's natural resources, particularly in the north.

Bounced Back

In 1949 he began to bounce back. He took over the near-defunct and Red-ridden Saskatchewan section of the United Farmers of Canada, deserted out the Communists, changed the name to the Saskatchewan Farmers Union and has never looked back.

Mr. Phelps is a born organizer, an able speaker. He has wealth of energy, drive and enthusiasm.

Mr. Schulz, who at 53 is two years younger than his colleague, came into the public eye somewhat later. A native of Bessarabia, Romania he came to Canada

in 1930 and rented a farm at Grandview. He played an active part in local organizations, such as the co-operative, and was municipal councillor from 1945 to 1949.

First Venture

His first venture into province-wide organization came in 1951. He had helped to form the first local of the Manitoba Farmers' Union at Grandview in August 1950 and was its president. By February 1951, 50 locals were organized. At the first provincial convention, February 1, 1951, he became president of the new provincial organization and he has held the post four consecutive terms.

In five years these two men have set up organizations which numerically al strength and breadth of representation probably never equalled in the prairie farm movement except by the wheat pools.

With Alberta and Ontario they have set up the Interprovincial Farm Union Council. They have fought with provincial and federal governments, with the older and more conservative Federation of Agriculture, the Canadian Wheat Board — which they strongly support — and the Board of Grain

J. L. PHELPS

to come — they will be much more at home attempting to shape events.

When they joined in talks, under the authority of the IFUC, with the TLC and CCL last winter to form the Canadian Farmer-Labor Economic Council, some observers sensed an attempt to form a new Farmer-Labor Party. But this is unlikely at present.

Mr. Phelps has intimated that he has been urged by some to remain as chairman of the Interprovincial Farm Union Council but he added that this is a matter to be decided by the will of the directors and the future status of the council. Mr. Schulz said recently he would remain as the call of the MFU as a speaker or organizer, but that this, too, will be a matter for the directors.

Commissioners. They have made many enemies, but they have built up strong organizations.

Not Watching: Working

No one who knows them believes they will be willing to sit still and watch the events of the years

Copyright, Winnipeg Tribune, November 23, 1954. Reprinted with permission.

would come, ask the audience to name a chairperson, make his presentation, and attempt to establish a local association and have a board of directors elected.

One evening my father was to speak in the town of Carman. The hall was full but the audience refused to give him a chairperson — no one wanted to be seen on the platform with him. Finally it was enough: in his accented English he delivered his verdict: "You know folks, I have read much about your town of Carman and I always liked what I read. I have heard much about your town and I always liked what I heard. This afternoon I drove through your town and I liked what I saw.... But now that I have met the people I don't think so much of it anymore."

I was less diplomatic. At Boissevain, as soon as I finished my presentation, a man, thirtyish, rose: "What do you want here? We're getting along fine without help from you. We don't need people with foreign names coming here telling us what to do. Just because people like you cannot make it on the farm doesn't mean the rest of us can't. Go back to the country you came from."

This needed to be handled delicately: "Listen. When my parents immigrated to this country and brought me with them, they had to prove to the immigration authorities they were mentally and physically fit to support themselves and contribute to the country. In your case, you son-of-a-bitch, you were born here and the country had no choice but to accept you."

The silence was ominous — and lasted forever. Then someone began applauding. Slowly it spread through-out the hall. I was safe.

At Homewood, my local contact, Marcel, rode with me introducing me to farmers. Our last call, at dusk, was to a neighbour who coldly invited us into the well-lived-in house and the family sat down to supper. Unusual for historically hospitable farm homes, they did not even offer us coffee. The truculent, lanky, hawk-faced farmer in his early thirties was no friend and the family got his message: the two cherub-faced, under-ten, boys noisily masticated their food while surreptitiously making faces in our direction and his short, black-haired, ill-tempered wife fairly snarled at us. He was a *free-enterpriser* who needed no union: "I've bin gettin along nicely without you guys until now. All you gotta do to beat the system is be a good farmer."

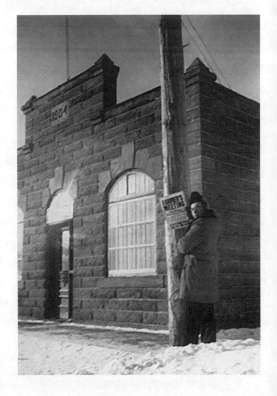

"But will you agree you would not be hurt by working with your fellow-farmers to collectively bargain for better prices?"

"'Collectively' means I gotta do like others want. I wanna do what I wanna do. I don't need nobody. I'm a good farmer."

"But the Crowsnest freight rates were won by collective action and surely you will agree they are of value to you?"[9]

Author at work posting MFU meeting.

MFU Annual Convention, Winnipeg, 1952, with 722 registered delegates plus about 400 visitors.

"No I won't. If it weren't for the Crow rates my neighbours would have to sell me their feed grain cheap for my cattle."

"You can't get rich by feeding cheap grain to cheap cattle."

"You can do it if you're a good farmer."

"What about the Canadian Wheat Board? It was won through the pressure of farm organizations and surely you benefit from it."

"If it weren't for the Wheat Board I could sell my grain at spot prices instead of pooling it with everyone else's grain."

"But how would you know when to sell it?"

"I would watch the market. You just gotta be a good farmer."

It was futile so we excused ourselves. He accompanied us to the door. It was a beautiful evening and the full October moon bathed the farmyard in light. It was not a prepossessing sight: the roof of the barn had collapsed; the machinery looked abused; a litter of pigs squealed piteously in the near distance; the dozen head of livestock were mooing for their next meal.

There, in the middle of the yard, needing only a beautiful young woman seductively draped over the hood to make it look like a General Motors' commercial, sat my brand new streamlined 1952 Chevrolet hard-top with the dark green lower panel and the white roof gleaming ethereally in the moonlight. The farmer stared: "That's a nice car you have there, Marcel."

"Oh, that's not mine. It's Mr. Schulz's car."

The farmer gulped: "Mr. Schulz's car! How did he get a car like that?"

"I got it because I'm a good farmer," I told him.

One bitter February day, on my way to a Bay Route Association convention in Prince Albert, two Saskatchewan farmers entered the train coach and sat facing me. We did not introduce ourselves. For an hour they spoke of farm problems, their conversation liberally spiced with references to "that son-of-a-bitch Schulz."

Finally they took note of me, introduced themselves, and asked my name. I tried to disappear into my parka hood: "I could not avoid hearing your conversation. I understand there are two Schulz sons-of-bitches. There's an old one and a young one. Which one were you referring to?

"Oh, the old bugger is not too bad. We've heard him speak and he makes some sense. But from what we have been told the young one is a real son-of-a-bitch." So I admitted: "Well, I'm the young son-of-a-bitch Schulz."

There were moments of reward. In the southern Manitoba Belgian-Catholic town of Dunrea one miserably cold evening the hall was full, and in the middle of the audience sat the local priest — an ominous sign for an organization which had been linked to communism. At the end of the presentation there were a few hesitant questions displaying some interest, but no one offered to sign a membership form. Then the priest stood up: "It is not up to me to say if an MFU association should be formed here, but if you people decide to do so you can use the Parish Hall for your meetings free of charge."

Almost every farmer in the hall signed up, an association was established, and a local board of directors elected.

There were moments of terror. In my home town of Grandview, with its strong loyalties to the co-operatives, there were serious tensions.[10] Many joined the MFU to gain a voice in their affairs, but others resisted strenuously because they felt their existing voice, the MFAC, was being cavalierly destroyed.

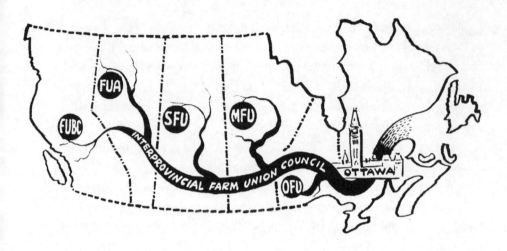

Cartoon depicting IFUC movement gathering strength as it sweeps out of the West toward Ottawa.

For several years after the advent of the MFU, loud arguments reverberated through the legion hall and monthly meetings were packed as people were drawn by the vigour of the debates and the implied promise of mayhem as to the bullring by the implied promise of bloodshed. Then, as the MFU prevailed, arguments became less vigorous — and attendance fell.

One evening, before the meeting, I visited Bill Lukie. He was a master farmer who usually looked like a slob in his greasy bib overalls, week-old beard and battery-acid-burned Mary Maxim sweater. He was pugnacious, the most profane man I had ever known (who never worked on Sunday) and loud — if he could not be seen on the street he could be heard. But he had a native intelligence, an innate sense of reality, and a razor-sharp mind. That got him elected president of the Grandview local of the MFU.

"Bill, we have a problem. Ever since we stopped having loud arguments at our meetings people have stopped coming. Tonight you and I will stage a fight to attract some attention."

Bill readily agreed. The meeting completed its agenda, and the audience of about fifty persons seemed ready to go home. I rose: "Mr. Chairman, I note the attendance at our monthly meetings is getting smaller and smaller and I am wondering if you, as president, are doing enough to build the local." Bill took his cue like a fish takes bait.

His voice rose several decibels: "Oh, so guys like you who wear suits and use big words think I'm not doing enough to build the union. Every day I talk to farmers. What the hell have you done for the union lately?"

"Well, Mr. Chairman, I'm not … I was only just saying.…"

"You were saying shit. You were saying I am not doing my job. Step outside and tell me that." He advanced down the centre aisle toward me, fists balled. He was about to reduce me to a grease spot right there in front of an audience. He had misunderstood: he had taken my word "fight" literally when I had merely meant that we should have an argument. I apologized abjectly and he, disappointed, returned to the podium.

But it worked. Within minutes the beer parlour and the poolroom emptied and the hall filled. For several meetings after that we had people virtually hanging off the rafters. When attendance began to drop off, we went through our act again — but with a more explicit understanding of our roles.

There were moments of revelation and muted triumph. In the autumn of 1951 much of the bumper crop of barley in west-central Manitoba was covered by an early snowfall in the swath stage. The next spring, as though to compensate, was early and hot, and combines were brought out to retrieve what was possible. The quality of the grain was good, but the weathering and spring heat caused a high percentage of kernels to crack while harvested. On delivery, my pool elevator agent explained anything with much more than 6 per cent cracked kernels must be down-graded to #2 feed. The price differential was seven cents a bushel. My neighbours reported the same experience. We groused but resigned ourselves. One day I hauled a load of barley to town. My MPE agent was at lunch but had left the elevator open. I parked my truck on the scales and, while waiting, crossed the street to say "hello" to the United Grain Growers agent whom I knew socially.

He was not in his office. Lying on his countertop, where I could not avoid seeing it, was a letter, addressed to all United Grain Growers agents, from their head office.

The letter informed them the Board of Grain Commissioners had, at a special meeting in late April 1952, ordered that tolerance of cracks in #1 feed barley be increased to 30 per cent. This meant automatic upgrading and a price increase of many thousands of dollars on many hundreds of thousands of bushels of barley. I knew the function of the board was to police the grain trade and that, on such matters, their word was law.

Returning to the pool elevator, I asked the agent: "Dave, did you receive such a letter?"

"No." To confirm his statement, I asked the four other agents in the Grandview Pool Elevator Association. None had received it.

I wrote to the MPE head office inquiring if they had received such an order and, if so, had they circulated it to their agents. They replied they had not considered the order important enough to circulate to their agents. The increased prices from the upgraded grain had gone to the company instead of to the farmers.

I was furious. But how to force compensation?

In February, the Inter-Provincial Farm Union Council met with the board of Grain Commissioners, and I attended.[11] The three commissioners, led by the authoritative-appearing chairman, D. G. McKenzie,[12] sat on a dais. Below were several dozen Farmer's Union people, led by jut-jawed, trigger-tempered Joe Phelps.

Phelps presented the union brief. It contained a veiled suggestion that the board was overly sympathetic to the grain elevator companies. The board chairman stopped him: "Mr. Phelps. That is not correct."

"I say it is and I say we have plenty of evidence...."

Phelps was challenging the integrity of the board. Visibly annoyed, the chairman interjected, but Phelps was adamant: "Mr. McKenzie, I have the floor."

"Mr. Phelps, the chairman of a meeting always has the floor."

Phelps stood and leaned forward like a leashed Doberman: "Mr. McKenzie, I have the floor now and what the hell are you going to do about it?"

It was an embarrassing exchange. The patrician McKenzie attempted to disengage, appearing confused. It was my moment: "Mr. Chairman. You stated your board polices grain grading and that in so doing you do not favour the grain buying industry."

"That is correct."

"Then if I brought you evidence that a certain grain company improperly took advantage of farmers, you would prosecute?" He appeared momentarily uncertain, but then: "Yes!"

Next morning I took my letters to McKenzie. He was uneasy: "But you are a member of Manitoba Pool Elevators. Do you want us to prosecute your own company?"

"I want you to do your job. This company took advantage of the farmers by paying them less than they were entitled to."

On my next visit to Winnipeg, I went to McKenzie's office and asked what action had been taken. He was visibly embarrassed: "I think it better that you inquire of the pool management."

MPE General Manager Bob Steele admitted to being contacted by the board but would say no more. I went back to McKenzie: "I want to know and I want to know now. Did you take any action against MPE?" He was clearly under strain: "Yes." His voice was weak, as though wary of the word.

"So what did you do?" He looked around as for an escape route: "We fined them."

"How much?"

"Twenty-five dollars."

There were moments of exasperation. Along the 150-mile crescent from Roblin to Neepawa, 1953 and 1954 were "the summers of rain." In areas with run-off from the south slope of the Duck Mountains or the north and east slopes of the Riding Mountains, crops were either not seeded or drowned out. I ploughed down seven hundred acres of crop that came up weeds. Others did likewise. Through no fault of our own, many farmers were desperate. To our appeals, the Government of Manitoba responded that we should apply to the Government of Canada for assistance under the *Prairie Farm Assistance Act*.

In mid-1953 a meeting of a number of MFU locals at Dauphin instructed Peter Burtniak from Fork River,[13] and me, to visit federal Minister of Agriculture James Gardiner who was at his home at Lemberg, Saskatchewan, during the summer recess. We took with us Gildas Molgat, newly elected Liberal MLA for the Ste. Rose area, and Raymond Mitchell, MLA for the Grandview–Gilbert Plains area since defeating my father in 1949.

Gardiner,[14] a short, stocky, gnome-like man, met us in the living room of his impressive farm home, Pleasantview. He had been premier of Saskatchewan 1926–29 and 1934–35, and federal minister of agriculture since 1935 — and creator of PFAA, designed to assist farmers with crop losses due to natural disasters.

In shirtsleeves and suspenders, rotund belly straining at the buttons of his shirt, slouched in his large upholstered chair, he was open, informal, unpretentious, forthcoming — and aware he must speak carefully because he was a minister of the Crown.

Burtniak and I made our case. Gardiner had informed himself: "You clearly have a disaster in the making, but it is spotty and limited to drainage basins rather than being general throughout large administrative areas. PFAA rules require assistance be applied only on a township basis. Your problem is that, while a number of townships are affected, there are areas within each that are not. Under the circumstances, PFAA is of no help to you."

We spoke at length. Finally Burtniak tried another approach: "Mr. Minister. We appreciate what you have told us about the limitations of PFAA. However, that does not alleviate the problems of the farmers whose crops have been totally destroyed and whose farms are going up for tax sale. It is my understanding the federal government has funds for emergency situations. We may not qualify for PFAA funds but, as you have said, we have disaster. Is it possible to obtain relief for the affected farmers through your emergency funding legislation?"

Gardiner thought a moment: "Yes, we have such funding available. But to get that you must have this declared a disaster area by your provincial government and they can then apply to us for emergency funds."

Tall, handsome, athletic, well-groomed, neatly dressed Peter Burtniak, looking more a school teacher than a farmer, glanced at me. Gardiner had virtually offered us a blank cheque and asked us to apply for it. And two Manitoba MLA's, of the same political party as Gardiner, had witnessed all this. We had it made.

During the discussion Mitchell and Molgat, whom we had brought as our heavy artillery, said nothing. On the way home they said little but there was no need to. Gardiner had told us what to do.

Several weeks later the four of us met with Premier Douglas Campbell and his minister of agriculture, callow, shallow, and abrasive Ronald Robertson. Campbell was not sympathetic and Robertson considered the

Farmer's Union temerity in even approaching government as a personal affront and the issue as a political argument rather than a natural disaster, was brutal. To them this was an isolated case affecting few *good* farmers and they saw no need for relief.

I resented their attitude: "Mr. Premier. I address myself to you directly rather than to this poor excuse for a minister. The fact is this will cost you little except the time to declare a disaster area and contact Ottawa. Mr. Gardiner virtually told us the funds are available subject only to Manitoba applying for them."

Campbell was irate: "I don't believe you. And if Gardiner wants us to declare a disaster area let him ask us to declare a disaster area."

Burtniak and I looked across the Premier's office to Mitchell and Molgat for confirmation of what Gardiner had told us to do.

They said nothing.

There were moments of wonder. I was driving to Winnipeg after an MFU meeting at Grahamdale, in the Interlake, at 2:30 a.m. A violent early-winter blizzard blew from the northwest, the road was invisible, the car weaved from side to side between the high snowbanks on both sides of the narrow highway, and I peered at the magic figures created by the swirling snow in the headlights, lurking like some gaseous *Fata Morgana* just beyond comprehension.

What a marvellous contrast! I was enveloped in this fierce, threatening maelstrom created by nature, inside the warm cocoon of my comfortable, powerful car, purring through the night and the storm. It was tempting to exclaim with Samuel F.B. Morse when he discovered his telegraph actually functioned, "What hath God wrought!" But clearly this machine was not wrought by God but by the protean genius of man.

How had it happened? Where had it all begun? When did the chemistry become the biology? What triggered the impulse in some ambitious molecule to crawl out of the primal slime and aspire, through self-replication, to immortality? Are we unique on this cosmic flyspeck?[15] And where do we go from here? …

The music on the radio stopped abruptly. The commentator spoke in hushed tones. The radio emitted a mysterious *beep, beep*. It was October 4, 1957. The Soviet Union had launched its Sputnik. Man had propelled himself beyond the gravity of Earth....

It ranked with Galileo's telescopic evidence which moved man from a geocentric to a heliocentric universe and changed our cosmology, and our view of ourselves, by a magnitude.

No one needed to tell me, alone there on that lonely road, in the middle of the night, far from home, threatened by the storm, that the world had changed forever.

In one fateful stroke the multi-billion dollar cross-Canada defence lines had become obsolete and the Strategic Air Command umbrella useless. The time needed to deliver a nuclear bomb by the Soviet Union to the United States or vice versa shrank from six hours to twenty minutes. This triumph of technology would make the Cold War hotter and trigger fingers itchier, but the superpowers would be constrained to fight wars by proxy and maintain the peace between themselves through fear of mutual extinction, while repeatedly testing each other's resolve.[16]

Psychology should have split the atom before nuclear physics but it had not, so our primal instinct for survival needed to cope with our genius for self-immolation. The atom bomb, first seen as making the world unsafe for war, soon bred scientists and spin doctors seeking to impose their nihilistic philosophy on:

> *...poor humanity's afflicted will*
> *Struggling in vain with ruthless destiny.*[17]

But Sputnik was also the first step toward what President Kennedy described as "the greatest adventure on which mankind has ever embarked": twelve years later men landed on the moon.[18] I had witnessed its beginning alone, on a blizzard-swept road.

❖ ❖ ❖

Most rewarding was observing the flowering of an informed public, with the MFU providing the educational thrust. One evening, at an MFU meeting in the little town of Ethelbert, I commented on some recent incident in Parliament. A man rose: "Dat vat you sed is not for true."

I was flustered: "What makes you say that?"

"I haff here da Hansford." He pulled a copy of *Hansard* from the hip pocket of his worn bib overalls and read a passage.

He was right. And I was overwhelmed that this gnarled, shock-haired, unshaven farmer with a grade-five education, who a year earlier did not know *Hansard* existed and still could not pronounce its title properly, had read it. It made the efforts worthwhile.

For the MFU the real problem was the South. Then, as now, a schism ran diagonally through Manitoba roughly along number one highway. The south was established, comparatively prosperous, settled, politically connected, Anglo-Saxon and Conservative. The north was new, raw, economically struggling, politically fluid, mostly central and east European and CCF/ Liberal. The south, with its sturdy folk in well-ordered communities, felt no need for the MFU — they had not yet realized they had more to lose than those with little. Farms were in the third and fourth generation, and their owners were loyal to spokesmen in the co-operatives and the MFAC and suspicious of strangers presuming to have ideas they had not thought of — especially strangers with an accent.

My father raised the issue one day:

> The MFU will never be an effective voice for farmers unless we can bring in the south. Those people have been here for several generations. They have the preponderance of voting strength and the political connections. But the south will never join the union while we have a president with a German name and accent. Go find an Anglo-Saxon to succeed me as president.

I found James Patterson, a gaunt, intelligent, reflective, successful dairy farmer, lay preacher and member of the local UGG board, from Neepawa. He was elected vice-president and on my father's retirement in late 1954, as

James Patterson, MFU President, 1955 – 58 (c. 1958).

president. Three years later he either misunderstood or misjudged. Six days before the 1958 federal election was called, Patterson endorsed Prime Minister Diefenbaker's *Agricultural Prices Stabilization Act* which appeared to support the MFU's main policy, parity prices for farm products. It proved to be a hoax and Patterson paid the price. The MFU began to fray. It achieved a substantial renaissance under its next president, youthful, ebullient, kinetic Rudolph Usick from Erickson, but it never fully recovered its early attraction and a decade later folded itself into the National Farmer's Union, which still maintains a vigil on behalf of the rural community.

And much of its effort was for naught. Short of a *parity price* structure in the marketplace, the MFU saw marketing boards as a mechanism for improving farm prices. We had an example. A generation earlier most farmers produced milk, or cream, picked up at the farm gate by processor's trucks. As the Depression intensified, markets shrank. Each farmer, desperate to sell his product, under-bid his neighbour. They competed each other out of business. The government feared there would be insufficient milk for the children. Today's children might be advised to drink Coke — or beer, but then parents saw some virtue — and food value — in children drinking milk. In 1937 the Bracken government, aware of the destruction wrought by unfettered competition among desperate people, established the Manitoba Milk Marketing Board which set the price of milk and limited production to the available market by issuing individual farm production quotas.

The conventional market system of a handful of buyers and many sellers was stood on its head: there was now a handful of buyers but only a single,

collective seller. It made milk producers the princes of the agricultural
industry, and established the prototype. The MFU made prodigious
efforts to extend this principle into
other areas of monopsony markets
with many sellers and few buyers
(beef, hogs, eggs, chickens, turkeys)
to improve prices.

Just as the MFU began popularizing the idea of collective marketing, governments, both federal and
provincial, began establishing
agencies to lend farmers money.
Farmers found it easier to borrow
money than to establish boards, and

Left to right: Manitoba Agriculture Minister, George Hutton; Manitoba Premier, Duff Roblin; MFU Secretary, Joe Galonsky; MFU President, Rudy Usick. (courtesy Manitoba Archives).

by the time they *were* established the profile of agriculture had changed
radically. Farms were fewer and larger, and many of their owners were
swimming in debt they had been lured into by the illusion of easy loans from
governments and banks alike.

Then they needed more credit to pay interest on existing loans. This
dichotomy of thinking between Depression-moulded fathers and their credit-
hungry sons became expressed in the aphorism, "never live beyond your means,
even if you must borrow to do it." Soon, deep in debt, they left the farms.

This psychology came into sharp focus at the annual convention of the
Manitoba Dairy and Poultry Co-operative in 1958. A debate on the efficacy
of marketing boards for eggs and poultry was sidetracked by a proposal for
the co-op to lend money to egg and poultry producers instead. I argued the
co-op was not a lending agency, that lending money to members meant more
bureaucracy to appraise the financial status of applicants and administer
the loans, and that the natural tendency would be to make most of the loans
to established farmers, thus using the small farmer's money to eliminate
him by supporting the larger farmer. Jim Kitching from Carman followed
me at the microphone:

"We do not need marketing boards to sell our products. We need money to produce more and we will find our own markets. The cost of administering loans is negligible. You just make the loans to the right borrowers. Take me for example. I have eight hundred acres of the best land in Manitoba ..." and he reeled off a list of assets. "If the co-op lends money to me it does not need to waste time administering it or worry about recovering it."

Ray Siemens from Altona, son of "Jake" Siemens who virtually created the Co-operative Movement in southern Manitoba, was faster than I to the microphone, and more succinct: "If Mr. Kitching has those assets he does not need our money."

But the psychology and the credit hunger prevailed. For a time many farmers farmed the banks: then the banks farmed the farmers.

Maxwell Hofford from Swan River, later elected president of the Dairy and Poultry Co-operative (fifteen years later he became first president of the producer-controlled Manitoba Hog Marketing Board) put it all into perspective:

> Mr. Chairman and fellow farmers. The disagreement here is between those who want to preserve the farm as a home for the family and an enterprise in which they can prosper by husbanding the land as a family heirloom, and those who see land as a trade commodity on which they can enrich themselves by eliminating their neighbours and capturing the market in both land and farm products. Farm product marketing boards *will* be established. That is entirely predictable. But instead of it being done now to protect the family farm, because of the nature of the opposition we are seeing here today, it will be done when there is only a handful of producers left in each sector of our industry and they can use the monopoly of the boards to rip off the consumers.

Boards were established, one by one, too late for most farmers. By late 2001, the number of Manitoba producers was approximately: eggs — 180; chickens — 124; turkeys — 67. And the problem was not that this increased consumer prices — marketing boards are intended to get income from the consumer rather than from government — but that the *family farm* had become a memory and the benefits accrued to a handful of farmers and agri-business investors.

The damage was permanent. Joe Phelps, a successful farmer and president of the Saskatchewan Farmer's Union, predicted in 1954: "The yeoman farmer who opened the West and built the community is being reduced to a serf. If vertical integration of agriculture continues, he will end up as a hired man on his own land working for tax-subsidized, non-resident investors."

"Iron Man" Maxwell Hofford (c. 1962), a Bowsman farmer, District MFU Director, Provincial MFAC Director (1955 – 58), Chair of the Manitoba Agriculture Credit Corporation and first Chairman of the Manitoba Hog Marketing Board (1971 – 76).

Forty-five years later, many of what is left of family farms are facing the obscenity of having investments of as much as half a million dollars, but needing off-farm income to pay the bills. Meanwhile, tax-subsidized agribusiness has moved in. Instead of farmers owning the processing facilities as envisioned by some farm leaders, processors acquired the farms and hired the farmers to operate them. In 2001, when Maple Leaf Foods purchased several huge hog farms and Schneider's meat processors, their vision was reversed: we had many sellers – but a single buyer.

It was so predictable. But the MFU was unable to counter the myopia and/or political agenda of established spokesmen. The *family farm* became the victim of opinion-moulders and policy-makers who paid lip service to the idea, but whose policies — by design or inadvertence — emanated from a different vision.

❖ ❖ ❖

5

The Campaign for Cash Advances

Nothing is as difficult as initiating a new order of things;
the reformer has enemies in all who profit from the old order
and only weak defenders among the public, who do not believe
in anything new until they have had the experience of it.
NICCOLO MACHIAVELLI, *The Prince, 1513*

THE MANITOBA FARMER'S UNION had much energy sapped by its endless fight with the Manitoba Federation of Agriculture and Co-operation and the commercial co-operatives that fed it. The founding of the MFU led to instant warfare with the MFAC on the question of which would be the farmer's spokesman. This led to enormous economic, political, and social complications. While the MFU was a direct-membership organization — a farmer had to pay to get in — the MFAC was the creation of, and funded by, the co-operatives. Any member of a co-operative was automatically a member of the MFAC. Since most MFU members were also members of at least one (and sometimes half a dozen) co-operatives, they were in the invidious position of having one organization, on their behalf, stating they favoured some policy, while the other, also ostensibly speaking for them, claimed they did not.

Much venom would have been drawn out of the conflict had the MFAC accepted the MFU's challenge to go to a direct-membership basis. But the MFAC leadership feared their organization would not survive such an attempt, and the co-op leaders, the real policy makers, needed the MFAC as a conduit for presenting their farm policies and as a front through which to fight the MFU's claim to be farm policy spokesman. Therefore, while the fight was ostensibly between the MFU and the MFAC, the battleground became the co-operatives everyone supported but which were being torn apart in the internecine struggle. It led to misunderstandings, a lamentable waste of time and energy, shattered friendships, and intense intra-community conflicts "until the third generation."

As a member of the MFU, but having been active in the MFAC and become friends with many fine young persons in it, I saw myself as a bridge between the MFAC and the MFU. But disenchantment with my self-assumed role came quickly. I was seen as a "traitor to my class." My efforts ended tastelessly when the daughter of a friend attended the MFAC summer camp, Wannakumbac: "I am Camp, I am sunlight; A sheen on the waters, a mist on the mountains, and stars,"[1] at Clear Lake, Manitoba, and reported that all the cabins there were named after well-known persons in the Co-operative Movement – and the outdoor biffy was named "SCHULZ."

Almost perversely, policy positions of the leadership of the MFAC and the MFU were frequently opposite to each other. Since the needs of the farmers appeared to be the same regardless of which organization they were in, MFU members concluded that the reason for this divergence lay in the independence of the MFAC as a vigorous farm advocate being limited by its dependence on the co-operatives for funding. They also concluded this relationship was unwittingly dragging the co-operatives, which all supported, into the mire of the MFAC–MFU conflict. They conceded that the co-operatives, as commercial organizations, needed the goodwill of governments and should be wary of advocating radical farm policies that offended governments.[2] But a farm organization must do so, so they pleaded for separation of the MFAC from the co-operatives. They pleaded in vain.

There was only one apparent solution: MFU members who were also members of the MFAC must take over the MFAC conventions and make policy more to their liking. But the local co-op associations controlled the credentials: a maximum of ten each — depending on membership — to district, and three each to annual conventions of the MFAC. Throughout Manitoba, wherever the MFU had strength, its members began infiltrating annual meetings of local associations of co-operatives and voting credentials to themselves.

This required hundreds of quiet little meetings and thousands of phone calls. Those attending these little *klatches* knew "loose lips sink ships." Being on party telephone lines, we devised code names to identify individuals. The president of the Grandview MFU association was "Violent" because his eyes bulged and his voice rose menacingly when he spoke on any subject. The MFAC district director, a middle-aged woman of good heart but questionable competence, became "Babe," because of her tendency to weep when she lost a vote. The Manitoba Pool Elevator Provincial Director was "Apollo." The secretary of the UGG local association, a surly, officious type,

Edward Puchalski, Grandview farmer, MFAC District Director and MFU Provincial Director, with his wife, Mary (c. 1956).

through a chance remark that "this man was once a Justice of the Peace — back in the days when they wore three-cornered hats — of course he had the head to fit it," became known as "the man with the three-cornered head." My primary fellow conspirator, erudite, articulate Edward Puchalski, though fifteen years my senior, because of his six-foot two-inch frame became known as my "bodyguard" but in our code he was "Slats." I, for no discernible reason except that the acronym for the word resembled that of a popular scatological term, was "Buckshot."

So we planned and plotted like guerrilla warriors. Slowly MFAC conventions were swamped by MFU members and policy resolutions began assuming an uncanny resemblance to those of the MFU.

It was not easy. Whenever it appeared the MFU people would win a point, an MFAC director would quote some obscure section of the MFAC constitution to impede us. So we memorized the MFAC constitution. Then they began quoting the constitutions of the various co-operatives — until we memorized those. When that failed they quoted *Robert's Rules of Order*, which was always interpreted against us. So we memorized *Robert's Rules*. Then they quoted at random from the *Companies Act* — so we memorized it.

The boards of the co-operatives inimical to the MFU responded with tighter control of the agenda and of credentials to the MFAC policy-making conventions. They simply handed the convention credentials to their friends, shutting out the dissidents. We strenuously pointed out the MFAC constitution stated delegates "shall be elected," which, to us, meant being chosen at a membership meeting instead of being *appointed* by the directors. Gradually, many boards were forced into reluctant agreement, and throughout west-central Manitoba MFU members took control of the meetings and captured an increasing number of credentials.

At a meeting of the Dairy and Poultry Pool Association at Grandview, my hometown, we elected the *wrong* delegates. The secretary, defending the status quo, refused to surrender the credentials. That led to some harsh dialogue, and almost mayhem.

The meeting ended and we dispersed. We were on the second floor of the Dairy and Poultry building. I was about to take the first step down to the ground floor on a steep, temporary stairway, with no handrail, where a misstep could lead to a broken arm — or neck, when I felt a tap on my shoulder.

I turned, with my back to the large opening above the rickety stairs — and a ten-foot drop. The secretary's husband, a large, powerful, middle-aged man, his face beet-red with fury, stood two feet from me. He shook his huge fist in my face, and roared: "I wish to Christ I had let you drown in that damn creek before you could speak English."

At age four, a very recent immigrant unable to speak English, I had fallen into the creek that separated our farm from his. I would have drowned had he not, by sheer accident, passed by and pulled me out. I had forgotten that incident of thirty years earlier, but now memory came flooding back. I owed him my life. But this was war. My reply was a model of taunting arrogance: "Mr. Evans, I have long known you resent the fact that I speak better English than you do." He blustered but retreated and, for a second time, probably saved my life.

Puchalski and I, who shipped our grain through MPE, bought United Grain Growers membership cards just to be able to vote for their delegates to the MFAC conventions. We asked the chairman of the board to call a membership meeting to elect MFAC delegates. He promised. We soon realized he would not. So we placed an ad in the local newspaper, stating the time and place of a meeting to be held, and sent the bill to the board secretary.

On the appointed evening, eighteen men, all MFU as well as UGG members, attended. The only board member present was the secretary, *the man with the three-cornered head*, who had become almost a caricature of an elected official. He refused to participate. So I was elected chairman, and Puchalski secretary, of the meeting. We explained the purpose of the meeting, discussed several resolutions, and elected ten delegates.

And then the board secretary, having sulked silently apart throughout the process, pursed his lips and smugly, in his usual precise manner, asked triumphantly: "Well, Mr. Schulz. Now that you have elected your delegates to the convention, how do you propose to obtain the credentials?"

"Well, Mr. Britton. Since you graced this meeting with your august presence, we assumed you brought them."

"Well, Mr. Schulz. That would have been impossible. Our directors had a meeting last week. We appointed our delegates to the convention and distributed the credentials."

Trumped!

But we had anticipated this.

"Well, Mr. Britton. we assumed as much. Therefore I manufactured ten credentials on my trusty portable typewriter."

I drew the credentials from my shirt pocket, signed them as chairman of the meeting while Puchalski signed them as secretary, and distributed them to those elected. The *man with the three-cornered head*, aghast, muttered darkly that such mischievous Machiavellian machinations would get us nowhere.

Three weeks later, at the MFAC district convention at Dauphin, the Grandview UGG Association was entitled to ten delegates. But it had sent twenty: ten *appointed* by the board but with official credentials, and ten *elected* at a membership meeting but with homemade credentials. Ten had to go. Quoting relevant sections of the MFAC constitution, we convinced the convention chairman, a member of the old guard, he must rule that those *elected*, despite their unorthodox credentials, were the official delegates. Then, to ensure there would be no retractions in the event of an authoritative

John Zaplitny (Fred's brother) an Oak Brae farmer, MFU Director, and the first person to break the hold of established leaders with his election as MFAC Provincial Director, 1954.

phone call from head office in Winnipeg, we replaced the chairman with one of our own.

Other MFU activists, in other areas of Manitoba (among many others, Max Hofford at Bowsman, George Higgs at Swan River, Ed Diziak at Dauphin, Eggert Siggurdson at Kenville, John Zaplitny at Fork River, Rudy Usick at Erickson, Ray Spencer at Russell, Sam Uskiw at Selkirk, Clarence Baker at Beausejour, Mike Sotas at Oakburn, George Henderson at Manitou, Russell Barnlund at Sanford, Nick Manchur at Starbuck, Ray Siemens at Altona — the last four in southern Manitoba) likewise infiltrated the MFAC. Soon we controlled the delegate body. We controlled the district conventions. We controlled the provincial convention. We wrote the resolutions. We made the policies.

It gained us nothing. The provincial board of the MFAC, relying on the support of the incumbent boards of the many co-operatives, simply ignored the mandate of their conventions.

So, with almost military precision, we began taking over the boards of local co-operatives. This was intended to end their financial support to the MFAC and as a first step towards taking over the provincial board of the MFAC. In late 1951 four MFU members, including myself, were elected to the board of directors of the Grandview MPE Association, giving us a majority. The same was done elsewhere, and not exclusively in west-central Manitoba. Then I and a number of other MFU members were elected delegates to the policy-making annual convention of Manitoba Pool Elevators; Manitoba's largest co-operative, established in 1923 to buy farmer's grain and keep the profits in the farmer's hands.

This was to bring me into direct, and permanent, conflict with Manitoba's pre-eminent spokesman for agriculture, the internationally respected, powerful panjandrum of Manitoba's largest and most successful, multi-million dollar commercial co-operative, This was the contemplative, soft-spoken, aristocratic president of Manitoba Pool Elevators, William J. Parker.[3]

Parker had been elected to the board of MPE in 1930 and become president in 1940. He shepherded Manitoba's primary co-operative from a near-bankrupt upstart to a thirty-five-thousand-member organization handling more than half the wheat and coarse grains delivered in Manitoba. It gained an international reputation and had a series of profit statements almost boring in their predictability. I saw him as much like my father: a successful farmer with wider interests who knew what he wanted to do and how to get it done and who, in his contemplative moments, had the look of a visionary. Parker took both his job and status seriously, and I, like all who knew him, was in awe of him.

He knew his stuff and was not to be trifled with. The prospect of challenging him to verbal combat on a convention floor made the blood run cold and the eyes glaze, and was contemplated only by the brave or foolhardy. And I was neither. I had no intention of trifling with him — or with anything relative to MPE. For me, the green country kid, attending the vaunted MPE convention — and as a delegate yet — was like a novitiate priest allowed into the sanctum sanctorum of the Vatican, and seemed the nearest to Heaven I would ever get.

Until I introduced my resolution.

Parker's response made us mortal enemies, changed the direction of my thinking, and made me the *bête noir* of half the province.

A year earlier, two incidents had affected me deeply. The second made me a lifetime conditional cynic about how good men could be corrupted by peer pressure or desire for power. The first gave me a lifetime profound respect for how ordinary people with common sense could find solutions not dreamed of in the philosophies of the technicians and the bureaucrats.

Our basic problem was wheat: we had too much of it. We could not sell it so we could not convert it into money. And we were powerless to change the situation. It mattered not if we had frozen wheat, or wet wheat, or no wheat, or a half crop, the stocks of surplus wheat kept growing.

In 1952 we had a bumper crop and, in the autumn, farmers' grain bins were full but their pockets empty. The banks would not take stored grain as collateral and the farmers faced the paradox, metaphorically, of starving while the pantry was bursting; and literally, of having a bounteous harvest but being unable to pay their bills or property taxes, leading to long lists of farm tax sales notices. Because we could not pay our creditors — the fuel agent, the fertilizer distributor, the grocer — entire communities verged on bankruptcy. Bulging bins and tall cones of grain heaped like pyramids attested to our productive capacity: we were crop rich but cash poor. We could not pay our bills until we converted the inventory into cash, which we could not do until we delivered the grain to the elevators, which we could not do because the elevators were full. The paradox caused some wag to muse:

> Here lies the body of farmer Pete
> He starved because he produced too much to eat

Even when the grain pipeline began emptying and we should have been able to sell, we could not ship: there was invariably a maddening shortage of boxcars. They were hauling other goods, or being repaired, or in the United States, or parked on some siding, but they were not available for hauling grain. Sales orders were cancelled and ships lay at anchor in Canadian ports at great cost in demurrage charges paid by the farmers, or they moved to American ports and Canadian sales were lost.[4]

Farmers were desperate. And our leaders had no solutions.

At a meeting of the Grandview MFU association, one evening in the autumn of 1952, a tall, lean man in his early forties, stood up: "I subscribe to several American agricultural magazines. The Americans have had, for twenty years now, a method of coping with this problem. Perhaps it is worth considering."

He concisely explained how the government of the United States advanced to the farmer an interest-free loan to be recovered on delivery, a percentage of the value of his grain in storage on the farm. If that were instituted here the costs would be negligible but benefits immeasurable. It offered early infusion of money into the semi-morbid corpus of the rural economy.

I listened and my metabolism raced. What a marvellous scheme: no fuss, no muss, no cost, no risk, no loss, only gain for all. It was a *win–win* situation before the term was coined. Because of the delivery quota system imposed years earlier by the Canadian Wheat Board, the central selling agency, every grain farmer's acreage and production record was registered on the delivery permit books filed in the offices of the grain elevator agents across western Canada. Each farmer would apply through the elevator agents and receive an advance on 50 per cent of the grain he claimed to have in storage. The bins need not even be inspected.

The Government of Canada would loan the necessary funds to the Canadian Wheat Board, which would administer them through the commercial elevator system. The government would be repaid when the Wheat Board sold the grain. The only costs were the interest on the money borrowed by the Wheat Board, and the time needed to make the applications and write the cheques.

The proposal was breathtaking in its scope and simplicity. I approached its author: "Your proposal is so simple and practical and promises such economic benefits that I curse myself for not having thought of it. Why have we not heard from you before? Who are you?"

"My name is Ed Puchalski. I farm ten miles directly west of town and you farm eight miles directly south of town, which is probably why we have never met. I have been to several MFU meetings and liked what I heard. But you need help. Count me in from now on."

I did. We became bosom companions. We travelled many miles together and mentally reconstructed the world many times, until his death forty-two years later. But that evening, with his proposal, Ed Puchalski actually reconstructed the economy of western Canada.

The MFU immediately adopted the proposal of cash advances for farm stored grain and it instantly became a political issue. The policy, once in place, became so popular among both farmers and rural businessmen that today there would be a revolution if it were terminated. But getting it put in place was another matter.

My other experience, a month later, was different. I stood for nomination as delegate for the Grandview Association to the policy-making annual convention of Manitoba Pool Elevators in October, 1953.[5] Two others were also nominated. By then tensions between the MFU and the MFAC had divided the community.

About 250 MPE members were in attendance. I knew most by name and knew how they would vote. I knew the membership would split on the rock of myself: people would vote either for me or against me. But I had been elected to the board of the local MPE association so I obviously had some support. I would get most of the votes south of town, Alex Morran would get most of the votes north of town, and Bob Wilson, a very fine person but with no particular constituency either for or against him, would get a handful. I knew that I would win or run a close second.

I ran third.

I would be neither the delegate nor alternate delegate who would receive the convention credentials if the delegate was unable to attend. I would not be attending the convention in any capacity to promote my new obsession with the policy of cash advances on farm-stored grain.

When the meeting adjourned, I left the hall deeply disturbed by the inexplicable discrepancy — less by the loss of the election than by my apparent misreading of the mood of the community and my influence in it. Two neighbours approached me: "Herb, we believe you lost because Mr. Crossley did not count the votes properly."

MPE Provincial Director Watson Crossley had counted the ballots. Earlier, to aid in his presentation of the annual report, he had set up a large blackboard, on a tripod, on the stage at the front of the hall. He had taken the ballots behind the blackboard to count them.

"I don't believe you."

"We were sitting against the wall of the hall. From that angle we could see him past the edge of the blackboard. We saw him stuffing ballots into the pockets of his suit jacket."

Watson Crossley of Grandview, in his fifties, was a large, quiet, rumpled man with no intellectual pretensions, unassuming in both his personal life and his public persona. He was a charter member and long-time provincial director for MPE District No. 7, the largest in Manitoba, and active in other co-ops. He was initiator of a local farm implement museum, founding member of the local CCF association, Sunday school teacher, competent farmer, holder of a diploma in agriculture from the University of Manitoba, and had an earned reputation as a righteous citizen.

And my idol. For half a dozen years I had raptly listened to his low-key annual reports. This was the kind of man I aspired to be. To me Watson Crossley was a model of personal rectitude and public morality. No, Mr. Crossley could not have done that! But in my heart I knew he had.

After this incident Ed Puchalski, who had read Homer, code-named Crossley "Apollo," the sun god who betrayed Hector at Troy.

"When the votes are being tabulated always watch the guy with the pencil. He decides how the vote count is recorded," my boyhood chum, Fred Kempf, had said to me at a meeting a year earlier. At the time I considered it a cynical remark. Now I learned to watch "the guy with the pencil."

I spoke of the incident to only my wife and Puchalski. Next year I was again nominated as delegate to the annual convention of MPE. Just before the ballots were distributed, I moved a motion that each nominee appoint his own scrutineer. The howls of protest were deafening: "Don't you trust Mr. Crossley to count the ballots?"

It was precisely what I had anticipated: "This is not an issue of trust in Mr. Crossley. But losing candidates sometimes raise ugly questions. It is precisely to protect trust in our provincial director, who must be seen as above reproach, that I move my motion. I should think Mr. Crossley would be the first to support it and relieve himself of potential future criticism."

It worked. Each candidate appointed his own scrutineer to count the ballots. I was elected delegate to the 1954 MPE convention. To the end of the decade I was re-elected whenever I chose to run. So I was delegate for the Grandview MPE Association — the largest in Manitoba — during the turbulent 1950s, while the resolution on cash advances was working its way into MPE policy.

But how to even get the resolution to the policy convention? Differences of opinion make the world go round and life exciting by their extreme unpredictability. What appears an irrefutable proposition to one may appear a travesty to another. Not every farmer immediately saw — or wanted to see — the value of the proposal: it was something new; it was not *their* idea; they feared cheating; they misunderstood it; they feared hidden costs; it might encourage farmers to overspend; they suspected that anything sounding so simple must have internal defects. Some did not like it because of the politics: the proposal was being promoted by the "wrong" people — known members of the CCF and of the MFU.

The bi-section of Manitoba by Number One Highway was replicated in many communities as settlers sought to be near their own kind. In Grandview, the CNR (which on its initial run in 1896 brought the legendary passenger who alighted from the train, observed the verdantly treed valley sloping down from the foot of the Duck Mountains and up the foot of the Riding Mountains twenty miles south, and uttered the incantation "This a grand view!" and had thereby given the place a name) was paralleled by Number Five Highway. In general terms, they marked an approximate division. To the north were the original settlers, arriving in the 1890s by wagon train, mostly Anglo-Saxon, Anglican/Presbyterian/United Church, and Conservative/Liberal. To the south were those arriving a generation later by railroad train, mostly from the territories of the disintegrated Austro-Hungarian and Czarist Empires, Lutheran/Catholic/Orthodox, Liberal/CCF, and some touched by the various "isms" of Europe. Over time, all became the best of neighbours, but initially there were the invisible divisions of race, nationality, religion, language, history, psychology, geography, and the relative *status* of pioneer vs. parvenu.

So the obscenity continued. Because of the limited markets and congested grain elevators, the Wheat Board established delivery quotas for farmers in western Canada. Periodically, as the market permitted, the board, usually on short notice, would announce a quota opening allowing farmers to deliver perhaps one bushel per seeded acre. That caused an immediate rush to the *sentinels of the Prairies*, the tallest structures in most towns, where the grain was dumped and a cheque received. But elevator space was limited. Those near town, or friendly with an elevator agent who alerted them in advance, would get there first. Others would wait in long lines, hoping there would still be space when their truck arrived, tortoise-like, at the grain elevator door.

Some had to haul their grain home and shovel it back into the bin. Some did not learn of the quota opening until the elevators were full. To beat their neighbours, farmers got up earlier and earlier in the morning, or spent the night sleeping in their trucks, parked on the street, waiting for the elevator to open.

For some perverse reason it seemed whenever the quota opened I was away from home, at an MFAC convention, or an MFU meeting, or a CCF conclave, promoting the concept of cash advances. By the time I returned it would be too late: the elevators were full.

"We are fools," I would say to anyone within earshot. "We are so busy attempting to survive financially that we are destroying ourselves as social beings. We work all night seeding, we drive our combines through the night, and now we are even reduced to delivering our grain at night. We never even get to see the damn grain, the fruits of our labours. This is stupid. We are destroying each other and ourselves. Do you not understand all this can be avoided by the payment of cash advances?"

But for some, as for Sophocles, "the remedy was too strong for the disease." My increasingly strident pleas got no support and little sympathy from those, particularly north of town, who still had the political power and still set the economic agenda: "If you weren't so lazy you'd get up earlier in the morning and get your grain to the elevator just like we do, and you wouldn't need those silly cash advances," several said to me.

And then they said it once too often.

I was at an MFU meeting, promoting cash advances, at Manitou, on a Saturday evening. Sometime after midnight I returned to my hotel room. My wife had phoned and left a message: "A one-bushel quota is opening Monday morning."

In the night I drove the three hundred miles to my home.

On Sunday morning I loaded my own and three rented trucks. My three hired men and I drove the four trucks into town, parked them on the ramp against the grain elevator door, locked the brakes and doors, and rode home comfortably in the car in which my wife had followed us. Monday morning, after the deep sleep of the just, we dressed in clean clothes, ate a hearty breakfast, and then my wife drove us the nine miles back to town.

A half-mile-long line of trucks was parked bumper to tailgate, along the streets and the highway, their owners stiff, weary, and hungry after spending the cold late October night in their greasy cabs. And there on the ramp, in plain view of everyone, in front of the elevator door just about to open at 8:00 a.m. were the four trucks carrying my entire quota of 1,160 bushels.

That did it! There was no more talk of laziness. Attitudes changed abruptly. Shortly after, the Grandview Association of MPE almost unanimously passed a resolution requesting the Manitoba Pool Elevator organization to ask the government of Canada to establish a system of advance loans on farm-stored grain.

And I was elected delegate to the annual provincial convention.

"When you go out in public, dress properly. It shows respect for others and for yourself," my father often told me. At times I almost hated him for insisting I wear a suit and tie when others seemed so comfortable in slacks, open-necked shirts and windbreakers. But, at twenty-eight, I had grown into the habit. I arrived at the convention looking as I thought all delegates would look: dark blue suit, colour-coordinated tie, white shirt with starched collar and French cuffs displaying silver-framed onyx cufflinks, black mirror-polished slip-on shoes with socks to match, and carrying my trademark black briefcase. Inadvertently, in the crowd, I became the cynosure of quizzical glances. My suit could not be ignored or easily dismissed. Not so my arguments.

The Grandview resolution was on the floor. Despite believing the idea was so good it could not be opposed, and that if I was capable of understanding its benefits everyone could, I had learned this was not necessarily so among the farmers. But now I was among the elite; those who would understand immediately. Nevertheless, in the event of any vagueness in the resolution, I planned my arguments carefully, point by point:

> First, this proposal asks the Government of Canada to institute a
> system of advance loans on farm-stored grain, to the value of 50 per
> cent of the initial payment, through the elevator system, administered

by the Canadian Wheat Board, with the government absorbing interest and administrative costs.

Second, such advances are not new nor radical. It has been done in the United States for two decades and is supported by all its political parties and farm organizations.

Third, there is nothing mysterious here. This simply gets the farmer his own money sooner than is now the case. The Wheat Board replaces the banks and accepts stored grain as security.

Fourth, it is risk-free. The grain-delivery permit book of every farmer in western Canada is in the office of some elevator agent, who knows each farmer's land and practices. And in any case, the advance will be on only 50 per cent of the stored grain, so the farmer who overestimates gets less upon delivery.

Fifth, this requires no administrative apparatus. The Wheat Board already has all the cheque-writing capacity it needs.

Sixth, the only costs are interest charges which should be paid by Ottawa. It is the tariff and fiscal policies of the Government of Canada, and their refusal to take foreign currencies or trade goods as payment, that have made it difficult for the Wheat Board to sell grain. If the government wishes to use stored grain as a political lever to keep food costs down in Canada, or as a "food bank" to affect foreign policy, it has the obligation to pay costs from the national treasury, not the farmers' pockets. Also, requiring the government to pay the interest costs will induce it to seek more markets.

Finally, it will be a great boon not only to farmers, but to the entire rural community and those who have commerce with it.

Reaction among the delegates was better than expected. Farmer after farmer, including those from southern Manitoba, trooped to the microphone, commented on the marvellous proposal, and endorsed it. My resolution was about to be adopted as policy by Manitoba's premier co-op and largest grain buyer, guided by good, solid businessmen not known to support radical proposals. Best of all, men with personal influence and political connections.

MPE President William J. Parker, fifty-ish, medium height, sturdily built, square-jawed, ruddy-cheeked. sandy hair precisely parted, always appropriately dressed — medium-grey or powder blue pencil-stripe suit with vest by day, and midnight blue pencil-stripe suit with vest for evening functions — always sat on the stage in front of the delegates, with access to the microphone. When he was concentrating his eyes had a tendency to focus inward and in our code he became Cyclops, the one-eyed giant Ulysses encountered in *The Odyssey*. Nothing escaped his laser gaze.

Cyclops rose. As was his habit when rationalizing, the little finger of his left hand was inserted into the corner of his mouth, and he spoke as though he had a mouthful of hot potato: "Gentlemen, this is your convention. I do not want to tell you what to do. But ..." and he rambled about potential problems: some farmers might cheat and thus take advantage of their neighbours; it was ridiculous to believe the government would pay interest costs; the Wheat Board would need to borrow the money to pay the cash advances and the consequent interest charges would reduce farmers' final payments; the Wheat Board might be damaged; the Americans would consider it a subsidy; there would be problems and costs of administration; those taking the advances would have an advantage over those who did not; if the government paid the interest charges on the money advanced, it would cost the Canadian taxpayers; the grain elevator companies, including Manitoba Pool Elevators, did not want to become involved in such a scheme, etc., etc. And finally, his voice rising: "And gentlemen, if you had all that money, what would you do with it?"

God almighty! He was wondering what we would do with the money? I was speechless.

But not others. They had heard their master's voice. One by one delegates, mostly from southern Manitoba, including several who had ten minutes earlier supported my proposal, some in aging wedding-and-funeral suits, scuffed shoes, wilted shirt collars and garish, Christmas-gift ties, trooped to the microphone: "Well, if Mr. Parker thinks we should not have that money then perhaps we should not have it...."

I was stunned. The stupid buggers deserved to go bankrupt.

From that moment, Parker and I saw each other across an unbridgeable gulf. We became two characters in a Greek play, caught between pride and fear, between vanity and common sense, emanating a sense of foreboding as we revolved around a fixed set of circumstances from which there was no escape.

It seemed clear the reasons he gave had little to do with farmer's wants. They desperately wanted the advances. It was the government that did not want it. I heard my father's voice: "In the last analysis, everything is politics...."

And we in the Grandview MPE Association, and others who agreed with us, were disturbing the accepted theology.

At the MPE convention in October 1955, the delegate body rebelled and passed a Grandview resolution instructing the MPE provincial board of directors to: "Petition the federal government to take immediate steps to make available advance payments on farm-stored grain through the Canadian Wheat Board, with the interest and administrative costs to be borne by the federal government."

Similar resolutions were proposed by the MPE associations at Erickson, Birdtail, Belleview, Makaroff — and Baldur. This indicated a new attitude: Baldur was in southern Manitoba.

At a country meeting, Parker had told his audience that MPE meetings "are the essence of democracy in action. They are unlike political meetings where the platform dictates to the floor."

But when the "floor" spoke in favour of cash advances through the Canadian Wheat Board with Ottawa paying costs, the "platform" proceeded to kill "the essence of democracy in action."

On August 14, 1956, a meeting was held in Saskatoon to devise some form of interim financing on farm-stored grain. Attending were representatives from the three prairie farm unions, wheat pools, federations of agriculture, and the UGG. Vice-President George McConnell represented MPE. He supported a proposal for bank loans on applications approved by municipalities, up to four dollars an acre on a maximum of eight hundred acres, with farmers paying interest charges. McConnell proposed that "the interest rate on loans be no higher than that paid by the Canadian Wheat Board."[6]

This proposal, initiated by the federal government, would guarantee banks a percentage of money lost on loans to farmers. The banks decided who got loans. It guaranteed farmers nothing.

On September 8, 1956, a second meeting was held in Saskatoon for the same purpose. The same organizations were represented but the personnel had changed. I replaced former MFAC President Jack Wilton who had been defeated as a provincial director by MFU member George Henderson. I had also been elected a provincial director and the provincial convention had armed me with a resolution favouring "a permanent plan for cash advances on grain in reasonable storage, intended for sale, with interest and administrative charges borne by the federal treasury." A modified version of this proposal was adopted, with support primarily from the three farm unions and the Saskatchewan Wheat Pool.

But not from McConnell who again represented MPE and again supported the bank loan plan. I reminded him of the 1955 MPE resolution favouring cash advances. McConnell admitted such a resolution had been passed but: "The board was reluctant to go along [because] we could not expect to get interest-free money or have administrative costs absorbed [and we] oppose having either the Wheat Board or the grain elevator companies involved."[7]

At the district meeting of MPE at Dauphin, I raised the issue of cash advances. McConnell, on the MPE board since 1931 and VP since 1940, attended. He was a lean, hard-eyed, harsh-voiced, irascible, bombastic, dark-suited farmer, an intellectual lightweight with an authoritarian cast of mind. He responded sharply that President Parker had already stated his opposition to cash advances and that satisfied him they were bad. I was prepared: "Mr. McConnell, at the convention in 1954 Mr. Parker asked what the farmers would do with the money if they got it. I suggest the farmers know exactly what to do with it, like pay their fuel bills and taxes. But perhaps the issue is that Mr. Parker does not need the money so he thinks others do not either. So would you be good enough to tell us what Mr. Parker's salary is?"

"That's none of your damn business."

His barking shout rattled both the hall and the fifty-odd farmers present: "Well, Mr. McConnell, I intend to make it my damn business. We need the money and we intend to get it with your help or without it. Perhaps Mr. Parker does not need the cash advance because he has sufficient income from non-farming sources, but for most MPE members our farm sales receipts are our only income."

Further questions about Parker's off-farm income, or about why the MPE board opposed cash advances, elicited only verbal abuse. It was time, figuratively, for the kick in the testicles.

6

We Win One

The play's the thing,
Wherein I'll catch the conscience of the king.
SHAKESPEARE, *Hamlet*

FARMERS HAD NO CASH WHILE GRAIN STOCKS GREW. Total grain deliveries in the first six months of the 1955–56 crop year were 31 per cent of total deliveries, down from 54 per cent in the 1951–52 crop year. On August 1, 1956, the beginning of the new crop year, carry-over of wheat from the previous year was 527 million bushels (165 million on western farms), 11 per cent higher than the previous year and 95 per cent of the ten-year average. And the new crop year was expected to add another 534 million bushels. In Manitoba total grain carry-over on July 31, 1957, was 55 million bushels compared with only 15 million a year earlier. Farmers desperately needed a program for obtaining cash while their grain was working its way through the labyrinth of being sold on the world market.

Yet Parker had stated cash advances were not needed, and the board of directors even refused to honour the resolution in favour of cash advances adopted by delegates at the 1955 convention. After McConnell's refusal to support cash advances at the Saskatoon meeting, and my confrontation with him at the Dauphin district meeting, I decided to do something drastic.

My plan was a bit disingenuous. I wrote a long resolution that was adopted by the Grandview MPE Association board of directors and forwarded to head office for inclusion on the agenda of the annual convention in October 1956.

And I was elected the delegate from Grandview.

Manitoba Pool Elevator conventions were august affairs. In the 1950s, many farmers were still uncomfortable in the big city. They were awed by the ornate opulence of the Royal Alexandria Hotel, the pride of Winnipeg, and of the Canadian Pacific Railway. They were intimidated by the galaxy of impeccably dressed executives and bureaucrats seated on the high dais in front of them or lounging along the dark-panelled walls in the huge, high-ceilinged room, looking as though born to power and influence. And I too was awed and intimidated. But I had a job to do.

It took three days to arrive at the Grandview resolution. But there it was, on the printed agenda, in front of every delegate. I had palpitations whenever I glanced at it. Slowly we worked our way through the business and other resolutions. The moment of truth was approaching. I was sweating. Do I really want to do this and increase the existing animus between the old guard and myself? Do I really want to risk offending delegates whose support I might need on other issues, by insulting their revered president? Why do I not just refrain from moving the resolution when it is read? Better still, why not go to the secretary, and ask that the Grandview resolution be deleted from the agenda....

"Mr. Schulz. Could I speak with you a moment?" Startled, I almost fell off my chair. I looked up into the clean-shaven, handsome face of an MPE fieldman leaning over me: "Mr. Schulz. You really don't want your resolution to be read to the convention, do you." It was more assertion than question.

Jesus Christ! They had read my thoughts. And they were afraid. Surely this man had not come of his own volition — he must be Parker's emissary. It was just what I needed to restore my resolve, to remind me of Parker's opposition to cash advances and of why this resolution was written. The fieldman's propitious intervention saved me from a display of cowardice and a betrayal of the trust of the community that had me sent me to the convention. Adrenalin replaced sweat. I snarled: "Yes. I do!"

An hour later, the man charged with reading the resolutions to the delegates took a long drink of water, stepped back to the microphone on the high stage in front of the delegates, cleared his throat several times, appeared embarrassed, apologetic and as though hoping someone would take this cup from him, and read:

> "Whereas Mr. W. J. Parker, as president of Manitoba Pool Elevators, has a salary of $14,000 plus expenses,[1] and, "Whereas Mr. W. J.

Parker, during his term as president of MPE has held directorships in the Canadian Federation of Agriculture, the Canadian National Railways, Trans-Canada Airways, the Canadian Broadcasting Corporation, the University of Manitoba, the Natural Products Marketing Board, the Advisory Council to the Canadian Wheat Board, the Bank of Canada, and, "Whereas these directorships pay salaries and expense accounts.

"Therefore be it resolved that this convention is opposed to our president being on boards with no direct connection with Manitoba Pool Elevators."

It was a stratagem! I did not know if all the positions listed in the resolution were correct, or what they paid, so I had concocted the figures and added them up to a tidy total in my presentation. Whatever Parker's off-farm income was, I was certain it would be more than most delegates realized — and much more than their own farm income.

The sound of the reader's voice stopped. No one breathed. We were as though in a vacuum. The convention chairman stepped to the microphone, hesitated momentarily, and asked: "Is there a mover for this ... er ... resolution?"

Through the silence of the tomb I went to the floor microphone: "Yes. Schulz. From Grandview."

There was a great sound of indrawn breath.

"Is there a seconder for this resolution?"

I was certain none of the 212 delegates would touch this with a long-handled pitchfork. That was good. With no seconder it would not be on the floor and could not be debated. Parker could not respond. The *facts* stated in the resolution would be left, like a flashing light, in the subconsciousness of the delegates when they returned home. Parker would be permanently impugned. If only no one seconds this resolution I am home free....

"Yes, Mr. Chairman. I second this resolution." It was an old friend, Eggert Siggurdson, from the Swan River Valley: "Mr. Chairman. I want to make it clear I do not support this resolution and I do not know why it is on the agenda. But I know this young man who has moved it, and I know he does not do such things lightly, and I think so highly of him that I second his resolution just to get it on the floor to hear his argument."

Good old Eggie. He wanted to help me, and he ruined my ploy.

In the vast chasm of reproving silence I spoke briefly, reviewing the proposal for cash advances, and stating that it can be logically opposed only by those with sufficient off-farm income to not need them. If Mr. Parker's opposition is for that reason, perhaps it is time his income, including his salary as president of MPE, is reduced. Also, as one who helps pay MPE operating costs, including executive salaries, I resent being told that my president's salary and perks are "none of my damned business."

Parker took the microphone — and the bait. He was furious. For once he did not have his finger in his mouth and his voice was not muffled. He fairly roared. And he fell neatly into my trap.

To counter my fictitious income figures, he had to reveal the real ones. When he finished defending himself, all knew his off-farm income. While not as high as I had stated, it was much higher than most delegates imagined, and higher by a magnitude than that of most farmers. He skilfully deflected some of my attack by explaining "I was never on the board of governors of the Bank of Canada," as erroneously reported in the press, so my resolution was not the kick in the testicles I had hoped for.

The revelations in my resolution, and the angry exchange that followed, left some convention delegates wondering if Parker was indeed opposed to cash advances because he did not need them, and in their eyes his status as a demigod was strangely diminished. However, in my expectation this would diminish his authority, or change the thinking of the MPE provincial board on the issue of interest-free cash advances, I was to be sadly disappointed.

The MPE leadership never saw the grain delivery crises as anything but temporary and would go no further than to support the temporary measures of the Government-proposed, partially guaranteed bank loans with the banks deciding who would get what, and with farmers paying the costs. Why offend a government seemingly determined to go no further?

The attitude that there was nothing wrong with agriculture that time would not cure and farmers had nothing to complain about, permeated the leadership of the producer co-operatives, their satellite farm organizations, their official news organs, and elected Liberal members, and was reflected in their statements:

> Farmers of western Canada should not receive more than fifteen cents a bushel on the final payment on the Canada-UK wheat agreement. (MPE President W. J. Parker to the founding convention of the Manitoba Farmer's Union, January 1951).
>
> Farmers of this country were never better off and should not complain. (MPE Vice-President George McConnell to the MFU district convention at Dauphin, June 1951).
>
> Farm Union statements to the effect that farmers are going broke does not apply to [my] constituency. (Liberal MLA from the Constituency of Gilbert Plains, which included Grandview where the MFU was born, to the Manitoba Legislature in March 1951)
>
> The agricultural picture looks brighter for the coming year. (Press dispatch from the Canadian Federation of Agriculture convention, Montreal, February 1952)
>
> We must take a new International Wheat Agreement at any price. (J. T. McLean, MFAC executive secretary, to a meeting at Grandview, April 1952)
>
> We must not charge anyone a higher price for wheat in the new International Wheat Agreement. (Mrs. Florence Harkness, MFAC provincial director, to annual convention, Winnipeg, June 1952)
>
> The coming year looks brighter than the last. (G. F. Habing, MFAC president to annual convention, Winnipeg, June 1952)
>
> We are looking forward to another prosperous year. (H.H. Hannam, president, Canadian Federation of Agriculture, at annual convention, Victoria, January 1953)
>
> Farmers do not need advance payments or loans on farm stored grain and those who advocate it are doing so against the best interests of the farmer. (Roy Marler, president, Alberta Federation of Agriculture, in telegram to C. D. Howe, federal minister of trade and commerce, November 24, 1953)

> We [farmers] must be prepared to take lower prices for our
> products. (J. T. Monkhouse, president, Manitoba Dairy and Poultry
> Co-operative, to MFU annual convention, Winnipeg, December 1953)
>
> The banks claim there are less than two percent of the farmers
> that are squeezed by the market situation. (Editorial, Camrose
> Canadian, reprinted in Manitoba Co-operator, official organ of the
> Co-operative Movement in Manitoba, December 24, 1953)

It was reminiscent of J. M. Keynes memorable statement during the Great Depression that: "In the long-run the economy will cure itself, but in the long-run we will all be dead." It was this attitude on the part of those to whom farmers looked for leadership that had led to the founding of the Farmer's Unions, and to the fierce fight that followed.

And the leadership of MPE and its satellite, the MFAC, never understood — or wilfully ignored — the politics of using cash advances as a tool to force policy changes. They would not accept the fact — or feared offending the government — that if the government were required to lay out millions of dollars to pay for storage of unsold grain, it would force government to adopt new policies to accelerate grain sales. This would automatically reduce the fabled surpluses and allow market prices to rise.

In October 1956, the MPE annual convention debated a resolution from the Bowsman Association, almost as much *persona non grata* as Grandview, favouring "a plan of cash advances on grain in reasonable storage intended for sale, *with interest and administrative charges to be borne by the federal treasury*."

At Parker's suggestion, "*with interest and administrative charges to be borne by the federal treasury*," was deleted.

Then the entire resolution, including the amendment deleting the above phrase, was defeated.

On March 1, 1957, a third meeting was held in Saskatoon, with representatives from the same organizations as in the previous September. I again attended as the representative of the MFAC, and again presented their convention request for interest-free advances through the Wheat Board. The representatives supported my proposal for the MFU and the SFU, but the meeting actually retreated from its September position and essentially accepted the Liberal government plan with modifications.

McConnell had been appointed to the Canadian Board of Grain Commissioners by the government of Canada, and Manitoba Pool Elevators was represented by its new vice-president, T. H. Wilson, who opposed the cash advance program. When I reminded him of the resolution passed by his convention 1955, he replied that there was little demand for cash advances among the farmers, and echoed Parker's statement to the annual convention that interest-free cash advances was "pie in the sky."[2]

Four months later, on June 10, 1957, the Conservative Party won the federal election. The Liberals, in office for twenty-two years, were out. Old political friendships ended. New alliances were formed.

Two months later Prime Minister Diefenbaker announced his government would institute a permanent system of cash advances on farm-stored grain, made by the Wheat Board through the grain elevator system, *with interest and administrative charges to be borne by the federal treasury*.

Despite the opposition of the leadership of the farmer-owned wheat pools and federations of agriculture, and their obstinate refusal to act even on the resolutions passed by their own conventions, it was "an idea whose time had come."

Southern Manitoba suddenly woke up. Graysville and Brunkild, MPE associations in Parker's administrative district and next door to his hometown, sent a joint resolution to the 1957 annual convention. It requested that: "The federal government make immediate provision for cash advances to farmers on farm-stored grain … all administrative and interest charges to be borne by the government of Canada."

On October 21, 1957, as soon as the above resolution was moved, Parker strode purposefully to the podium and waxed almost rhapsodical explaining

the new cash advance program. He assured delegates the cost to the Wheat ·
Board would be "negligible," that "it will not cost [MPE] much money for
administration and we are glad to pay this to help," and, triumphantly, urged
farmers to: "Take all the cash advances you can get. And if you do not know
what to do with the money, you can lend it to MPE."

Again, my father's voice, "Everything is politics...."

A delegate raced to the microphone to burble enthusiastically: "Mr.
Chairman. I want to move a motion of gratitude to Mr. Parker for having
worked so hard to get us cash advances."

The entire delegate body jumped to its feet. Wave after wave of applause
swept across the hall. Parker graciously accepted the kudos, looking pleased.
Then a voice was heard at the microphone: "Mr. Chairman. I too wish to
move a motion of gratitude.

The applause subsided and the delegates waited in anticipation: "But
my motion of gratitude is not to Mr. Parker."

The delegates looked confused.

"Mr. Chairman. I wish to move a motion of gratitude for having worked
so hard to get us cash advances — to Herb Schulz."

Some delegates, innocently caught up in the congratulatory spirit, began
to applaud, realized their apostasy, and stopped.

Parker, appearing apoplectic, strode angrily from the stage.

George Henderson, the slim, soft-spoken, unassuming farmer and MPE
delegate (later Conservative MLA) from the pleasant, picturesque, southern
Manitoba establishment town of Manitou, had administered the kick in the
testicles.

On October 30, 1957, the House of Commons enacted *The Prairie Grain
Advance Payments Act* by a vote of 188 to 6 (all Liberals). Hundreds of millions
of dollars were pumped into the rural communities in the early autumn when
it was needed most.

Newspapers suddenly discovered the need for, and simplicity of, the
program. The *Calgary Albertan* wrote: "The elevators are full so the

government is giving the farmer a little of his own money in advance; that's all." The *Winnipeg Tribune* saw it as: "A boon to the farmers on low delivery quotas, and it will give a lift to the whole prairie economy." The *Globe and Mail* editorialized: "Cash advance will provide income to farmers when they need it most … it is not a gift or subsidy or loan. It is a payment to farmers which would come to them sooner or later."[4]

Characteristically, the Liberal-oriented *Winnipeg Free Press* found this program an obstacle to their solution-of-choice to the farm problem — get the farmers off the farm: "Farm prosperity and average farm size are intimately related. Government should not throw up roadblocks to the expansion of efficient farmers. The cash advance measure certainly works in that direction."[5]

And the reasoning of the early supporters of cash advances that required the government to pay interest and administrative costs would force policy changes and increase grain sales, proved correct. Following enactment of cash advances in 1957, with the Treasury laying out $40 to $45 million annually in costs recoverable only when the grain was sold off-shore, the Government of Canada, through the Wheat Board and other initiatives, undertook a veritable blizzard of activity to escalate grain sales.

On August 30, 1957, on the eve of the legislation, the *Winnipeg Tribune* carried a banner headline: "*The Wheat Surplus: Canada's Biggest Headache*," and the surplus hung like a shroud over the entire agricultural economy. In the first three years of the cash advances program, grain exports shot up and total stocks dropped from 722 million to 536 million bushels. Fifty million dollars was contributed to the Columbo Plan to buy thirty-eight million bushels of wheat for those who needed it, and Canadian wheat became a weapon in the Cold War. The enormous market in the Soviet Union and Communist China were opened to Canadian wheat, $175 million was extended in export credits, and foreign currencies were accepted in payment. The federal Rural Development and Rehabilitation Program took marginal land out of grain production for recreation urban development, reforestation, community pastures, and forage crops. An unexpected benefit was the ending of the isolation of China, bringing her back into the international community.

The proposal for cash advances on farm-stored grain by a farmer who had done some reading and thinking and familiarized himself with grain marketing policy in the United States, speaking at a Farmer's Union meeting in the little town of Grandview, had not only changed the face of agricultural communities in western Canada, but had both national and international ramifications.

In October, 1960, three years after the program came into effect, the MPE annual convention resolved, "That Manitoba Pool Elevators send a note of appreciation to the federal government for interest-free cash advances on farm stored grain, which has been a benefit to the farmers."

President W. J. Parker found no fault with the resolution.

7

Uncivil War

The time is out of joint; O cursed spite,
That ever I was born to set it right.
SHAKESPEARE, *Hamlet*

PARKER'S IMPLACABLE OPPOSITION TO A PROGRAM with no discernible disadvantages, and the MPE convention's rejection of a policy most farmers desperately wanted, energized the MFU. "Cash advances on farm stored grain" became our metaphor for rural renewal. The call went out. MFU members by the thousands attended annual meetings of co-operatives throughout Manitoba, replacing directors and capturing credentials to MFAC conventions. One year, the co-operatives at Grandview were entitled to sixty delegates to the MFAC convention, and all were MFU members. Old MFAC stalwarts fell like overripe grain. MFU supporters gradually entered the MPE delegate stream, won majority control of the board of directors of the Manitoba Dairy and Poultry Co-operative and replaced long-time president John Monkhouse with an MFU member, and won election as delegates to the annual conventions of United Grain Growers.

And, after the ballot count incident at Grandview, we determined to remove Watson Crossley from the MPE provincial board of directors. Ed Puchalski and I approached several persons to stand for the position. No one would.

"We have been looking in the wrong place," said Puchalski one day. "Realistically, you are the logical successor."

Administratively, the MPE was divided into seven districts. Each district was entitled to one director to the provincial board. The delegates elected each director from the associations in that district. Each association had one vote. The election of directors took place during the annual convention, by the delegates separated into their respective district groups.

District Seven, represented by Crossley, was the largest in Manitoba, comprising roughly a triangle with a base of a hundred miles from Minnedosa west to Russell, and then two hundred miles north to the Swan River Valley. It had thirty-three associations. I needed seventeen votes to win. In the autumn of 1955, in the six weeks prior to the MPE annual convention, I added six thousand miles to the odometer of my car visiting board members and convention delegates and alternates from each of those thirty-three associations.

On the evening of the first day of the convention I was approached by two older friends, Jake Sicmens and Charles Hunt: "Do you have enough delegates to elect you?", Siemens asked.

Jacob J. Siemens, Altona farmer and "Sunflower King". Inducted into the Agricultural Hall of Fame for developing the oilseeds industry in Manitoba.

"I have sixteen. I am not sure of the seventeenth."

J. J. (Jake) Siemens took over the family farm at Altona in 1929 and expended himself prodigiously in the services of farmers, locally, provincially, and nationally. He played a leading role in the organization and development of the Rhineland Agricultural Society, the Rhineland Consumers Co-operative Ltd, the Federation of Southern Manitoba Co-operatives, and the Manitoba Co-operative Wholesale Ltd., which expanded into the interprovincial Federated Co-operatives Ltd. He inspired the Western Co-op College at Saskatoon and served as long-time director of the Co-operative Union of Canada. Significantly and enduringly, he virtually singlehandedly, in the face of fear among his neighbours and the hostility of government, created the Manitoba Vegetable Oils Co-operative which in turn virtually created the oilseeds growing industry in Manitoba and gave farmers a cash crop they were to treasure. He was a confirmed and practicing socialist and was greatly — and justifiably — suspicious of the elitist leaders of Manitoba's establishment farm organizations and co-operatives. He was, in his activities, a dedicated, determined, one-man powerhouse, never deflected from his goals by opposition (at his funeral in 1963 at age sixty-seven, the Unitarian church minister eulogized that "Jake Siemens won lasting fame for the enemies he made.") He was my hero and friend, and I looked to him for help: "Then why don't you withdraw and let Charlie run. With your votes and those he can get himself, he can win."

I was stunned: "Listen, dammit, I made a three hundred mile trip to ask Charlie to stand for director and he refused. Now that I have lined up the delegates to support me you want to cash in on my work."

"You're right. Forget we mentioned it." Siemens was contrite.

But I was haunted by the fear that, if I did not get that seventeenth vote, my nemesis would be re-elected. So, as always when faced with an insoluble problem, I took it to my wife.

"Your quarrel is with Crossley, not with MPE. Hunt is much more respected in the Co-op Movement than you are and may be more effective than you. And he is solid. He will not sell out."

"But I did all the work. I have earned this opportunity."

"Moses did the work but was not allowed to cross the Jordan."

Wanting no one to know my intentions, I said nothing except to hint to Siemens that Hunt should enter his name as a candidate for the directorship. All around me were knots of delegates and directors, looking sidelong at me, and becoming instantly silent when I walked by. They were plotting against me. Let them!

On the final day of the convention, the District Seven delegates gathered in a room allotted to us. Crossley, Hunt, and I were nominated. Crossley supporters could hardly restrain their joy. They knew Hunt and I would split the votes not committed to Crossley, and he would win. We were each allotted five minutes to make our case. I spoke of my commitment to the Co-operative Movement and particularly to MPE. Crossley supporters smiled smugly at each other. My ambition would give them victory. Then: "Mr. Chairman and fellow delegates, having said all that, to the regret of some and to the joy of others, I withdraw my name and ask the delegates committed to me to vote for Charles Hunt."

The smug smiles ceased. The thirty-three votes were carefully counted. In October, 1955, *Apollo* was defeated by my friend, Charles Hunt, who was MPE provincial director until he retired sixteen years later.

Charles C. Hunt, from the town of Swan River, was raised in the Southern States and still spoke with a Missouri twang, but settled in the Swan River valley during the Depression. He was a successful farmer with a high degree of moral rectitude (he once proved to Revenue Canada that he owed more income taxes than they had assessed him for) and refused to grow malting barley, for which his land was particularly suited, because it would be used to make beer. A lean, five-foot nine-inch, sharp-featured, acerbic man, his mind was incisive and his speech trenchant. In his mid-fifties, he moved as though thirty. A teetotaller, he smoked like a chimney. A cautious man, he drove his car — always a large, powerful car — like a stock-car racer. He was an active member of half a dozen co-operatives, including having been a long-time member of the boards of directors of the Consumers Co-op and the MPE association at Swan River. He was highly esteemed in the Co-operative Movement, and was on the board of directors of Manitoba Co-operative Wholesale and Federated Co-operatives Ltd. He travelled widely, read avidly, had a large private library, and could converse knowledgably on any subject. He was also a member of the MFU and a long-time member of the CCF, the only political party that supported the policies of the MFU.

As the farmers struggled heroically to free themselves from the vicissitudes of nature and the vagaries of the market, the core policies of the MFU essentially reduced themselves to four. These were: cash advances against the collateral of stored grain to alleviate the cash crunch in the autumn of the year; producer-controlled marketing boards to give farmers collective bargaining power in the marketplace; a system of publicly administered but voluntary crop insurance to protect the farmer against natural disasters; parity prices for agricultural products, with built-in limitations on the amount to individual farmers, to provide a return commensurate with production costs.

But there was no apparent need for the Government of Canada or the Official Opposition in Ottawa, or their counterparts at the provincial level, to pay attention to the plight of agriculture. Because of the continuing internecine warfare between the farmer's unions and federations of agriculture and co-operation (and their national voice, the Canadian Federation of Agriculture), the farmers spoke with a forked tongue.

The unions supported cash advances on farm-stored grain with Ottawa paying the administrative costs; the federations ridiculed the proposal. The unions supported parity prices on farm produce; the federations sought a *percentage* of parity. The unions wanted a livestock marketing board to end the monopsony of many thousands of farmers bargaining individually with four meat-packing companies; the federations questioned it. The unions wanted to increase aggregate farm income and supported the *family farm*, which they saw as both an efficient economic unit and an essential social ingredient in the future viability of rural society; the federations, particularly the CFA, seemed content to let the number of farmers shrink to fit available income.

Daily it became more evident that, to command the attention of the public and the fear of the politicians, there must be only one *voice* for agriculture. To MFU members, the atrophied MFAC had to go. And they concluded that, as a farm organization, the MFAC would collapse in a heap except for its indirect funding.

Most irksome to MFU members was the funding of the MFAC by the co-operatives. To kill the MFAC we must kill the funding.

Local co-operative associations began instructing their head offices to stop funding the MFAC. In 1953 the Grandview Consumers Co-op voted to stop contributions. In 1954 the annual convention of Manitoba Co-operative Wholesale, recognizing the inequity of the funding and the impropriety of having its preponderance of urban members voting on farm issues, ignited a firestorm among the old guard by voting to withdraw from the MFAC. In 1959, the annual convention of the Manitoba Dairy and Poultry Co-op endorsed a Grandview resolution to end its contributions to the MFAC.

The largest single contributor was Manitoba Pool Elevators. In 1956, Grandview and four other MPE associations (Swan River, Bowsman,

Makaroff, Erickson), sponsored resolutions requesting ending contributions to the MFAC. At the annual convention, other delegates and I spoke in support. We pointed out one-third of the delegates present were MFU members. We explained as most MFU members were also members of co-operatives, that this automatically made us members of the MFAC, and that the MFU and the MFAC were in conflict, which placed MFU members in the invidious position of having to pay the MFAC to attack them. Currently their only way out of this dilemma was to quit doing business with the co-operatives, which would be damaging to both themselves and the co-ops. This was unfair and unacceptable. The obvious solution was for the co-ops, beginning with MPE, to stop funding the MFAC.

The resolution was debated at length. Again, we had attacked dogma. Cyclops merely had to purse his lips and the herd instinct prevailed. Our resolution was soundly defeated.

Then, to add insult to injury, they passed a resolution that, "MPE continue to give financial support to the MFAC."

Later I was informed that some delegates in southern Manitoba, when asked by their local associations with considerable MFU content why this resolution had not passed, had replied it might have passed had "Schulz" not entered the debate. They explained my presence was like waving a red flag and delegates had turned against me, and against the resolution I supported, on instinct.

The following year, the resolution to withdraw funding for the MFAC appeared on the agenda again; again sponsored by several associations. The debate was a replay of the previous year. So was the defeat. Another resolution proposing that the current grant to the MFAC be split with the MFU was also defeated. I went to the microphone to speak on a point of privilege:

> Mr. Chairman, and fellow delegates to the convention of Manitoba Pool Elevators. My name is Schulz, and I am the delegate for the Grandview Association.
>
> The resolution just voted on was debated at length last year. It was defeated. I am informed some delegates reported to their

associations that it might have passed if I had not spoken on it. The resolution was defeated again a few minutes ago. You will have noticed I did not speak on it so the mess you people have just made cannot be blamed on me. But I intend to speak now.

You are all aware that the current situation forces MFU members to pay tribute to an organization we have learned to despise. But I do not intend to debate the issue because all that needs to be said has been said. Anything more is futile. Every delegate here knows this is unfair and an insult to those MPE members who are also members of the MFU. But you have chosen to listen to your master's voice and risk the future of MPE rather than cut adrift that whited sepulchre, the MFAC. So the time to talk is over.

You are all aware that MPE associations are independent entities owned by their local members. Our adherence to the central organization is voluntary and can be withdrawn at will.

It is now 11:30. Unless by two o'clock today you change your decision and agree to either withdraw funding to the MFAC or to contribute funding to the MFU, I will phone the president of my MPE board at Grandview. I will tell him to proceed with the plan we discussed to sell the Grandview Pool Elevator Association to United Grain Growers. And I remind you Grandview handles over a million bushels a year and is the largest MPE association in Manitoba. Mr. Chairman and gentlemen, I leave you to think.

There was not a whisper.

I stalked out of the convention and went to lunch – alone. No one approached me, nor did I encourage anyone to do so. I needed time to think. I had thrown down the gauntlet. I was frightened witless. If my challenge was accepted, I could not possibly win.

The convention adjourned for lunch immediately after I had spoken. It reconvened at 1:00 P.M. As soon as it was gavelled to order Keith Alexander, delegate for Roblin (later a Conservative MLA), strode quickly to the microphone: "Mr. Chairman and delegates. In view of what Mr. Schulz said before lunch, I suggest we better give him something."

He stated "this does not mean we endorse MFU activities," but it should be done in recognition of support for MPE by MFU members and "I move we contribute five thousand dollars annually to the MFU."

The motion was seconded by George Henderson of Manitou, from Parker's district.

The resolution was carried without debate. I did not look up to see if it was unanimous. I did not care. I had not really wanted a contribution to the MFU: I had hoped to trigger termination of grants to the MFAC, and the five thousand dollar contribution to the MFU was more insult than salve compared with thirty thousand dollars to the MFAC. But it was a beginning. The dam was broken and logic would force either equal contributions to the MFU or end those to the MFAC.[1]

The MPE hierarchy and the leadership of the MFAC had been put on notice their picnic was over.[2] And I had been relieved of the need to attempt to implement my impossible threat.

But the small victories did not match the large defeats.

Since most MFU members were also MFAC members, it was self-defeating to have two organizations ostensibly speaking for the same people. It was decided to effect a united voice by merger.

This had been attempted in 1951 when the MFAC annual convention resolved that "everything possible be done to amalgamate the Farmer's Union and MFAC and build one strong farm organization." MFAC President Jack Wilton, who had opposed the resolution, sent a letter to the newspapers extolling the virtues, power, and popularity of the MFAC, and inviting the MFU to become a member of the MFAC. MFU President Jake Schulz responded this was not an invitation to negotiate but the action "of a warrior chieftain … beating his chest about the virtues of his tribe … [In the interests of farm unity] our executive is ready to meet yours any time and anywhere you suggest, but the invitation should be made by letter and not by a province-wide publicized lecture."

In early June, 1954, Schulz wrote to Wilton proposing serious discussions on farm unity. Three weeks later the MFAC convention resolved: "That the MFAC board appoint a negotiating committee of three and invite the MFU to name a committee of three, to prepare a plan for amalgamation and present it to producers."

Patrician, distinguished-appearing, immaculately dressed Wilton, a farmer from Carman where the MFU was seen as some form of virus, faced a dilemma: if he agreed he would be accused of apostasy; if he refused he would be seen by the many MFU members in the co-operatives as a barrier to unity. This had to be treated delicately. He agreed to discussions. Then he appointed a committee of three persons (former MFAC president Gerald Habing, G. E. Wardle and W. G. Landreth) to whom the mere mention of the MFU was anathema, and guaranteed the negotiations would fail. They did.

The position of the MFAC negotiating committee became a moving target. They insisted the new proposed organization (to be named the Organized Farmers of Manitoba) include the three producer co-operatives (MPE, UGG, and the Dairy and Poultry Co-operative). Conversely, a firm tenet of the MFU was that co-operatives, being commercial entities, would not — and indeed, could not — be strenuous advocates of farm policies without inviting the danger of government legislation — such as tax laws — damaging to themselves. Indeed, the basic purpose of organizing the Farmer's Unions had been to establish a farm *voice* without commercial interests so it could be strident when dealing with government.

In a desperate effort to negotiate a united farm voice, the MFU committee (John Canart, Neil Simonsen, and Rudolph Usick) agreed to include the three producer co-operatives. The MFAC committee raised its stakes to include seven co-operatives — including consumer co-operatives, credit unions, and Co-op Life Insurance which were more urban than rural in membership — and that these be given seven of fifteen positions on the executive. Again, the MFU committee conceded. Then the MFAC committee demanded that the new OFM adopt the Canadian Federation of Agriculture as its national spokesman and that the Inter-Provincial Farm Union Council be terminated. The MFU committee proposed that the question of national and international affiliations be left to the members of the new OFM to decide. The MFAC committee rejected this. By March, 1955, negotiations had collapsed.

In late June the MFAC convention voted against amalgamation and in favour of the MFU becoming an affiliate member of the MFAC.

Essentially, the MFAC proposed to swallow the MFU.

It was like Israel being invited to become part of Palestine.

But we had anticipated this, and MFU members who were also MFAC members began taking over the MFAC. Between 1954 and 1956 we replaced four long-time directors. Florence Harkness was defeated by John Zaplitny, a Fork River farmer and brother of CCF Member of Parliament Fred Zaplitny. Rossburn farmer and MFU stalwart Michael Sotas defeated MFAC vice-president Percy Burnell. Ben Reimer, an MFU member but also a notable in the Co-operative Movement defeated Burnell's replacement as vice-president, Paul Turko. In 1956, the conflict became so heated that one district convention voted that: "The MFAC wind up its affairs and cease to exist." And the rebellion was no longer confined to north-central Manitoba: in the deep south, in the MFAC district coterminus with Parker's MPE administrative district, MFU-member George Henderson, a Manitou farmer, defeated MFAC President Jack Wilton.

Control of the MFAC was slipping out of the hands of the old conservative-Conservative element of southern Manitoba.

In early 1956, Manitoba became a battleground as contending forces fought for and against the concept of unity. At meetings of MFAC member co-operatives, the fight for credentials to the MFAC annual convention became fierce, unrelenting, and devious.

Some old guard MFAC supporters in Grandview, including Watson Crossley and Florence Harkness, seeing themselves and their resolutions defeated at the conventions in 1954 and 1955, formed a new *MFAC association*. The official report on their organizational meeting explained this was necessitated because the "dissidents" (MFU members) within the MFAC espoused: "Dictatorial philosophies, intolerance of views, use of intimidation and threats to achieve objectives, and unethical methods to obtain by compulsion rather than mutual consent. Concern is caused by a close working relationship with the CCF Party and linking with labour Unions. To freedom-loving citizens this is alarming. It is desirable to have an organization based on democratic philosophy, tolerance of views, and opposed to the use of intimidation, threats and unethical procedure."[3]

We saw the new *association* as a transparent ploy to obtain credentials to the MFAC convention. They were sent. Two friends and I immediately applied for membership in this *democratic* association. As expected, we were refused because, "You are not true MFAC members." So much for *tolerance*. We reported this to the MFAC provincial secretary. Their credentials were revoked.

MFU members took control of many MFAC and co-operative local associations. Those referring to the MFU members in the MFAC as "dissidents" were now the "dissidents." They did not like it.

In late June, I was seated peacefully at the MFAC annual convention at Brandon, relaxed, minding my own business, momentarily not in the eye of the storm. MFAC Provincial Secretary Jim McLean approached me: "Mr. Schulz. Someone wants to see you in the hotel lobby."

Mrs. Harkness awaited me, her face a mixture of fury and triumph. She waved two pieces of paper in my face: "You forged the signatures on these two convention credentials."

They were from the Grandview Dairy and Poultry Co-operative, showing signatures of its president and secretary.

"What makes you say those signatures are forged?"

"Because Cameron McBride and Mrs. Evans did not sign them."

"So what makes you think I forged them?"

"Because you are the kind of person who would do that."

At a meeting of the Grandview Dairy and Poultry Co-op the *wrong* delegates were elected to the MFAC convention. The president and secretary refused to sign the credentials. The unsigned credentials were obtained and the two elected persons, also MFU members, registered at the convention. The signatures of the president and secretary on their credentials were forged.

I knew the credential bearers were not the forgers, but I suspected who the forgers were. I took them to lunch: "Why did you do this?"

"They were properly elected and had the right to be delegates."

"Then they should have challenged the credentials committee and asked for a convention ruling. Forging signatures is not done. At the next meeting we'll kick McBride and Mrs. Evans off the board. But meanwhile you have caused the MFU a serious problem."

"We just wanted to help you."

Fortunately, my accusers were less interested in finding the forgers than in pinning the forgeries on me. Charges were laid. The RCMP came to see me twice, asked if I had signed the credentials, and left when I said I had not.

Then they came a third time. I was helping a neighbour build a barn. It was a very hot August day. I was wearing nothing but shorts and boots. The police car stopped a hundred feet from me. A large, neatly uniformed, officious-looking officer got out: "Come over here. We want to talk to you."

"Just give me a minute to get my shirt on."

"No! Just come over here and get in the car."

I felt embarrassed sitting there, my sweaty skin against the cushions of the rear seat. And I suddenly knew how vulnerable a person feels when questioned by police while virtually nude.

"Write your own name ten times." They gave me a pad and pen.

"Now write 'J. C. McBride' ten times." I did.

"Now write 'Mrs. R. S. Evans' ten times."

The officious officer examined the signatures and then turned, leaned into the back seat, and half shouted: "We have all the evidence we need. We know you signed those credentials."

I resented his attitude: "Officer. If you had said you *believe* I signed them, or that you *believe* you know who else might have signed them, I would be worried. But you said you *know* I signed them and since I know I did not, I know you have nothing. I suggest you either get some evidence or stop making accusations."

"Then tell us who did sign them."

"You have already said you *know* I signed them. Therefore obviously no one else did." I got out of the car.

"We will be back to see you again."

"You know where to find me."

They did not come again. But it was a stressful summer.

❖ ❖ ❖

By mid-1956 four of the seven MFAC districts had elected MFU members: John McCallister, George Henderson, Max Hofford, and myself (I replaced John Zaplitny, who retired). Also, Mrs. N. R. Jasper, long-time director as the representative of the women's section, was replaced by MFU supporter Nena Woodward, giving us a majority on the MFAC provincial board. Nena Woodward was a long-time worker in the vineyards of the Co-operative Movement and farm organizations. She and her husband, Bert, an accountancy graduate from Regina College and now secretary of the Red River Consumers Co-op in Winnipeg, were old Saskatchewan hands from Yorkton, who had been through both the economic wars of the Depression and the political wars to get the CCF elected, and she needed no instruction on what we wanted to accomplish.

Nena Woodward, MFAC Provincial Board Member (1956–57), with husband Bert, Secretary of the Red River Consumers Co-operative.

Then MFU supporters took over the 1956 MFAC annual convention. They voted to accept the terms of merger agreed to by the two negotiating committees, but with two changes: to delete the co-operatives from the new organization; to leave the decision about national affiliations to the future members of the OFM.

The new MFU-controlled MFAC executive moved quickly and with precision to implement that resolution. We notified the MFU we had removed the two obstacles on which earlier negotiations had foundered, invited them to appoint a new committee to help tie up whatever loose ends remained, appointed a three-person committee to work with its MFU counterpart, and announced a special MFAC membership meeting to vote on the merger terms to be negotiated.

Now the MFU would swallow the MFAC.

I was ecstatic. I phoned my father, then president of the Inter-Provincial Farm Union Council: "We did it. We appointed a committee to negotiate a merger and we called a special convention for February to ratify it."

"Who are the members of your committee?"

"Max Hofford, MFAC President John McCallister and W. L. Landreth who was on the previous MFAC negotiating committee."

"You have made a serious mistake. Two of the three are MFU. You cannot expect the proud people of the MFAC to be taken in by a tactic that has MFU people negotiating with MFU people."

"But if we appoint those MFAC shitheads to the negotiating committee we will have the same results as before."

"Then we will try again. We will keep trying until the farmers take this out of the hands of the leaders and do it themselves."

"But they did that in June by voting to exclude the co-ops from the OFM and electing a majority of MFU members to the MFAC board."

"We will not have a united farm voice until the co-op leaders agree, and they can only be directed by their own members. You cannot force these people to amalgamate. You can only try to persuade them. Without that, a forced merger would simply lead to the formation of another farm organization. What you have done will be seen as a move to kill the MFAC."

Later that evening, at my hotel, I received a phone call from Southam newspaper's heavyweight reporter Charles Lynch: "I note two of the three appointed to your MFAC committee to negotiate a merger with the MFU are members of the MFU."

"So what! There are millions of us. It is difficult to find an MFAC member who is not also an MFU member."

"But you will have MFU members negotiating with MFU members."

"For all practical purposes they are the same people."

"That's not a merger. It's absorption of the MFAC by the MFU."

"But the MFAC claims to represent practically every farmer in Manitoba, so why could this not just as easily result in an absorption of the MFU by the MFAC?"

"That is sheer sophistry. Most MFAC members don't even know they are members. The MFAC is an empty shell propped up by pool elevators. The point is that you are not planning a merger. You are inviting the MFAC to dig a grave and throw itself in."[4]

The walls were closing in. The earlier euphoria evaporated. The process needed to be rethought. Time for a new tactic.

At the next MFAC board meeting Hofford pleaded "shortage of time" and resigned from the negotiating committee. I proposed he be replaced by another board member, old guard MFAC supporter Dave Barclay, a rather harmless-looking bachelor from Souris. I had greatly underestimated his intelligence. He saw the hole we had dug for ourselves. He declined for "reasons of health."

Hubris, and a few minor tactical victories, had caused me to go a coup too far. The MFU, and I were to pay the price.

The two committees met many times. Terms of the proposed merger were hammered into place. Both committees made an honest effort. If anything, too honest to suit me. I had no desire to see a dead horse revived just to negotiate the manner of its death. At the next MFU convention, I railed against the proposed terms being too favourable to the MFAC. But the convention delegates accepted them. The merger now rested with fate — and the MFAC membership.

Almost a decade earlier, in 1948, at an MFAC Leadership Training School, I had met a man. Tall, imposing, mid-sixties, with a leonine head that might have graced a Roman coin, Fawcett Ransom was a member of *old family* pioneer aristocracy in Boissevain. He was a successful farmer, a notable in the Co-operative Movement, a charter member of the Manitoba Wheat Pool and provincial secretary of Manitoba Pool Elevators 1924–49, and much more. He had authored a little booklet entitled *Heritage of the Prairies*,[5] a rhapsodic tribute to the soil and those who tended it: "I have lived here forty-seven years with men who tilled the soil — people from different lands. They are great people."

In his late teens, before the turn of the century, he had come from Ontario to southern Manitoba and fallen in love with *the good earth*. He was now retired and spending much of his time on the lecture circuit, speaking of the farmers who had come from the ends of the earth to work in harmony opening the virgin land, building the Co-operative Movement through which to assert some control over their economic and social future, and educating themselves through such media as the leadership schools.

He stood before us, in his black suit — he always wore a black suit — speaking in a deep, resonant, almost melancholy voice:

> The purpose of these schools is to teach citizenship, the art of living together.... In these schools you will meet young people who are becoming the warp and woof of society, which is faith in man and the common good, learning mutual understanding and tolerance.... The task of education is to inspire and to develop a love for what is good in life ... to make communities a better place to live.... They teach that one can be noble-minded even though he clean stables.... They teach working together for the good of the whole.... They teach democracy and ideals.... Ideals will create machinery; machinery without ideals will rust into decay.
>
> "Without vision, the people perish."[6] There is a lesson to learn from Naziism and Communism — that they represent definite goals fairly well understood by their followers. If their opponents are without a blueprint or definite aim, people will tend to follow those that have, however wrong they may be. Democracy must be given meaning through schools of adult education. Democracy cannot be measured in terms of dollars and cents. It is a human institution with a spiritual force.

He explained the world of pre-science ancients who saw nature as the giver of life, and named what they could not understand for the gods they propitiated (*cereals* derived from Ceres, the Roman goddess of agriculture) and opened to us a world we had never known. He quoted Sir Richard Livingstone's, *On Education*: "education is not a parade ground [but] a steady and continuous advance into an undiscovered country, where each step leads to a further step, and each corner reveals a wider view."

Here was a man! And my hero.

Now, eight years later an issue was rending the farm community: the proposed merger of the MFU and MFAC. The convention to decide the question was set for February, 1957, and I was worried. Could it be done? Was it possible or were the mutual hatreds too deeply embedded in the psyches of the decision-makers to allow it? If we could only line up a cadre of speakers who were influential, who would be listened to....

In late October, 1956, I was walking out of the meeting chamber at the annual MPE convention, deep in thought. There, right in front of me, sitting alone on an overstuffed chesterfield, in the ornate lobby of the Royal Alexandria Hotel, was Fawcett Ransom. In 1954, at the MFAC convention, he had moved a motion favouring the principle of a merger of the MFAC and the MFU and urged delegates to "keep down any prejudice and talk over this important matter and reach a decision from the standpoint only of the welfare of the farmers." Here was the man with the influence, and the dedication. Though we had met on a number of occasions, I approached the great man respectfully and with trepidation:

> Mr. Ransom. I know from having heard you on several occasions that you believe farmers need a vigorous organized voice. I assume you believe, as I do, this will not happen while the MFAC and the MFU are at each other's throats instead of attacking the conditions that injure the farmers. I have heard you speak on this subject and assume you support the proposed merger. But there is no certainty it will be accepted because too many nasty things have been said by too many people about each other to make them comfortable in each other's presence. If we want this to succeed, some persons with influence must be enlisted in its cause. I as a known partisan am not among those. But you are such a person. If you were to speak favourably at the forthcoming convention to decide on the merger people would listen.

I had assumed too much. He turned his classically featured head and looked at me with cold eyes:

"What makes you think I will support this merger?" He waited for the question to sink in, and continued: "That's the trouble with you central Europeans. You are not happy at home so you come over here and start telling us what to do until we stop you. You are either dictators or whiners. Your psyches require that you either have to order others around or that you kneel at their feet and beg for crumbs. I would not support a merger that would extinguish the MFAC, but even if I thought it a good idea, I would not support a German."

My anguish must have been visible. But he had talked too long. It had given me time to think: "Mr. Ransom. For years I have virtually worshipped you. I have told thousands of people what a great man you are. Now I see that I was wrong. And your analysis is wrong. There are some central Europeans who are not inclined to be either beggars or dictators. We just do not intend to be discounted and ignored. Not by anybody. Not even by you. In fact, especially not by you."

I was in tears: of anger, and frustration, but mostly because another mighty one had fallen. Another of my heroes had exposed his feet of clay. Fawcett Ransom's face went ash-white. His jaws worked but no sound came. I would like to believe he regretted destroying the illusions of a youthful idolater. He rose, walked slowly to the hotel door and boarded a bus. Next day I was told he was ill. Three months later he was dead.[7]

The campaign was bitter. Communities were ripped apart. Those who had long paid their dues to the MFAC and asked no questions, and then joined the MFU, suddenly became labelled *MFU sympathizers, quislings, infiltrators, stooges, subversives,* and *zealots.* Dave Barclay, from his position on the MFAC board, published a minority report attacking the MFU. MFAC President John McCallister, seeking to correct the misinformation and innuendo, was attacked for *attacking* Barclay.

On February 12, 1957, over 1,500 persons (the largest farm meeting in Manitoba history) including 1,142 delegates to the special convention of the MFAC, packed the old auditorium (now the Provincial Archives building) to capacity. People virtually hung off the balcony railings. The debate raged endlessly. And with studied ignorance, MFAC supporters complained bitterly about the terms agreed to by the two committees. They complained there was no youth rep on the new proposed OFM as there was in the MFAC (there had been no youth rep on the MFAC board since 1950). They complained the MFU committee had refused to accept a proposal for a new type of farm organization proposed by Sol Sinclair of the University of Manitoba (Sinclair's proposal had been rejected by the MFAC committee). They complained that the proposed OFM constitution was "undemocratic" because it permitted expulsion (the clause had been lifted directly from the MFAC constitution). They argued that MFU sympathizers should simply get out of the MFAC. (In 1954, when we pleaded to be allowed out, MFAC President Jack Wilton stated our only way out of the MFAC was to get out of the co-ops.)

A few speakers took a rational approach, but mostly the hall echoed with shouts, catcalls, mutual recriminations, and the exhumation of decade-old insults. The more intransigent MFAC supporters had determined to end the presumptions of the MFU. By mid-afternoon the calls commenced to "put the question."

MFU members, through their co-op membership, had worked hard to get convention credentials. But the old guard had worked harder. By early afternoon it began to appear we would lose.

But we had anticipated this and had planned for it like a marine operation, including, if necessary, a strategic retreat so we could fight another day. I gave the signal.

Peter Budlowski, from Ethelbert, went to the microphone:

> Mr. Chairman. I, like everyone else, have sat here for five hours listening to this debate. The more I listened the more confused I have become. And I am not alone. Like most delegates here, I feel the fighting between the two organizations must stop. The real losers are the farmers, and the longer the conflict continues the more we lose. The tragedy is that both organizations consist of essentially the same people with the major difference being the leadership. No wonder the Russians and Americans are suspicious of each other

when we, who are negotiating with ourselves, cannot agree. Therefore I would like very much to vote for this merger.

But, Mr. Chairman, it seems some delegates here believe the proposed terms of merger will revive a dead MFAC. Others fear the MFAC will be absorbed rather than become an effective partner in future farm policy-making. No matter how this vote goes, it will leave some very angry people. That is not in the best interests of agriculture. It would be tragic if we were to take a step this afternoon, in the heat of debate, which we may greatly regret later. We need more time, and more reasoned discussions.

Therefore, Mr. Chairman and fellow delegates to this crucial convention, under these circumstances, I move that the vote be postponed and we send our negotiators back to the drawing board to produce something we can agree on at some future date.

Peter Budlowski was a thirty-two-year-old farmer from the tiny Ukrainian community of Ethelbert, some thirty miles north of Dauphin. A marginal farming area, the community still displayed houses with low roofs covered with homemade, axe-hewn shingles, and walls of *Ukrainian stucco*, the dirty-yellow local clay mixed with lime to strengthen it, horse-tail hair and straw to bind it, and animal manure to keep it flexible. Peter was tall, narrow of shoulder, gaunt of body and face, thin dark hair slicked straight back — he looked like the stereotypical city image of an unsophisticated farmer feeling his way through life — and he had a razor-sharp mind (he was later hired as municipal secretary). I had hand-picked him for this impossible job: "Peter. When the call for the vote comes, I will assess the mood of the meeting. If we are winning, we will proceed. If we are losing, we will postpone. Watch for my signal."

"Peter. This may be the most important speech of your life. Your effectiveness will depend as much on appearance and demeanour as words. You must show you came to vote but changed your mind."

"And Peter, above all, you must plan your speech carefully to make it appear totally spontaneous."

Budlowski, the good MFU soldier, stood at the microphone, his dark suit wrinkled, his shoulders stooped as though bearing a great weight, his face reflecting melancholy and perplexity, his voice that of a man intellectually feeling his way through a maze. It took genuine courage:

> Courage is the price which life exacts for granting peace.
> He who knows it not knows no release from little things.[8]

I have seldom been so proud of anyone.

He was enormously effective. He had made his observations and his words were inspired. He had become convinced this was the only way. The play-acting had become the reality. He was for real. There were scattered shouts to "put the question," but the noise abated. The delegates recognized sincerity. They were thinking hard. We were going to snatch victory from the jaws of defeat.

It was time for the seconder of Budlowski's motion.

Eggert Sigurdson was a highly successful farmer from Kenville, fifty-ish, medium height, moon-faced, pleasant, soft-spoken and passionate. He was highly respected as a long-time labourer in the vineyards of the Co-operative Movement, the MFAC, and the MFU. He was always immaculately dressed, a *white-collar* farmer, erudite, well-read, the picture of sophistication, who knew his way around the world of business, politics, and organization. I had specifically sought him out and informed him of my plot: "Eggie. If it appears like a defeat, Budlowski will move to postpone. I would like you to second his motion. You and Peter will make a persuasive combination. People will listen. Be first in line at the mike."

He was: "Mr. Chairman. I wish to second the motion to postpone."

The chair gave him the floor. The world held its breath: "Mr. Chairman and fellow delegates to this significant convention of an old and honourable organization."

The audience was listening intently. We were going to pull it off: "Ever since three weeks ago when I was asked to second this motion...."

He paused. He had recognized his error.

A portentous silence, like that preceding a cyclone, pervaded the enormous auditorium.

Then, like a thunderclap, there was a great roar of whistles, shouts, and derisive laughter as MFAC supporters, genuinely moved by Budlowski, realized it had all been a contrived manoeuvre.

Budlowski's motion to postpone the decision was quickly defeated. So was the motion to merge which routinely followed.

President John McCallister, fearing return to the old warfare and desperately seeking to rescue something from the debacle, moved an amendment to include the three producer co-operatives in the new OFM. It was laughed and shouted into oblivion. The MFAC old guard had come to do a hatchet job on the hated MFU. They did it, adjourned, and went home. A grateful MPE gave the MFAC an *extraordinary* grant of six thousand dollars to cover costs of the meeting.

For me, it was the first of a long list of defeats.

MFAC supporters, delirious with joy, almost fell over themselves, and the mezzanine balcony railing, congratulating each other on their victory. I, with the taste of ashes in my mouth, waited for the boisterous crowd to thin and then walked slowly down the long semi-circular stairway from the mezzanine. Part way down I caught up with a very old, frail man, with two canes, working his way down, one cautious step at a time. I took his arm to assist him and noticed the delegate's tag on the lapel of his suit jacket: "This speaks highly for you sir, that at your age you should still take sufficient interest in the politics of agriculture to come to this important convention."

He stopped to rest, glanced at me through age-bleared eyes, gasped for breath, and quavered: "Oh, I don't give a shit about politics or agriculture or this damn meeting. I quit farming twenty years ago and couldn't care less. Somebody gave me this here red tag and told me to come here today and vote against that son-of-a-bitch Schulz."

I was caught in the coils of my own Machiavellian machinations.

❖ ❖ ❖

8

Parity Prices

And Sisyphus, with waning will,
Watched the rock roll down the hill.
AUTHOR UNKNOWN

WITH CASH ADVANCES IN PLACE, the concept of parity prices for farm products became the mantra of the MFU. Western Canada was a great world breadbasket, and 60 per cent of our wheat was exported. That was good for the general economy, gaining in both low food prices and export-earned foreign currency, but bad for the farmer.

Alfred Marshall's *theory of marginal utility* held true: the last bushel of wheat sold on the competitive market set the price for the entire crop. Worse, the price for the entire crop was set by our exports to war-ravaged Europe and underdeveloped Asia and dirt-poor Africa. Our farmer's prices were set by economic conditions in the world's poorest countries, but our costs were established by the Canadian economy, one of the world's richest. We either could not sell, or sell at a loss.

W. B. Beattie, Dairy Farmers of Canada president, explained: "A surplus of food is a national asset and who has a greater responsibility to carry this than the Canadian people through the government? To ask the farmers to supply Canadians their daily fare at world prices and buy their supplies under the protected conditions by which the other branches of the economy operate is rank discrimination."[1]

Canadian Wheat Board Chairman George McIvor, addressed the MPE convention in 1957: "United States exports constituted a gain of 200 million bushels over the previous year.... Every device at the command of the United States authorities was used to move grain to overseas markets ... at the expense of Canada."

However, brusque Industry and Trade Minister C. D. Howe refused to accept foreign currencies or trade goods. Proposals that food surpluses be used as a political instrument in the Cold War, and General MacArthur's plea, "the fight for the Far East will be won not with guns but with larger bowls of rice," were ignored.

American historian Richard Hofstadter wrote: "The United States was born in the country and moved to the city."[2] So it was also in Canada. The St. Laurent government, observing the accelerating exodus from farm to city and the declining relative importance of agriculture in both economic and political terms, and not wishing to offend urban voters with increased food prices or higher taxes to subsidize food exports, left any form of *food bank* the burden of the farmers. Presidential candidate Adlai Stevenson's pungent critique that inability of governments to use surpluses of food constructively represented "a breakdown of imagination and leadership," meant nothing to these political pragmatists.

Farmers attempted to compensate for decreasing prices by increasing production, but they were caught in a spiral: the more they produced the more it cost but the lower the price went and the poorer they became. Voltaire's Dr. Pangloss's prescription that the productive person was one who grows two blades of grass where only one grew before, was making them paupers.[3]

Jake Schulz, president of the Manitoba Farmers Union, asked: "Why did our government encourage us to produce during the hot war but not now when food is a weapon in the Cold War? If we cannot dispose of our wheat now when millions of people are hungry, does it not disgrace our intelligence? The price of hogs dropped two cents a pound yesterday. Does that mean the people of the world are less hungry today than yesterday?"

And Joe Phelps — the other *terrible twin* — raged:

> What in hell do they mean by a surplus of wheat? How can we have a surplus of food when most of the world is hungry? The problem is not overproduction, but under-consumption. Peoples are no longer isolated from each other. The extravagant waste during the War,[4] and modern communications, have opened the eyes of the underdeveloped world

to the wealth of the West. Our surpluses are what most of the world does not have enough of, yet our farmers are being technologically displaced while our governments are too stupid to understand what is happening elsewhere or too arrogant to care. The population of the world is exploding.[5] Our bounty is not a curse but a national treasure. Instead of curtailing food production, our government should be concentrating on getting it to those who need it.[6]

But raging, and arguing that the problem was not overproduction but inadequate distribution, did not help Canadian farmers. In 1953, net farm income dropped about 12 per cent to $217 million. In 1956, the GNP boomed from $26 billion to $30 billion but the farmers' share decreased despite increased sales and farmers, representing 13 per cent of the population and a $10 billion industry, received only 5.4 per cent of the national income. In 1957, DBS reported that in the previous five years net farm income dropped from $1,919 million to $1,053 million for Canada, and from $1,118 million to $448 million for the West. In the decade before 1958, the farmer's share of the consumer dollar dropped from fifty-one to thirty-nine cents, grain prices dropped 21 per cent for wheat, 37 per cent for oats, 27 per cent for barley, but costs of goods and services used by farmers increased 50 per cent.

"We are living off our depreciation," thundered Joe Phelps, and all agreed farmers were caught in an inexorable cost-price squeeze. But the solutions to the problem, proposed by the two opposing groups of farm organizations, represented two profoundly different views of agricultural economics: one advocated reduced production; the other, expanded markets.

Leaders of the federations and pools — with the sometime exception of the Saskatchewan Wheat Pool — seemed less concerned with incipient farm bankruptcies and destruction of rural communities than with the fear of high farm commodity prices. MPE Vice-President George McConnell told an MFAC meeting in 1953 the demand for $2.50 a bushel of wheat "will ruin the Canadian farm economy." The curse of the farm economy was overproduction and their prescription was to reduce prices, and consequentially, the number of farmers. Yes, they favoured some sort of price supports, but they must be low — and flexible.

Conversely, the farm unions argued this "economic law of business" does not apply to farming. The farmer cannot close his plant and lay off his workforce to go on public relief while unit prices are maintained through the creation of a shortage of supply. Farm production could not be adjusted by reducing prices.

On family-size farms, perhaps 75 per cent of costs were fixed, and the farmer could not reduce them by firing himself or letting part of his land lie idle, for it is the last few acres and the last few bushels of yield that bring the margin of profits over costs. As the price for his products decline, the farmer is harder pressed for efficiency, and the first and universal law of farming is that greatest profit comes from highest yields. Therefore, he strives for the highest possible productivity to maintain his living standard and meet his fixed costs. Those claiming that lower prices reduce farm production had not farmed or did not believe history.

Indeed, it may have the opposite effect. If a farmer nets two hundred dollars per cow one year but only $150 the next because of lower milk prices, would he cope with his 25 per cent loss of income by reducing his herd, or compensate for his loss by increasing his herd?

The answer, farm union leaders argued, was obvious. Flexible price supports will only flex downward as they will not reduce farm production. A formula for low and flexible price supports as advocated by the pools and federations would condemn the farmer to operate under the fictitious concept of a free market which, in practice, did not exist within the Canadian economy.

Ezra Benson, U.S. President Eisenhower's secretary of agriculture, verified that. Blaming farm surpluses on post-war fixed price supports, he had scrapped them in 1952 and instituted a system of flexible supports. In 1955, he admitted they were a failure: the overproduction he sought to control by allowing prices to flex downward had induced greater production.

So, why not switch to other products? What? Only shortages were keeping up the price of some farm products. When farmers moved into those products the bottom fell out of the market. That left only one choice: leave the farms. And they did. In 1940, 33 per cent of the population of Canada were engaged in agricultural production: by 1956 it was 13 per cent. And the number of farms had decreased 22 per cent.

Those who argued if grain production was unprofitable, farmers should take the advice of the *experts* to get out of it, did not realize — or ignored — the extent of farm diversification. From 1949 to 1957, wheat acreage was reduced seven million acres and about a hundred million bushels. From 1951 to 1960, cereal production decreased 12 per cent while conversely, other production increased: cattle – 68 per cent; calves – 22 per cent; hogs – 43 per cent; eggs – 56 per cent; milk – 12 per cent.

But this roused the objections of other *experts*. Professor J. R. Cavers, head of the Department of Poultry Husbandry, Ontario Agricultural College at Guelph (my professor at the University of Manitoba in 1946), told the CFA convention in Montreal, January 27, 1958, that prices must be reduced to reduce the number of egg and poultry producers. Professor J. N. Nesbitt, head of dairy science, University of Manitoba, warned "there is room for only a limited number of farmers in dairying, and plans must be developed to encourage farmers to leave the farm."[7]

Simultaneously, promotion began for providing farmers with borrowed money to replace the money they were not receiving for their products. Governments and some farm leaders argued price support policies must not favour the larger farmer, but policies proposed by *experts* and adopted by governments tended toward fewer and larger farms.[8] The philosophy of shrinking the number of farmers to fit available income, rather than increasing aggregate farm income to sustain the farmers, reached its logical culmination in the late sixties in two major studies — one federal and one provincial — which, obsessed with overproduction, recommended a drastic reduction in farm population "faster than the natural rate of attrition" and more sources of credit for those remaining. The recommendations, consciously or otherwise, seemed designed to make the world safe for agribusiness.

Farmers attempted to close the gap between costs and income by borrowing with a vengeance. From 1950 to 1960, farm indebtedness increased 88 per cent. Farmers borrowed from banks, the Farm Loan Board, the Farm Improvement Fund, the Manitoba Agricultural Credit Corporation, and the Federal Credit Corporation. By 1996, the FCC alone had outstanding loans of $4,066 million against estimated collateral of $3,919 million — a value gap of $146 million.[9]

Farm union leaders were not Luddites retarding change. They had lived through the world's worst Depression and most savage war, and witnessed change that would have staggered their grandparents. Indeed, they were the bearers and disciples of change who encouraged farm diversification and, in many cases, were personal exemplars of that philosophy. But they profoundly believed in the efficacy of the *family farm* as an economic unit from the perspective of both management and productivity. They saw no benefit for farmers, or the general economy, of farmers switching from one deteriorating line of production to another when they had no control over prices.

For almost a century farmers had championed free trade and fought against the national policy of protectionism, but were realizing the battle was lost. So their thinking changed. If the government protected industry with tariffs, import duties, trade restrictions, anti-dumping laws, and direct subsidies, agriculture was entitled to similar protection.

Joe Phelps slammed his fist on the table at an MFU convention:

> When industry receives generous benefits from the taxpayers, it is 'job creation,' but when farmers ask for a decent price, it is a 'subsidy.' And that comes mostly from those who already have price guarantees giving them cost-of-production-plus-profit returns. Our government subsidizes just about every industry in the economy.[10] Shipping, railways, banks, coal mining, gold mining, are on the public dole. Imagine! The gold mining industry was subsidized $13 million last year and what contribution does it make to human welfare compared with the food producing industry? We have minimum wage laws for those working and unemployment insurance for those who are not. We have fixed railroad, airline, and telephone rates to guarantee their owners a return on investment. Our government subsidizes newspapers, those great apostles of free enterprise, so we unwashed masses can read their propaganda that farmers must not have subsidies. Farmers operate in an international economy over which we have no control. Our government must recognize this.

Actually, the Liberal Government of Canada had recognized this. In 1946, they passed the Agricultural Prices Support Act which: "shall endeavour to secure … a fair relationship between the returns from agriculture and those of other occupations."

It had not lived up to its promise. Each year $200 million was allocated for price supports, but by 1952 spending totalled only $10 million. In its first decade, expenditures for supports (eggs, potatoes, apples, butter, beans, honey, skim milk, cheese, hogs cattle) totalled about $94 million — and of this $70 million was spent during the 1953 *emergency* foot-and-mouth epidemic which should have been paid out of other funds. During about the same decade (1948–57), subsidies to the gold mining industry — employing fewer than twenty thousand persons, one-third of the number of farmers in Manitoba alone — was about $102 million. Subsidies to industry in the form of tariffs was estimated at $4,000,000,000.

By 1955, purchasing power of hogs and cattle was about half that of 1951. Wheat, selling for $1.81, basis Thunder Bay, in 1945, was now $1.49 a bushel. Meanwhile (1955–56) support prices for wheat elsewhere was: Argentina – $2.72; Austria – $2.62; Chile – $4.50; France – $2.64; Belgium – $2.56; Finland – $3.93; Switzerland – $4.19; Norway – $3.43; West Germany – $2.72; U.K. – $2.30. The United States, our main competitor, did not fear *unmanageable* surpluses: their wheat support price was $2.30. In Canada it was $1.40. The Canadian farmer was forced to compete with the American treasury.

The farm unions argued that prices of farm products should not be based on what India or Liberia could pay, but on the "cost of production," or "parity" with incomes in other sectors of the Canadian economy. This could be achieved by the government of Canada either accelerating sales to allow market prices to rise, or by providing adequate support prices as was done by our market competitors. Thus was born the concept of "parity prices." Farm union members popularized it throughout the West.

Webster's defined "parity prices" as "a balance between prices received by the farmer and prices he pays for labour, equipment, etc." The Farm unions defined "parity" as "equality between the farm price index and the farm cost index." To Liberal Minister of Agriculture Gardiner it was "farm purchasing power equivalent to the purchasing power during a base period." Conservative

Minister of Agriculture Douglas Harkness saw it as "a relationship which is the same between prices farmers receive for commodities and prices for which the commodities are sold" — whatever that meant.

The concept caught fire. In May 1955, the CCF introduced a resolution in Parliament asking the government to establish "a parity price system for farm products." In March 1956, the Conservatives requested, "legislation to create parity of prices for farm products to ensure a fair cost-price relationship."[11] All opposition parties unanimously supported both motions. The Liberals were unanimously opposed.

Agriculture Minister James Gardiner defended his opposition to the resolutions by stating floor prices under his support program were "pretty well in line" with those advocated by the Canadian Federation of Agriculture.[12]

The CFA, established in 1935, was the national voice for the provincial Federations of Agriculture and affiliated co-ops. It was for fifteen years the only spokesman for Canadian agriculture. During that time it developed an easy — and seemingly incestuous — relationship with the long-reigning Liberal government.

It was sometimes difficult to distinguish between Liberal and CFA policies. Finance Minister Walter Harris told the annual meeting of the Ontario Federation of Agriculture: "Rising productivity of agriculture has important implications ... for government and the Federation.... Nothing can be accomplished by adoption of policies which will not permit economic forces to bring about readjustment."[13] That philosophy became the mantra of the CFA whose leadership seemed to be aspiring to be national statesmen rather than spokesmen for farmers who paid their salaries and gave them status.

Gardiner, in opposing the Conservative resolution for parity prices, continued: "[The CFA] say in their statement they do not want floor prices on cattle ... and support prices on hogs is much as they think it ought to be and as we think it ought to be."[14] In *Jimmy Gardiner: Relentless Liberal*, the minister is quoted stating: "I and my officials discuss every important matter concerning agriculture [with the CFA] before action is taken."[15]

The CFA, in a commendable effort to get rationality into farm price supports, appointed a policy committee to make a study and recommendations. In late 1954 the committee reported: "The most satisfactory base period for Canadian agriculture is 1925–29.... A general level of agricultural prices representing the same purchasing power per unit of production as obtained from 1925 to 1929 should provide fair returns to agriculture today."

They compiled a statistical formula of prices for nine farm products (wheat, oats, barley, corn, cheese, butter, milk, eggs, hogs) during that base period, multiplied those by the cost index increase since then, and calculated what current prices should be. This, they concluded, should be the *fair relationship price*. Then they committed the ultimate obscenity: in what appeared almost calculated perversity, they recommended support prices at: "A range of from 65 to 85 per cent of the fair relationship prices would, for the key commodities mentioned, appear to leave the price support program *with a maximum of flexibility consistent with minimum protection to the interests of the farmer*."

Canada's national farm organization, claiming to speak not just for active farmers but for virtually the entire rural community, proposed a farm products price support formula providing 65–85 per cent of what the farmer needed to survive. Then it boasted this would provide "minimum protection to the farmer."

Practically applied, the CFA formula indeed provided *minimum protection to the farmer*. In 1956 prices and supports were:

Livestock, good steers, Toronto, 100 lbs.

10-year average market price $21.38

Average market price in 1956 .... $18.30

CFA formula support floor $15.16

Hogs, grade B1, Toronto, 100 lbs.

10-year average market price $27.84

Average market price in 1956 .... $24.40

CFA formula support floor $20.28

Wheat, No. 1 Northern, Ft. William, per bushel

10-year average market price $1.75

Average market price in 1956 .... $1.49

CFA formula support floor $1.33

So, when Gardiner opposed the Conservative resolution for parity prices, stating his own support formula was "pretty well in line" with that of the CFA, he was being generous. His floor price on wheat of $1.40 a bushel, on which the farmers were going broke, was actually higher than the $1.33 proposed by the CFA.

The CFA defended the formula as proposing only a *floor* price, not a market price. But anyone with experience or with a modicum of intelligence knew a floor price almost inexorably tends to become the market price. Why would any buyer pay more than the price the CFA formula states a product was worth?

Even Agriculture Minister Gardiner admitted to Parliament: "Low floor prices tend to drag down the free market."[16]

Distributed CFA material stated: "The theory and methods for calculating basic prices, arrived at by the statistical formula, are complex and not as readily grasped as would be desired."

On the contrary, the farmers grasped it all too well. The delegate body at the CFA annual convention in Edmonton, in January 1955, rebelled. Headlines reported: "Price Formula Fails to Win Approval."[17]

Nevertheless, on March 3, 1955, the CFA executive presented the rejected price support formula to the Government of Canada as official policy. Their brief explained: "We do *not* believe it is practical to have a price support program to guarantee the farmers prices *which represent full, fair (or parity) relationship for each product*."

In his address to the CFA annual convention on January 24, 1956, CFA President Hannam praised this formula as: "Undoubtedly the most comprehensive and statesmanlike statement of national agricultural policy ever issued in Canada."[18]

In November 1956, Hannam told the annual meeting of the Ontario Federation of Agriculture: "A 100 per cent parity program would turn consumers and taxpayers against a government that tried it and lead to its downfall."[19]

At the same meeting, Liberal Finance Minister Walter Harris referred to the CFA as "good friends of the government."

It was understandable that the Liberal government and the CFA, their existence coterminus from 1935 to 1957, should think similarly, but the thinking of the federations, frozen in amber, did not change with the change in government and in the thinking of both government and farmers. Tragically, the CFA presented their formula as official policy for agriculture precisely when the Conservative Party, which became government on June 10, 1957, was vowing support for "parity prices for farm products."

The CFA, consciously or unwittingly, made itself a barrier behind which government could hide from the farmers when, after the 1958 election, Diefenbaker was asked to implement his promise.

Long the sole spokesman for agriculture, the CFA greatly resented the advent of the Farmer's Union. While fighting the union, it felt compelled to forsake its previous apologia and compete for rural support with the brash and aggressive newcomer. In doing so, it became a caricature of a farmer's representative.

In 1956, the CFA's major request to Cabinet was for more and easier farm credit. In practical terms, without improved prices this could result only in more farmers going bankrupt faster.

In January, 1957, the CFA national board resolved: "That the CFA generally adopt a more aggressive policy in making representation on behalf of agriculture."

Pursuant to this new *aggressiveness*, they passed a resolution requesting: "that the price support on spray process skim milk powder be increased to sixteen cents per pound."

The government raised the support to seventeen cents. The next year, a resolution thanked the government and requested that supports be kept at that level. So much for the CFA's new *aggressiveness*.

In early 1957, the formula's 65 per cent floor was raised to 70 per cent. At the meeting of the national board, December 5–6, 1957, Saskatchewan CFA Director T. G. Bobier moved: "That the 70 per cent be raised to 75 per cent." Parker, the CFA's Manitoba director, argued "this is the back door to parity and I do not want it." The motion was defeated.

To ensure no further tampering with the formula, the same meeting passed a motion, moved by J. B. Lemoine, CFA director from Quebec, and seconded by Parker: "That our CFA policy on price supports (at 70 per cent of the cost of production) shall be based on the philosophy outlined by the policy committee (in 1954)."

This was occurring precisely while a ferocious debate on the possibility of including *parity prices* in the Conservative government's Agricultural Prices Stabilization Bill raged in Parliament.

On August 1, 1957, as though to ensure "that no good custom should corrupt the world," the CFA surpassed even itself. President Hannam wrote to Prime Minister Diefenbaker: "In reply to your enquiry ... as to the policy of the CFA on cash advances on farm stored grain ... my reply [is] that beyond ... implementing the *Prairie Grain Producers Interim Financing Act* ... the federation has no policy on this question. We have no request that cash advances be made.... We believe there is little demand for cash advances on grain."[20]

Seven weeks after the election of the Conservatives committed to cash advances and only a few days before Diefenbaker announced a permanent program of interest-free cash advances, *the CFA still supported bank loans instead, with farmers paying the interest.* In his address to the CFA Annual convention, January 28, 1958, President Hannam described cash advances, already enacted, as "an emergency measure." That *emergency* has lasted forty-six years.

In January, 1958, the Western Agricultural Conference (the western division of the federations and co-operatives), meeting in Winnipeg, debated a resolution: "That the price for wheat for *domestic* consumption be at the cost-of-living index standards." It passed only after "domestic" was changed to "human," reducing the amount of wheat to be sold at parity prices by two-thirds.

The same meeting debated a resolution that: "The government of Canada purchase stocks of grain held on farms ... *at prices which will give a fair and equitable return to the producers in relation to the cost of production* ... for a national food bank." It passed, but only after being redrafted to read: "that the Government of Canada institute a national food bank, through the purchase of farm held grain." Reference to the purchases being made at "a fair and equitable return to producers" was deleted.

But one resolution, with a long and tortured history, passed: "that the government of Canada establish a price support program based on the cost of production on agricultural products."

Farm Union members had, through infiltration and publicity, carried their message about *parity prices* to meetings of the co-operatives and the federations. As with cash advances, it was a slow, frustrating process. Again we had to fight the producer co-operatives and the federations of agriculture, provincially and nationally, and those farmers who did not want to waste time discussing price problems — they just wanted more programs to borrow more money to produce more goods — for less.

Nonetheless, in October, 1954, delegates to the MPE annual convention endorsed a Grandview resolution that: "the federal government set the price of wheat for Canadian consumption on a parity level with our Canadian economy."

Even a two-price system, limiting a parity price to the portion of wheat sold on the domestic market, offended Parker. He phoned U.S. Senator Frank Carlson, who was promoting a two-price system, upbraiding him for having stated that "Canadian farmers had no objection to a two-price proposal."[21]

In October, 1955, delegates to the MPE annual convention almost unanimously endorsed a Grandview resolution that, "We go on record favouring 100 per cent parity prices for all agricultural products."

That afternoon Gerald Habing, former president of the MFAC, moved to rescind the resolution. The delegate body that had voted for the Grandview resolution in the morning now voted 107 to 37 to kill it. Then they passed Habing's motion that, "we endorse the support price formula of the Canadian Federation of Agriculture." That was the *65 per cent of parity* formula.

The 1956 MPE annual convention debated a resolution sponsored by Erickson and Grandview: "That we go on record as being in favour of full parity prices for all agricultural products."

It passed only after it was amended to read: "That we work toward a higher degree of parity."

But in 1957 we got our revenge. In addition to the MFU, resolutions supporting parity prices were adopted at the annual conventions of the three producer co-operatives and the MFAC.

In March, the annual convention of the Manitoba Dairy and Poultry Co-op supported a Grandview resolution, "that the MDPC go on record as favouring parity prices for farm products."

In June, the MFAC annual convention endorsed a Grandview resolution urging "the government of Canada to establish a price support program based on equality with the cost of production on all agricultural products."

In November, the United Grain Growers annual convention endorsed a Grandview resolution, "that we favour parity prices for farmers."

In October, the MPE annual convention passed a resolution from several associations including Grandview: "Resolved that the Government of Canada establish a price support program based on the cost of production on all agricultural products."

Resolutions going from the western federations and co-operatives had to be cleared through the Western Agricultural Conference before going to the CFA annual convention. On January 25, 1958, despite opposition from MPE board member George Franklin because, "I do not know how to establish production costs," the WAC approved that resolution. To me it was magic. The resolution on parity prices adopted by the policy-making annual convention of Manitoba Pool Elevators was endorsed by the Western Agricultural Conference and sent on to the policy-making annual convention of the Canadian Federation of Agriculture.

It was a fateful resolution. Four days later it would create havoc at the national convention of the CFA.

And I, having been elected by the MFAC, was a director from Manitoba on the national board of the CFA.

It was the premier farm organization. It had the ear of government. It met in convention annually to establish policy by vote of its delegate body — theoretically.

In January, 1958, the annual convention was held in Montreal. The affairs of the CFA were conducted by the twenty-five-member national board of directors representing all provinces but Newfoundland. In 1958, the allotted three national directors from Manitoba were Manitoba Dairy and Poultry Co-operative President John Monkhouse, Manitoba Pool Elevator President William J. Parker — and I.

I had arrived.

There I sat in my beautiful, new, fine-textured, grey Donegal-tweed suit, white starched shirt, and red knitted tie that picked up the subdued red flecks in my suit. In all of Canada, I was one of twenty-five. I was a member of the elite.

The day before the convention, this elite board met to decide which resolutions, submitted by member organizations, would go to the open convention. Indeed, that is why we were the elite — to decide what we should allow the common herd to discuss and vote on. Clearly, democracy in an organization is fine so long as it is not allowed to spread to the ordinary delegates.

One by one, resolutions were disposed of: "This one will go in. Agreed?" "Agreed." "This one is on the books from last year and redundant. Agreed?" "Agreed." "This one is self-contradictory and should not be taken to the convention. Agreed?" "Agreed."

The drone became routine and I became relaxed. Everything was in order. I had made it to the top. Nothing can go wrong....

"We won't take this one to the convention." It was the voice of W. J. Parker, MPE president and first vice-president of the CFA.

"No. We will not take that one to the convention," agreed John Brownlee, the tall, austere, thoughtful, courteous, cautious, distinguished, bespectacled man with grey-brown hair parted down the middle of his skull and a lugubrious expression of perpetual melancholy, former premier of Alberta, president of United Grain Growers Company since 1948, and long-term UGG representative on the national board of the CFA.[22]

The resolution before us was brief and clear: "Be it resolved that the Government of Canada establish a price support program based on the cost of production on all agricultural products."

It had originated in the little town of Grandview, won approval of the delegates at the MPE annual convention, and was endorsed by the WAC despite the opposition of the MPE delegate to the WAC. Like a salmon surviving the hazards of ocean, lake, shoals, dams, eagle-eyed birds, predatory animals, hungry humans, and the river, to return to its source, it had survived. There was only one more obstacle in the raging torrent....

It was now before this august body....

And the powerful CFA directors around the table were about to consign MY resolution to the garbage heap of history....

I was jerked out of my self-congratulatory reverie....

"Mr. Chairman. Mr. Chairman. May I ask your indulgence. I wish to discuss this resolution on parity prices. I believe it should go to the convention." I heard my own voice quaver.

"Mr. Schulz. You have been daydreaming. Disposition of that resolution has already been agreed to."

"Nevertheless, I want to return to it." The bile was churning and, as though in a dream, I heard myself shouting.

Dr. H. H. Hannam, CEO and chairman of the board of directors of the CFA, had an honorary doctorate from St. Francis Xavier University, was chairman of the National Agricultural Advisory Committee from 1943 to 1957, president of the International Federation of Agricultural Producers from 1949 to 1951, member of the Canadian government delegation to the United Nations Food and Agricultural Organization since its inception, and a Companion of The Order of the British Empire. President of the CFA since its inception in 1935, he was the premier spokesman for Canadian farmers (made a fellow of the Agricultural Institute of Canada in June, 1958). He was a short, sturdy, educated, always impeccably dark-suited, executive-type, soft-spoken, genial man — unless contradicted. Then his eyes became icy and his voice steel-edged: "As you wish. But I remind you we do not have time to waste."

"Mr. Chairman. I remind Mr. Parker a resolution supporting parity prices was adopted at the annual convention of the MPE of which he is president. I also remind Mr. Brownlee a resolution supporting parity prices was adopted at the annual convention of the UGG of which he is president. I suggest these two gentlemen are required to take this resolution to the floor of the convention for debate and disposition."

Hannam was not mollified: "Nevertheless, we are not taking it to the convention."

"Mr. Chairman. A resolution for parity prices was adopted in the past year by every farm organization and producer co-operative in Manitoba and by the WAC. This board has no choice but to take this resolution to the delegate body of the convention."

In desperation, I looked around the mirror-polished table in the large, dark-panelled, high-ceilinged, opulent room in the Windsor Hotel. There was no word or glance of encouragement.

"Mr. Monkhouse. The Manitoba Dairy and Poultry Co-operative of which you are president endorsed parity prices at your last convention. Surely you will want to take this to the delegates here so it can be presented to government if agreed to?"

Tall, well-built, ruggedly handsome, always smiling, pleasant, John Monkhouse had told the MFU annual convention in 1953, "We farmers must be prepared to take lower prices for our products," but now he had a resolution from his membership requesting parity prices, so what would he do? He looked at me and smiled: "No. I do not know what *parity* is."[23]

I felt like Samson, "eyeless in Gaza, at the mill with slaves."[24]

Parker, Brownlee, and Monkhouse were refusing to support the resolutions passed by their own conventions.[25] And there was nothing I could do about it. Or was there?

"Mr. Chairman. If this board refuses to present this resolution to the open convention tomorrow I will do so myself," I shouted.

"Hah! You won't even get a seconder." Parker stated the obvious. The balance of the board meeting was a blank....

I was finished. So near but so far. All was for naught. The Sisyphusan rock had rolled back down the hill.

"The labour and the wounds [were] vain."[26]

9

Victory — and Defeat

Success is only delayed failure.
GRAHAM GREENE, *A Sort of Life*

T HE PEREMPTORY KNOCK ON MY HOTEL ROOM DOOR startled me.
It was after 11:00 p.m. I was lying, fully clothed, on my bed, fatigued but too angry to sleep, seething with helpless fury against those I believed were betraying the trust of the farmers, pondering on how to get my resolution before the convention next day, and knowing I could not....

The *deus ex machina*, the device classical dramatists created to extricate their heroes from impossible conundrums, had arrived.

Charles Hunt stood at my door. I almost wept: "Charlie! Your presence almost makes me believe there is a God. I have never been so happy to see anyone, except my wife, and right now I need you more than I need her."

Hunt was on his way home from Europe. Knowing of the CFA convention, he stopped in Montreal. Knowing I would be attending, he sought me out. As a director of Manitoba Pool Elevators he had accreditation as a delegate at the CFA convention. Quickly I explained what had transpired at the board meeting: "Charlie. If I move the resolution on parity prices at the open convention tomorrow, will you second it?"

"You're damned right I will." Charles Hunt was a practising Christian who never used profanity. The depth of his anger was registered by the fact that he made this an exception.

"Charlie, you know what we are contemplating cannot be done?"

"So we will do it anyway."

The following day we reduced the normal decorum of these usually smug, self-congratulatory and relaxed affairs to a shambles. Hunt was magnificent, standing in the middle of the convention floor smiting about him like a Viking berserker determined to go down surrounded by a circle of slain.

Like stalking tigers, we patiently awaited our opportunity.

A resolution, forwarded by the CFA national board, was read:

> Be it resolved that support prices be established according to a formula which takes into consideration living and production costs, as well as the fluctuations of demand, as is contained in the CFA policy statement on price supports.

We pounced.

I moved, and Hunt seconded, an amendment, innocent but lethal: "That we delete the phrase: 'as well as the fluctuations of demand.'"

I explained: "Market demand has no connection with production costs. We currently have a surplus of wheat and the price is decreasing, but production costs are increasing. If price supports are set according to 'market demand' they would be absolutely useless just when we need them most."

Convention Chairman Hannam immediately recognized the danger: acceptance of our amendment would gut the CFA support formula.

He called on Dr. Hope, CFA staff economist and author of the "65 per cent support" (already changed to 70 per cent) formula, to explain why the amendment was not acceptable.

Both Hannam and I were stunned by Hope's response: "What Mr. Schulz says is correct. I see nothing wrong with his amendment."

Hannam, visibly embarrassed, spoke sharply: "But removing that clause would mean *parity* in our formula."

Hope was not helpful: "Parity is the cost of production. That is what the farmer needs to survive."

Hannam, a picture of consternation, decided he should do the explaining himself. Parity prices, he argued, was a ridiculous concept. It was impossible to define and even more impossible to persuade governments to accept. The CFA support formula was far superior because it allowed for "a large measure of flexibility" consistent with fluctuations in market demand.

Hunt was scathing: "Mr. Chairman. You say *parity* cannot be defined, but Dr. Hope has just defined it as 'the cost of production.' Also, your own formula states farmers are entitled to price supports of 70 per cent of cost of production, or parity. If, with the acres of statisticians available you are not able to define *parity* how did you manage to arrive at a definition of '70 per cent of parity'?"

Hannam was adamant: "Our formula is based on cost-price relationships during a particular historical period. We have worked from there. But how does one define *cost of production*? What would that include and how would we persuade government to accept it?"

Hunt was merciless: "If they need to have *cost of production* defined for them, just tell them we will accept the definition they wrote for the *Gold Mining Act*, in which they have defined it lucidly."[1]

The dam was broken. Unexpect-

Charles C. Hunt. Credit: University of Manitoba Archives and Special Collections, MSS 24, Winnipeg Tribune Collection.

edly, others from whom we had not expected support rushed in like a flood.

A. R. Stewart, from Ontario, chairman of the CFA committee on unemployment insurance for farm labour, was appalled: "We have here an executive that seems intent on doing everything possible to stop the farmers from getting that $250 million [appropriated under the new Conservative *Agricultural Prices Stabilization Act* enacted four days earlier]."

Another Ontario delegate repeated a statement made earlier by Gordon Greer, president of the Ontario Federation of Agriculture: "Our policy of 70 per cent of cost of production is not meeting favour with farmers. We must do better. Cheese producers are receiving 93 per cent of parity and that is not enough. Farmers are going broke."

Fred Milne, a Saskatchewan Wheat Pool director, stated: "We have spent the last fifty years trying to *get away* from support prices set according to market demands."

And another Saskatchewan delegate added: "Implementation of this formula would decimate the farmers."

Hannam fought back: "Farmers are capable of producing 50 per cent more than they are producing today, and would if we made it profitable for them. This would cause unmanageable surpluses as in the United States."

Clearly, he was less concerned with low prices than with high production. A delegate interjected: "If high, rigid support prices have caused these *unmanageable* surpluses in the States, what has caused the even higher per capita surpluses in Canada?"

Another delegate was even more succinct: "High prices *may* increase production but low prices *force* it."

A delegate recalled that, at an earlier meeting Hannam had admitted that he, a dairy farmer, faced with reduced prices but no commensurate reduction in production costs, would be forced to compensate by getting another cow and increasing production.

Parker weighed in. He could not support the amendment because: "Any price support formula must consider 'fluctuations of market demand.' We used to produce Timothy hay for horses. Now tractors have replaced horses, so what would we do with the timothy hay if price supports encouraged its production?"

He sat down, embarrassed, when someone shouted: "Cows also eat timothy hay."

Relative to the expressed fear that high prices would cause surplus even the Treasury could not bear, a delegate stated that the cost of supports to American farmers was actually a fraction of what we kept reading in the newspapers, which used gross rather than net figures. He added that the total cost of farm price supports was a very small fraction of the costs of storing military surpluses, recently revealed by the Hoover Commission, which was a direct subsidy to industry. He concluded by explaining that the American farmers were not fools intent on pilfering the Treasury; to reduce costs and save the smaller farmer they had voted in several referenda to limit production in return for fair prices.

A delegate, obviously persuaded by Hannam, argued that "Parity" was an impossible dream. But another, in an oblique criticism of Hannam (a dairy farmer), replied it was interesting to note that many of those opposing parity for the general farming industry already had it for themselves, such as dairy farmers.

To the charge that price supports at the parity level would inevitably lead to "total government regimentation," an Alberta delegate agreed imposed production controls should not be encouraged, but argued he would be better off producing a hundred bushels of wheat at two dollars a bushel than two hundred bushels at one dollar a bushel.

To Hannam's statement that: "Parity would cost the taxpayers of Canada $60 million a year," a Saskatchewan delegate responded: "The small subsidy the Canadian consumer pays is his cheapest guarantee that he will have enough to eat and a consequent high standard of living."

Another delegate stated that, considering the market structure, if consumers were not paying enough to give producers adequate returns, then farmers were actually subsidizing consumers.

To suggestions by several delegates that parity prices must have limits, Hunt responded that those promoting parity supports have proposed a two-price system for wheat, which would favour the smaller farmer and limit the supports to individual farms: "But surely it is silly and self-defeating to begin promoting limitations before we establish the principle of parity."

A Nova Scotia CFA director opposed our amendment: he feared an imminent surplus of eggs "because prices are too high."

Hunt shot back: "There is an easy cure for that. We will just charge you more for our western feed grain."[2]

Hunt's Missouri twang, as always when angry, was pronounced, and an exciting novelty to the many francophone Quebec delegates, who encouraged him with boisterous laughter and applause.

We took the convention by storm. We savaged the authority of the CFA hierarchy.

The delegate body of some three hundred persons cheered us loudly.

Then they voted for our amendment by a substantial majority, destroying the entire basis of the CFA formula.

Lorne Hurd, editor of the *Country Guide*, official organ of the United Grain Growers Grain Company (UGG), accosted Hunt and me at our coffee table. His naturally red face even redder with fury, he glared at me and shouted: "You have been saying the leaders of the CFA cannot properly represent farmers because some are themselves not actual farmers."

I shouted back with equal fury: "I didn't say they *cannot*. I am saying they *are not*."

Hurd mumbled that it appeared to him the criticism of the CFA formula was an attack by "Farm Union people."

Hunt silenced him: "If the attack on your ridiculous formula can be attributable only to Farm Union people, then God help the CFA. And if the ideas expressed by those defending this formula permeates the CFA, then God help the farmers."

Hunt said to me, with an expression more of sorrow than anger: "What manner of men are these that our farm newspapers have hired to be our opinion-makers?"

Indeed, and ironically, much of the more virulent opposition to parity prices for agriculture came from farmer-owned publications. At the precise time the debate was raging in Parliament to force the Diefenbaker government to honour its pledge of farm price parity in its *Agricultural Prices Stabilization Act*, the *Country Guide*, owned and operated by the United Grain Growers Grain Company, carried a year-end article by W. H. Haviland stating: "The Diefenbaker government has, I think wisely, withdrawn from its original position of all-out support for parity."[4]

A month later, the *Country Guide* editorialized: "Price supports should not create incentives to production which perpetuate surpluses and prevent desirable adjustments," i.e., get farmers off the farm as the Liberals, joined by the Conservative since they had become government, were saying repeatedly.[5]

While farm families were bankrupting themselves buying state-of-the-art machinery, the *Country Guide* editorialized: "The greatest threat to the family farm is either the inability or unwillingness of farm people to keep in step with mechanical and technological innovation."[6]

Another *Country Guide* editorial criticized the Farm Union leadership because: "Guaranteed prices based on parity, or costs of production, which they advocate, could amount to subsidies running into the hundreds of millions of dollars."[7]

A year later an article by editor Lorne Hurd again criticized the Farm Unions for proposing to government that "the issue is not how to reduce the number of farms, but how, through pricing and marketing policies, to maintain an adequate standard of living for those on the farm." The same article approvingly quoted Agriculture Minister Harkness: "The problem with price supports is to provide needed help to the farmer, but in a way that will not serve as an incentive" — just what Liberal Minister Walter Harris had told the CFA three years earlier.[8]

And two months later *Country Guide* editor Lorne Hurd criticized Harkness for keeping supports too high: "It is high time the government ... [realized] its mandatory price levels on eggs and hogs under the *Stabilization Act* are too high.... The CFA has called for action [to have] eggs and hogs either removed from mandatory supports or have the supports lowered."[9]

Clearly, with friends like that....

Perhaps even more vigorous than the *Country Guide* in opposing parity prices for farmers was the *Manitoba Co-operator*, owned by MPE and paid for by its farmer-members. It reprinted articles by the American Farm Bureau (U.S. equivalent of the CFA) and editorials by anti-parity media such as the *Christian Science Monitor*, and the *New York Times*. It also did its own editorializing: "As a fundamental section of the overall economy, agriculture is entitled to considerations similar to those granted to other segments [but] it seems extremely unlikely the Canadian economy could support the high cost of any scheme that would act as an incentive program."[10]

Maddeningly, no matter how often the farm unions stated they would deal with *incentives* caused by price supports by trading production limitations for remunerative prices, the media, particularly the farmer-owned papers, considered anything suggestive of *parity prices* for farmers as anathema.

The *Manitoba Co-operator* editorially boasted that the CFA (65 per cent) formula was superior to the American formula because it is "free from rigidity … and recommends support prices that never become incentives."[11] And again: "The hardiest of perennial weeds is the idea that the farmers should receive their costs of production.… The general rule by which production of any product is determined is that price is set very largely by what the consumer is willing to pay."[12]

Clearly, the editor of the *Manitoba Co-operator* did not apply that criteria to newspapers, heavily subsidized by the federal post office. But if both the *Country Guide* and the *Manitoba Co-operator* were merely expressing the opinions of the presidents of the organizations that owned them, why blame the hirelings?

But the farmer-owned papers were not unique in indifference to farm problems and ignorance of what was happening elsewhere. In mid-January, 1958, two weeks before the CFA annual convention, at the beginning of the next federal election campaign, and exactly when the Farm Unions and the Opposition in Parliament were attempting to flush out the Diefenbaker government on precisely what they meant with their reference to *parity prices* in their *Agricultural Prices Stabilization Act*, the *Edmonton Journal* wrote an editorial entitled "A Fantastic Suggestion," asking: "What group is guaranteed a profit, payable by the taxpayers, based on cost of production?"

Obviously, the editor had never read the *Gold Mining Assistance Act*. Obviously, neither had the editor of the *Winnipeg Tribune,* which reprinted that editorial on January 15, 1958.

Both Hunt and I had read that editorial and were reminded of it by our tiff with *Country Guide* editor Lorne Hurd. To avenge ourselves, and just to see if we could do it, we returned to the convention floor and exhumed the resolution which had made it here all the way from Grandview, but which the board had rejected the previous day. *My resolution.*

Miraculously, like some vagrant sperm that survives its fellows to fight its way up some errant fallopian tube, it was about to create new life. We moved and seconded the resolution stating that the CFA convention resolved that: "The Government of Canada establish a price support program based on the cost of production on all agricultural products."

And it too passed.

We had finally won.

Next day was my last on the national board of the CFA.

But *my resolution* had been adopted by the delegate body. It was part of policy. Nothing could change that: One week later, On February 5, 1958, the national board of the Canadian Federation of Agriculture presented its annual brief to the Government of Canada.

My resolution had disappeared. So had the resolution Hunt and I had amended.

The brief to Cabinet did not mention the two resolutions on parity prices Hunt and I had proposed, and which had been adopted by the CFA convention delegates.

In their place was the anaemic: "The price of wheat milled for *human* consumption [should] be raised to a level more in line with general Canadian price levels and living standards," and there should be *"reasonable* deficiency payments" on grain sold.[13]

It was painful to note that wheat for *domestic consumption* represented about 10 per cent of total Canadian wheat production.

Other areas fared better in the brief to the government. This included fully one-and-one-half pages (of a total of seventeen) on requests for more and easier farm credit.

The brief contained requests for action on estrogen-treated poultry, TB-free areas, feeding garbage to hogs, vibrosis in cattle, cereal plant breeding, treatment of condemned animals, disinfecting of trucks, reducing the value of the Canadian relative to the American dollar, hiring of farmers as PFAA appraisers, allowing tariff-free entry on beekeeping equipment, study and promotion of nickel alloy in ploughshares, a 20 per cent depreciation allowance on farm granaries, asking the media to reduce emphasis on grain surpluses (as though that would make them disappear). There were requests for protective tariffs on imports of lamb, mutton, potatoes, hatching eggs, honey, and dehydrated grasses, and a quarter-page urging protection of B.C. bulb growers from competition of American and Japanese imports.

There were expressions of gratitude to the government for price supports and import controls on wool, eggs, turkey, butter, skim milk, and cheese, and the warning that: "The dairy industry must be kept in a healthy condition and this cannot be done if it is subject to being undersold or undermined by imports from countries with lower costs of production." At that time, the dairy industry was barely feeding the people of Canada while the grain industry was pumping several hundred million dollars annually into the Canadian economy from the sale of exports.

There was one interesting resolution.

At the board meeting the day before the open convention, J. B. Lemoine, president of L'Union catholique des cultivateurs, second vice-president of the CFA, and a member of the committee that had concocted the monstrous 65 per cent formula three years earlier, had challenged his colleagues on price supports for maple syrup: "We could here, for once, make an exception to the CFA formula. We must have at least the cost of production for this product."

At the warning, from Parker and other directors, that high support prices would inevitably lead *to strict government regimentation* of farmers, Lemoine had exploded:

> We always worry about production controls. We always worry for fear the government might legislate down the production pattern in conjunction with price supports. There are more bankrupt farmers in Quebec than in all the rest of Canada. They still farm with a walking plough and a horse and ox hitched together. They have never been beyond their own fences. They have never developed beyond the stage of agriculture in feudal times. They would probably be happy if the government took over their farms.

So there, stated boldly in the CFA's brief to the Government of Canada on February 5, 1958, was Lemoine's resolution: "That a support price of twenty-five cents per pound be established on maple syrup."

On the basis of the above grab bag, the next Manitoba Pool Elevator annual report, October, 1958, informed MPE members that: "The CFA delegation met with the prime minister and Cabinet on February 5, 1958 … requests and recommendations approved at the annual meeting were presented.… The brief attached first importance to price support guarantee legislation."

But my resolution had disappeared.

On January 29, 1958, Hunt and I did not know that a week later the CFA Executive would consign our efforts to the garbage can, so we proceeded as though our work was of value. We took over the CFA Convention and turned it into a policy-making body for its delegate body instead of an annual outing for its directors.

Hannam's attempt to stop us was crushed like a tin can by Hunt:

> Dr. Hannam, the American government is subsidizing its farmers by buying up surpluses at fixed prices and dumping them on the world market. In payment, they take strategic goods and local currencies. That is the policy of the American government and their Treasury is picking up the tab. Here it is government policy to sell only for hard currency and to not take goods in trade. That means the Canadian farmer is left alone to fight the American Treasury and we are taking a massive loss. You, Sir, have stated adopting the American policy here and giving our farmers parity prices would cost the Canadian Treasury $60 million a year. Are you so dense that you cannot understand that, if there is a gap between farm income and farm production costs, and if that gap is $60 million, and if the Canadian Treasury is not paying it, then the Canadian farmer must?
>
> Canadian farmers are the victims of national policy. Our government is unloading problems and costs on a vulnerable economic group. That is understandable. But that you, the leader of an organization ostensibly representing farm interests accepts this, and states almost boastfully how little our support program has cost our Treasury, is inexcusable and unforgivable.

Then Hunt skewered the CFA itself: "Dr. Hannam. The real problem with this organization is that it is bankrupt. And not in the pocketbook. I mean in the head."

Hannam, deeply distressed and desperately attempting to regain control of the convention and policy, again called on his hit man.

Dr. Ernest Hope had a PhD in agricultural economics and a personality so outwardly calm and pleasant, almost insouciant, that few would argue with him. He was of medium height, slender, sallow-faced, bespectacled, fifty-ish, with a small moustache and thinning hair carefully combed from a neat part on the right side of his head. He often wore tweeds, and his progress anywhere was preceded by a long, ever-lit pipe on which he puffed contentedly while discoursing on any subject. As the author of the CFA price support formula, he now attempted to redeem himself in the eyes of his employers for his earlier heresy by explaining how he could define *70 per cent of parity* but not *parity*.

It was my turn. I stopped him in mid-sentence: "Dr. Hope. In our earlier exchange you admitted that the farmer needs cost-of-production prices to survive, yet the CFA policy advocates a support floor of only 70 per cent of cost of production. How do you expect the farmer to survive on that?

Again, I was stunned by his answer: "We do not expect him to survive on this. Many of those who have left the farm because of low prices have never been better off. Some are making eight thousand dollars a year for part-time work."

It was too much:

> Dr. Hope. You are a fine person but a classical example of one who gets the best education and remains ignorant. Clearly you are not making your living farming or you would not defend this ludicrous formula. You know nothing of farming except statistics. The only advice you give us is how to produce more for less. The fact is, the harder we work the less we get paid per unit of labour, and the more we produce the faster we go broke. We need a pricing plan for farm products that will protect us from the vagaries of the market, just like the corporations from which we buy our supplies. Obviously you are

not the man to provide it. All you need to do to win our support for your formula is to show us how it is good for farmers. You have been unable to do that and I suspect by now even you must know it is a farce. Instead of telling us what you think is good for us why don't you just sit down and listen to the farmers here tell you what we need.

Hope, visibly distraught, laid his pipe on a nearby desk with shaking hands. He attempted to regain self-control. His face was very red. He looked the parody of a *tweedy Englishman*. That night, in his hotel room, Dr. Hope died of a heart attack. While not knowing until a week later that the "Parity" resolution passed by the delegate body, with or without the help of Hope, had been in vain, my bitterly disillusioning experience at the Board meeting the previous day had determined me, like Milton's Satan, to "not give Heaven for lost."[14] I wanted another confrontation. I phoned a friend in Manitoba.

10

Cyclops Triumphant

Once more unto the breach, dear friends....
SHAKESPEARE, *Henry V*

Nick. I WANT YOU TO ARRANGE A PUBLIC MEETING in the heart of Parker's district. I want you to invite Parker. Then invite *me*. Fill the hall with people. Most important, I want you to put an ad in the southern rural papers advertising the meeting and put in BLOCK LETTERS *that I will be there to attack Parker*. Put it on the radio too. That should draw his crowd to defend their hero."

Nick Manchur was a successful farmer just south of Winnipeg, a member of MPE residing in Parker's administrative district, a capable and energetic organizer, a spokesman for farmers, a participant in all things political, a tough customer — he once personally ejected a heckler from a political meeting at which he was speaking — and a provincial director of the MFU. There was no need to explain to him twice.

I would eviscerate the lion in the den of his home district. I would incapacitate the one-eyed Cyclops as when: "Ulysses bunged his eye up with a pine torch in the dark."[1]

A week later the hall at Morris, Manitoba was filled to bursting. In a dispassionate manner, supported by reams of meticulously annotated documents, I made the case against Parker. I showed how the farmers were being treated by their own leaders; that if governments were not responding to farmers' problems it was less the fault of governments than of the fact those problems were not being presented by the farm leaders.[2]

Parker did not attend the meeting.

He did not need to.

Toward the end of the meeting a man rose: "This was a rigged meeting. We have heard only one side of the story. Perhaps Mr. Parker is not here because he is busy.[3] I make a motion that another meeting be called to hear Mr. Parker."

Raymond Siemens, of Parker's district, moved an amendment: "That Mr. Schulz also be invited to attend that meeting."

The amended resolution passed. No second meeting was called.

Cyclops was safe within the cave of his constituency. And he had made, and would continue to make, farm policy.

In 1954 the MFU, promoting farmer control over prices, proposed a Livestock Marketing Board. MFU President Jake Schulz asked for MPE support pursuant to a 1952 MPE convention resolution proposing "that we proceed to organize marketing boards to handle different commodities." Parker responded swiftly. He called a meeting of all MPE associations, at Brandon, to hear Schulz explain his plan. Prior to that meeting Parker sent a three-page letter, dated March 4, 1954, to each association, stating: "The Manitoba Pool Elevator Board is not endorsing any particular plan.... This [1952] resolution cannot be interpreted to mean the delegate body unconditionally supported creation of a marketing board for all agricultural products."

In case of any doubt among delegates, another letter to all MPE associations, dated April 6, 1954, clarified: "We must advise that Manitoba Pool Elevators will not support the proposal for a livestock marketing board at this time."

The MFU proposal was soundly trounced at the meeting.

Five years later, as the farm unions were having some success popularizing parity prices to get farmers cash instead of credit, the MPE board decided to make credit available to farmers to buy livestock: "W. J. Parker, president of MPE announced that the Pool will launch a program to establish feeder cattle associations throughout the province."[4]

The demand for the loans was overwhelming, and once again farmers' attention was diverted from cash to credit. The crunch came when it was time to pay it off — with money they had not earned on the sale of the livestock.[5]

By late 1958 it was clear the Diefenbaker government *Agricultural Prices Stabilization Act* was a farce. In October, 1958, after a speech to the MPE annual convention by Jack Wesson, president of the Saskatchewan Wheat Pool, the Manitoba Pool delegates agreed: "Whereas the deficiency payment to farmers (one dollar per acre, maximum two hundred dollars) announced by the government is totally inadequate, be it resolved we get together with other farm groups and march on Ottawa."

During the debate on the resolution, Parker was cautiously reluctant. As with cash advances and parity prices, he found lions in the way: what organizations would go; who would go; how would they be chosen; how many would go; who would pay, etc?

The resolution was passed but he remained cautiously reluctant: "In the event that western farm organizations should go to Ottawa — I say this pretty carefully — my recommendation would be to use your own money, not that of the local MPE associations."

The Diefenbaker government must have been greatly comforted by a *Free Press Weekly* headline "Farmers Split on March"[6] under which Parker was reported stating there was little public enthusiasm in Manitoba for a "march on Ottawa."

A petition being circulated at precisely that time in support of the march, was signed by 53,820 Manitobans.

On January 16, 1959, at a joint meeting of the MFU, the UGG, MPE, and the National Farmer's Union, called by MFU President Rudolph Usick to coordinate the march on Ottawa, Parker's reluctance became clear. Fred Cleverly, covering the meeting for the *Winnipeg Free Press* wrote a report with the headline, "Parker Cool to March."[7] This aroused Parker's fury, and elicited a rewrite by the paper. While questioning the march in private sessions, it was not politic to have that publicized.[8]

But southern Manitoba did not care. Their hero was immaculate. That was to be a salient factor in another fundamental dispute.

In the summer of 1957, the *loyal MFAC supporters* began taking back their organization, ending the reign of terror we had conducted against them. They plugged district conventions to recapture majority control of the provincial board, one director at a time. Then they plugged the provincial convention to recapture control of the political agenda.

The MFAC, recaptured, immediately reverted to type. At the 1957 convention — *a month before Prime Minister Diefenbaker announced enactment of interest-free cash advances* — they defeated a resolution for cash advances. The convention *did* resolve that "The government of Canada establish a price support program based on the cost of production on all farm products ... with deficiency payments from the federal Treasury."

The minutes of the convention were signed by the new president, Percy Burnell. At the next MFAC board meeting, in support of that resolution, and at a time when Diefenbaker was promoting *parity prices* for farm products, Max Hofford and I — the two remaining MFU supporters on the MFAC board — moved that: "Whereas the wheat price of $1.49 is 56 cents less than the $2.05 the Canadian Federation of Agriculture has established as the cost of production, we favour deficiency payments to give farmers a price at the cost of production."

All six *good MFAC* directors (A. Guild, J. F. Warburton, D. L. Barclay, Mrs. N. R. Jasper, G. E. Franklin, C. C. Dixon) voted against it. When Hofford and I pointed out the delegates at the annual convention endorsed this position, they were scornful. Burnell commented: "We cannot possibly get it." Barclay added: "There are always dreamers at conventions."[9]

On January 18, 1958, MFAC President Burnell met with the provincial government. His brief asked for price supports at "70 per cent of fair relationship prices" — 70 per cent of the cost of production. Three weeks later he approved the Diefenbaker government's *Agricultural Prices Stabilization Act* but expressed regret the government had not adopted the CFA's 70 per cent formula (instead of 80 per cent in the government's formula).[10]

At the Western Agricultural Conference, the annual policy-making meeting of all the western federations and co-operatives, on January 24–25, 1958, the *good MFAC* directors again revealed their thinking. Burnell explained that "Cost of production is the same as parity. This resolution passed our convention but I don't favour it. I am obliged to support it but if someone rewords it I have no objection." The resolution was promptly tabled.

But one resolution did pass the WAC: "That the government of Canada establish price supports based on the cost of production on all agricultural products."

It had been endorsed by the MPE annual convention, was opposed by MPE representative George Franklin because "I do not know how to establish costs," but endorsed by the WAC. *It was the fateful resolution* that, four days later, Hunt and I persuaded delegates at the CFA convention to adopt.

In February, 1958, I reported to the MFAC board, now controlled by *good MFAC supporters*, that despite the MFAC, MPE, UGG, Dairy and Poultry Pool, and WAC conventions having passed this motion, Parker and Monkhouse, the other two Manitoba directors on the CFA board, had opposed it at the CFA convention in Montreal. I then moved that they be removed from the CFA board.

Instead, the good MFAC supporters *removed me*.

But the end of their good works was not yet. On March 10, 1959, a mass delegation of farmers descended on Ottawa demanding Diefenbaker make deficiency payments as he had promised during his election campaign a year earlier. The march on Ottawa was supported by the farm organizations of western Canada — but the MFAC opposed it. After their board meeting new President S. E. Ransom of Boissevain, announced: "In opposing a mass delegation we believe, if government yielded to such pressure, the way would be open for all other groups to use the same tactics to gain their demands, and the result would be chaotic."[11]

But that was several months in the future. Meanwhile....

Until the MFAC annual convention in June, 1957, the MFU-member-dominated board of directors still controlled the agenda and administrative apparatus. We feared we would be overwhelmed at the convention, but we determined it must be done honestly.

The board was plagued by reports of inappropriate delegate selection. It appeared there would be many more delegates like the elderly man who had told me at the amalgamation convention the previous February: "I don't give a shit about agriculture or this damn meeting. I quit farming twenty years ago and I couldn't care less, but somebody gave me this delegate's tag and told me to come here and vote against that son-of-a-bitch Schulz."

At Grandview, the board of the Dairy and Poultry Co-operative had officially decided to send *no* delegates to the MFAC-MFU amalgamation convention, but moments after the meeting adjourned a board member handed a credential to a person of her choice.

At Gladstone, the local MPE board was asked to call a membership meeting to elect delegates to the amalgamation convention, but they refused because "it would just be an MFU meeting."

At Minnedosa, when an MPE member who was also an MFU member asked for a credential, the chairman reportedly stated: "As long as I am chairman no MFU member will receive a credential to attend an MFAC meeting." The same person reported that, when he told the Minnedosa MPE annual membership meeting the MFAC bylaws required convention delegates to its convention be elected by the membership, a representative from the MPE provincial office, in attendance, stated they need not comply because those bylaws were about to be changed.

At Arborg, the boards of three local co-operatives sent delegates to the amalgamation convention without the membership being informed of the convention, or that delegates would be sent.

At Roblin, the general membership meeting voted to support amalgamation, but later the board appointed three delegates and instructed them to vote against amalgamation. When the chairman was later reminded he had received a letter stating delegates should be elected at a membership meeting, he replied the instructions were not specific: they stated *should*, not *must*.

Clearly, the method of delegate selection was becoming crucial to the future direction of the organization. So, we on the MFAC provincial board decided to clear up the confusion.

The authority of the delegates selected was clarified by the *Companies Act* under which Manitoba organizations operated: "Directors shall be elected by the shareholders at a general membership meeting of the company.... Delegates can do any act respecting the resolutions, bylaws, and proceedings of the corporation in place of and as a representative of the members of the district so delegating them."

The bylaws of UGG, an affiliate member sending delegates to the MFAC convention, stated: "Delegates shall be elected at membership meetings." The UGG head office had so informed its local associations by letter.

The bylaws of MPE, also an MFAC affiliate sending delegates, stated a membership meeting shall be held, "for the election of directors ... and for the transaction of all necessary business."

Since the bylaws required election of directors by the membership, and since the *Companies Act* bestowed on delegates the same authority as on directors, surely it followed that delegates must be chosen by the membership.

The bylaws of the MFAC were crystal clear: "Those entitled to vote at any meeting of the Federation *shall be the duly elected delegates of the members*."

This was a fundamental principle, the guarantee of membership control of the policies and direction of the organization.

Accordingly, on April 22, 1957, the MFAC board of directors, at that time still dominated by MFU supporters, sent a letter to each affiliate local association, including the co-operatives, informing them delegates to the convention must be "elected" at a membership meeting. Anything else was not acceptable.

We knew in many areas there was a sharp divergence of opinion on policy matters between the membership, many of them MFU members, and the old guard executives who operated the associations as their private fiefdoms. And we knew the policies that emerged from the convention would depend on who made them.

Now, once and for all, while we still controlled the provincial MFAC board, we would put an end to incestuous *inner sanctum* control of the organization by *appointing* delegates and refusing to call a membership meeting in fear the *wrong* persons would be elected. We would also put and end to the even more nefarious practice of individual board members quietly slipping delegate's credentials to the *right* people.

The response to our challenge was not long in coming.

On May 10, MPE President W. J. Parker notified all his local associations they need *not* comply with the MFAC board directive.

On June 7, Dave Barclay, an MFAC provincial director, told the board he refused to comply with the board's directive on delegate selection passed at the previous board meeting. He was from Souris, in a part of Manitoba that seemed to consider democratic election of delegates a communist — or at least an MFU — plot, and which feared losing control if this was done. The board promptly removed Barclay from the convention credentials committee to which we had earlier appointed him.

On June 19, in a letter to the *Winnipeg Free Press*, two Barclay supporters, Percy Burnell (elected MFAC president a week later) and D. M. McNabb, stated, bylaws notwithstanding, affiliated associations could choose delegates any way they wished.

The determined fight for control of the MFAC and farm policy made MFAC convention credentials, often simply filed in the wastebasket by association secretaries two years earlier, into prizes contended for. The MFAC annual convention, attended by seventy-five persons in 1950, attracted more than five hundred in June, 1957.

MFAC defenders came in droves. And they were *loaded for bear*. They had tasted blood in February when they killed amalgamation of the MFAC and MFU, and their determination remained unabated. They now came to rid the MFAC of the hated MFU elements within it. For the most part their contributions to the convention were "Shut up!", "Sit down!", "Throw him out!", and "Go back to Russia!"

Max Hofford was appointed chairman of the credentials committee and instructed by the board of directors to refuse a delegate's tag, carrying the right to vote at the convention, to anyone not properly accredited, i.e., not showing signatures of the local officers and the date of the membership meeting at which the delegate was elected. At noon of June 24, the first day of the two-day convention, he reported to the executive that his committee had lost control of the registration process. People were sweeping past the registration desk refusing to show their credentials but later displaying delegate's tags, and it appeared passers-by with no connection to the MFAC were being handed credentials. His hands were shaking: "Dropping bombs on Germany was a picnic compared with this. These people are making me a nervous wreck. I smoked three packs this morning. My mouth tastes as if someone shit in it."[12]

By mid-afternoon, six of the eight members of the credentials committee had resigned. Vice-Chairman Fred Tufford, an esteemed member and director of several co-operatives, and a member of both the MFAC and the MFU, resigned and told the convention: "There are delegates here whose credentials are not legal. If we are violating the constitution and a complaint is made to the provincial [government] secretary [responsible for policing the *Companies Act*] and upheld, it may end this organization."

George Henderson from southern Manitoba had not resigned from the credentials committee but was very unhappy. He took the floor, read the letter the board sent to all affiliates stating delegates must be elected at membership meetings, and stated: "People have been violating the board's decision. There is no misunderstanding on the interpretation of the directive to the associations.... As one of the two remaining members of the credentials committee, I will *not* go on record to say which delegates to this convention are legal."

Another person who had resigned from the credentials committee refused to act as a scrutineer because there was no way of knowing who were properly accredited delegates.

But the old guard had come to do a job and did not intend to be stopped by technicalities or legalities. A leather-lunged delegate from the south, shouted that only a few persons present were raising the issue of delegate accreditation: "They are throwing a monkey wrench into the works. It's happened at every convention during the last three years. Let's get our business done."

He was cheered to the rafters.

Russell Barnlund, quitting the credentials committee, retorted: "If we want to get on with our business, let's stick to the constitution." He was drowned out by catcalls and foot stamping.

Roy Gamey, from Strathclair, stated in frustration: "It all hinges around two words, 'duly elected,' because some feel it means elected at a membership meeting and others feel it means appointment by local boards."

He did not appreciate that the interpretation of those *two words* meant the difference between elite and membership control.

Neither did the majority of the delegates. They voted to ignore the board's instructions to the credentials committee, and that: "This convention accept any official credential signed by the president and secretary of the member association."

An amendment, that a membership meeting must be called in those locals where is it demanded by at least twenty-five members, was defeated.

The establishment feared losing control. They would defend *democracy* — so long as it was not taken seriously by the people.

Tufford stated some "alleged delegates" who had forced their way past the registrations desk, had credentials not signed by either one officer or the other. His challenge was ignored.

The media explained: "Although they were MFAC members, the first loyalty of many who opposed the admittance of appointed delegates was unquestionably to the MFU."[13]

Clearly then, it was the MFU members who were fighting for membership control. But the time for appeals to reason was long past. It was time for the hammer.

Next morning, as MFAC president and convention Chairman John McCallister was about to call for a vote on a resolution, I rose: "Mr. Chairman. The chairman of the credentials committee has informed the board a number of persons carrying voting delegate's tags are not properly accredited delegates. Therefore, before this vote is taken we must establish who has the right to vote."

Gentle, soft-spoken, self-effacing John McCallister, caught in a crossfire he neither welcomed nor knew how to deal with, did not immediately grasp the significance of my statement.

"Anyone who is a delegate is allowed to vote."

"But Mr. Chairman, that is precisely my point. Before we proceed to vote we must decide who the voting delegates are." John McCallister still did not comprehend: "Anyone wearing a delegate's tag is a voting delegate."

"But Mr. Chairman, the chairman of the credentials committee has informed us not everyone here wearing a delegate's tag is an accredited delegate. You must decide who is a delegate." John McCallister was now comprehending but unwilling to assume the opprobrium of deciding which delegates were delegates: "We will let the convention decide who the delegates are."

"So who is going to be allowed to vote on that question?"

"Anyone who is a delegate."

"Mr. Chairman. In the name of common sense, you cannot have delegates decide who the delegates are until you determine who the voting delegates are. Those who are not properly accredited delegates cannot vote to seat themselves as delegates just because they carry credentials. The decision about who are properly accredited delegates must be made by you, as convention chairman, and it must be made on the basis of what the MFAC constitution defines as an accredited delegate."

"I have not sought legal advice on this."

"Then you should get some before we proceed."

The crowd was roaring at me to "Sit down!", "Shut up!", and "Throw him out!" Those who rushed to the microphones to support the position I had taken were simply drowned out.

Chairman McCallister called for order among those at the microphone. I rebelled: "Mr. Chairman, you should call to order the noisy buffoons who want to shut up anyone who does not agree with them."

That elicited more shouts and threats. I stirred the pot: "You see how it is, Mr. Chairman. You get all kinds of scruff in an automatic membership organization."

"You are trying to make a fool of this convention," a leather-lunged delegate shouted. I replied: "No matter how hard I tried to make a fool of this convention, I couldn't possibly do as good a job as you have done already."

Bedlam! Then McCallister announced: "The convention decided yesterday that anyone with credentials, no matter how they got it, is a delegate."

But I protested: "Mr. Chairman, such a motion is an amendment to the MFAC constitution. That requires a majority of two-thirds of the delegates. The motion yesterday did not get anywhere near that much support. Therefore it is invalid."

But McCallister insisted: "The convention has decided otherwise."

Again I protested: "The convention cannot make a decision until you decide, based on the constitution, who is entitled to vote on the decision."

"I have decided. Accept it or get a new chairman."

I felt a tap on my shoulder: "My name is Frank Syms. I'm a reporter with the *Winnipeg Tribune*. You are absolutely correct. People cannot vote to seat themselves as delegates just because they are here. The chairman must decide on the basis of the constitution."

Tough, passionate, articulate, Frank Syms, a native of Nova Scotia and graduate of Dalhousie, of medium height, jet-black hair and moustache, always well dressed, had an expressive face and aggressive manner, and had seen much of the world from inside a Canadian army uniform during World War II. In the next twenty-five years he would be public relations officer for the Red River Co-op, president of the Manitoba NDP, chairman of the Manitoba Liquor Control Commission (one day he closed down fourteen Main Street hotels persistently allowing crowding beyond licensed capacity), development officer for the federal department of northern affairs, and assistant to the Governor General of Canada. But at that moment he was a stranger crouched at my elbow: "I know that. But how I do I persuade the chairman and the delegate body?"

"You get a court injunction to stop the convention."

McCallister, having consulted earnestly with several persons on the stage, was now back at the podium: "We will let the delegates decide who the delegates are."

"Mr. Chairman. If you do that I intend to obtain a court injunction to stop this convention."

The building almost burst from expelled air as many of the five hundred delegates jumped up and down and shouted themselves hoarse: "Hah, hah, hah, you just do that little thing."

The chairman put the question to the convention and the delegates voted to seat themselves. My challenge was answered. My wife and I left the hall almost floating on noisy taunts and insults. I turned to her: "What's an injunction?"

"I don't know, but I think you need a lawyer to get one."

We did not know any lawyers. We did not know anyone. We did not know where to go. We did not know what to do. We walked hand in hand down North Main Street. Suddenly, fixed to the front of an old but impressive two-storey office building, we saw a plaque: *Mitchell and Green — Barristers and Solicitors*.

We had read Leon Mitchell's name in newspapers and knew him to be a Labour lawyer. We went upstairs and asked the receptionist if we could see him on an urgent matter. He was busy: "But his partner, Mr. Green, is free."

That is how we met Sidney Green. He was to become a powerful minister in the Schreyer government a decade later and our lives and careers were to become intimately entwined.

Short, dark, intense, kinetic, in his mid-twenties, recently graduated from law school with a gold medal — and another from the University of Manitoba — he was already known as a *lawyer's lawyer* who had little tolerance for lack of intellectual acuity by man, beast, or supreme court judge. He took charge: "The convention ends today so it is too late to obtain a court injunction to halt its activities, but we can immediately proceed to court to nullify any decisions made by the delegate body."

"Very well. Remember, this is a political case but we must take it to court because those who should remedy it refuse to do so."

"I do not fight political cases. I fight legal cases."

"And remember also, we are going to lose this case. We are challenging the social and economic leadership of Manitoba's agricultural bureaucracy. They cannot afford to allow us to win."

"I do not fight cases to lose."

We moved swiftly. I was informed that, since the MFAC was not a direct-membership organization, only an affiliate association could bring suit. The board of the Grandview Pool Elevator Association promptly called a membership meeting. On July 10, a large majority of the 250 members present authorized the Grandview MPE Association to become the plaintiff in a suit to have business done at the MFAC convention declared invalid. They voted one thousand dollars to pursue the action and appointed me as their agent.

The Bowsman MPE Association voted five hundred dollars to support Grandview. Individuals throughout Manitoba sent several hundred dollars.

Russell Barnlund at Sanford, Parker's hometown, did the impossible. He had been on the convention resolutions committee ignored and disdained by the *good* MFAC supporters. To the fury of the old guard, he persuaded the board of the MFAC district, coterminus with Parker's MPE district, to resolve that: "We support the plea of the Grandview MPE Association for an injunction against the MFAC until this issue is cleared up and the delegates properly elected by the membership … and that we also give financial support in order to help defray the expenses of the plaintiff."

This fight would be for real.

In the next three months, I added eleven thousand miles to the odometer of my car scouring the province for information and witnesses. Eden, Minnedosa, Gladstone, Manitou, Morden, Melita, Killarney, Durban, Swan River, Bowsman, Benito, Snowflake, Oak Bluff, Oakburn, Sandy Lake, Altona, Erickson, Russell, Beausejour, Roblin, Darlingford, Baldur, Arborg, Sanford, Rossburn, Stonewall, Dauphin, Sperling, Elphinstone, Labroquerie, Oakbank, Petersfield, Portage, Gilbert Plains, Teulon, Homewood, St. Pierre, Teulon, Gimli, became zigzagging points of light in my memory as the roads between them blurred before my eyes.

I learned a lesson: friend or foe, take a written statement, have the interviewee sign it, and issue a subpoena immediately after the interview. After a time people *forget* what they said, and that they had promised to attend the trial voluntarily.

Most were co-operative. Some were not. The president of the Dauphin MPE local, which had *appointed* its delegates, and two of the three who attended the convention were not even those *appointed*, refused to accept his subpoena. I phoned Green: "Toss it in front of him in the presence of a witness."

I located the president in the local RCMP office and called a young officer over to witness me intimidating this local VIP: "No! No! I don't want to be a witness."

"But you are here, so you are." I dropped the subpoena on the floor. Harley Armstrong had to stoop for it. He came to court as a very hostile witness. So were most of the other crucial witnesses. The more persons I interviewed the more I became convinced of the rightness of our cause, but the less of victory: It was becoming increasing clear we were fighting the political, economic, and social establishment of the province.

Then I read Green's brief to the court.

"This is brilliant. It is irrefutable. If there is such a thing as *justice* we will win." But Green was the consummate lawyer: "There is no such thing as *justice*. In courts there is only *the law*. *Justice* is made by legislatures."

Then, on January 7 and 8, 1958, we were in court.

One by one eleven witnesses (including several association presidents), all of whom had voted at the convention, paraded before the judge. One by one they admitted they had not been elected at membership meetings, or had not been either elected *or* appointed, or their boards did not know they had attended the convention, or those appointed were not those who attended the convention, or the appointed person had given the credential to someone else. One by one they testified their credentials were not properly completed, or had been altered, or were not signed because even their boards did not consider them legitimate, or were signed by only one officer, or had been obtained by means unknown, or an appointed delegate *took along a friend* for whom a credential was procured. Convention Chairman John McCallister (since replaced as MFAC president by old guard Percy Burnell) testified he had refused to rule on whom were legitimate delegates because, "I did not wish to decide."

We had shown that, even if the convention resolution "That this convention accept any official credential signed by the president and secretary of the member association," was accepted, a number of delegates who had voted at the convention failed even that test. We had proven our case in spades.

It was time for the *big one*.

Earlier I had instructed Green: "I want Bill Parker on the witness stand. I want his unquestioning disciples to know if they are not capable of judging him, others will. I want him to know he is not immune."

"Most of all, I want the world to see I dragged him onto the witness stand in front of a judge."

If I could not destroy the invulnerability of Cyclops, I would let the court do it.

Dragging Parker onto the witness stand was not only the apex of my legal case, but also the culmination of efforts to expose him to rational questioning since he had opposed my resolution on cash advances at the MPE convention five years earlier.

Green called for Parker to come to the witness stand.

Parker was not in the courtroom.

I was quietly exultant.

He had been presented with a subpoena — a court document ordering him to appear. The judge would now be required to send the sheriff to bring Cyclops to the courtroom, in chains if needed, to stand submissively before the blindfolded figure of justice who, unlike the docile delegates to MPE conventions, would not be influenced by his rank or status: "Why do you want Mr. Parker here?" Judge Maybank asked.

Green had assumed the subpoena would be honoured or, if not, would be enforced by the court. The judge's question caught him by surprise: "I want him to identify this letter."

Parker's *special circular*, dated May 10, 1957, had informed all MPE associations that, "a local pool elevator board has the power and authority to *appoint* delegates." And several witnesses had testified their MPE association had intended to comply with the MFAC board directive to *elect* delegates by the membership until they received Parker's letter stating they need not do so.

And we had a transcript, dated October 4, 1957, of a radio announcement of the annual convention of Manitoba Pool Elevators: "Of all the events that happen to a co-operative organization … there is nothing as important as the annual meeting…. The thirty-five thousand farmers in Manitoba will be represented by *properly accredited delegates*. These delegates *were elected at the annual meeting of their associations … through this technique, the farmer exercises control and maintains an alert interest in the affairs of his organization*."

But Parker had negated application of those same criteria — to maintain the same membership control — to election of delegates to the MFAC convention. It seemed his letter to MPE associations informing them they need not elect delegates to the convention as required by the MFAC board, was patent mischief. Finally, we had him. He would be destroyed by his own letter. And the whole world would be able to read about it in the press.

But Cyclops was not about to be humiliated by this court: "I am sure Mr. Parker will admit to having signed that letter. You do not need to have him here for that."

Mr. Justice Ralph Maybank would not exercise the subpoena!

"Everything is politics…."

E. D. Honeyman, solicitor for the defendant, the MFAC, argued that the word *elect* was synonymous with *select*, or *appoint*, or *choose*, or *name*, and therefore has no particular significance; that the MFAC provincial board had no authority to tell the local associations in what manner to *elect* their delegates; that any problem that may have occurred within the organization should be solved by it and within itself. Then he cited a dozen precedents to support his case.

Sidney Green, solicitor for the plaintiff, the Grandview MPE Association, argued that the parade of witnesses had proven that a number of those attending the MFAC convention were not legitimate delegates because they were *not elected, selected, appointed, chosen,* or *named*; that illegal delegates cannot vote to seat themselves; that the convention chairman had failed to abide by the constitution; that the MFAC had violated the law and could not correct the problem it had created so this issue must be referred to the courts; that ruling the actions of the illegal convention delegates as legitimate would mean loss of membership control of the organization. Then he cited a dozen precedents to support his case.

We had an ironclad case. We had demonstrated the confusion within the MFAC, partly due to the intervention of Parker. We had demonstrated *elect* means exactly that. We had demonstrated the MFAC was no longer capable of remedying the dilemma it had created: For the organization to be returned to membership control, the courts must intercede.

We had surely won! No need to spend more time on this.

And by then other matters had engaged my full attention.

❖ ❖ ❖

11

The Ides of March

And we are here as on a darkling plain
Swept with confused alarms....
MATTHEW ARNOLD, *Dover Beach*

O N FEBRUARY 1, 1958, on my way home from the CFA national convention in Montreal, I was in the visitors' gallery in the House of Commons. The chamber was virtually empty, the debates desultory, and my thoughts elsewhere. Members began occupying their seats. All went silent and an air of expectancy pervaded. There was activity and agitated whispering on the government side of the House. Suddenly, the curtains parted and, like a magician appearing out of a puff of smoke, the tall, black-suited figure of Prime Minister Diefenbaker strode magisterially to his place in the front row, and was immediately recognized by the speaker.

"Ah-h-h, Mr. Speaker, Ah-h-h, Today I made an historic trip by air to the Citadel in Quebec City to, ah-h-h, confer with his excellency the Governor General of Canada...."

"This government is supported by 113 members of a total of 265. Its position as a minority government has become intolerable...."

"At the outset of the session assurance was given by the Leader of the Opposition (Louis St. Laurent) that the government might count on the Official Opposition not to place obstacles in the way of the government.... The present Leader of the Opposition (L. B. Pearson) has indicated ... we can no longer expect that...."

"Accordingly ... I now conclude by saying ..."

Stentoriously, determined to wring every drop of melodrama from the situation, relishing his power and displaying the egomania that later reduced him to a caricature of himself, he announced the dissolution of Parliament and an election for March 31, 1958.

I was dumbfounded! The Social Credit Party was imploding. The CCF was hunched over contemplating its collective navel and redesigning its philosophy. The last thing either party wanted was an election. As for the Liberals, on January 20, when Leader Lester Pearson made his bizarre proposal that the Conservative government resign in favour of his "natural governing party," Diefenbaker had disposed of him so mercilessly that CCF'er Harold Winch remarked he doubted the prime minister's commitment to the "humane slaughter of dumb animals," and the Liberals wanted no further duels with their nemesis. The Opposition parties held a majority of seats, but were intimidated in the Commons and terrified of an election. Effectively, Diefenbaker had the freedom of Parliament: he could enact any legislation he wished in the interests of the people of Canada.

So, why did he need an election?

Perhaps Diefenbaker had read Machiavelli's decree that the ruler is entitled to do whatever necessary to acquire and hold power. In practical terms, he needed an election to obtain a majority so he could enact legislation, *not* necessarily in the interests of the general public but rather to pay off political debts. In Machiavellian terms, this was the best time to call an election — when the Opposition were demoralized and defenceless. There, in the gallery of the House of Commons, observing the performance, with Diefenbaker appearing as though selected by central casting, I learned another central principle of party politics: "The best time to kick an enemy is when he is down."

"Dief" stalked the land like a Colossus. He was a virtuoso playing on the strings of the public mood. Iron-grey hair curling above deep-set eyes ablaze with inner fire, staring into the distance above the heads of his audience, jowls shaking, he intoned in the affected, sonorous argot of an Elmer Gantry: "Ah-h-h-h, my fellow-Canadians. Ah-h-h, I have a vision."

To critical observers he was a phoney, at times resembling a dog in heat howling at the moon, but to true believers his cliché-ridden ramblings were sheer poetry.[1] After the dull grey image of McKenzie King (whom *McLean's* had revealed as having consulted with his dead dog on matters political), and emotionally emasculated " Uncle" Louis St. Laurent, Canadians had an exciting leader. For the general public he had that indefinable quality: charisma.

He scattered promises like Johnny Appleseed. Some were self-contradictory — sell more to but buy less from the United States; buy more goods from the U.K. so they will buy more wheat but provide more protection for Quebec textiles and Ontario tobacco — but these were not noticed. What caught the imagination of Canadians was the promises of roads to resources, a trans-Canada highway, reduction of foreign ownership, a NATO food bank, low-interest credit for farmers, a crop insurance plan, the South Saskatchewan dam, development of Arctic sea routes, "everything that can be done" for job creation through public works programs, a Hospitalization Plan to extend nationally what had been pioneered in Saskatchewan, and the ubiquitous P.E.I. causeway (promised by parties in every election since 1873 and finally built in 1996). Hordes attended the professionally stage-managed rallies to see the "Great Canadian" (as billed by Conservative election literature). Over 5,500 attended his rally in Winnipeg, 3,500 — half the population of the town — in Dauphin, 1,500 in the village of Steinbach where he had attracted fewer than two hundred a year earlier. "The Chief" was a locomotive that could not be stopped — not even by those prepared to throw themselves onto the rails.

In rural communities, especially among MFU members, the major election issue was agricultural policy because the late 1950s brought no respite from the cost-price squeeze that had accompanied mechanization and expansion of farms after World War II. The price of wheat was lower in 1959 than in 1950, and the mid-1950s brought a period of poor grades, due to adverse weather and poor harvesting conditions.[2]

Diefenbaker had won their support by enacting cash advances four months earlier. He now reached for the brass ring by appearing to embrace the MFU's ultimate policy. The Tories circulated a pamphlet touting their *Agricultural Prices Stabilization Act*, enacted on January 25, 1958, and claimed it provided "parity prices for farm commodities."

My father, an MP, whom I was visiting while in Ottawa, warned me that the *Act* was not what the government claimed. Indeed, he had so stated in a speech in the House of Commons when he had graphically described it as "the Minister standing beside hell and throwing snowballs to reduce the temperature." I protested: "But in 1953 and again in 1956 Dief introduced motions in the House of Commons asking the Liberals to enact legislation providing for parity of prices for agricultural products."

"I know, but it appears he has had a radical change of mind since he moved from the opposition to being the government."

"But farmers are depending on him. He cannot now reverse his position. He would not get away with it in the next election."

"He *has* reversed his position and he *will* get away with it."

"But two days ago I heard the minister of agriculture speak at the annual convention of the Canadian Federation of Agriculture in Montreal. I quoted from Douglas Harkness' speech: "This legislation will give farmers ... a yearly guaranteed price for all agricultural products ... set at a level having regard to the estimated average cost of production ... to ensure the farmer a fair return for his labour and investment and to maintain a fair relationship between the price received by the farmer and the cost of the goods and services which he must buy."[3]

"You are doing some wishful thinking. Stop listening to election speeches and read the *Act*." He handed me a copy.

It looked so good — and it was so clever: "to provide farmers with a fair share of national income" was only in the *preamble*.

The operative clause in the body of the *Act* stated price supports would be triggered when market prices fell to 80 per cent of the average prices of the past ten years.

No! They could not be doing this! But they were.

The Diefenbaker government had adopted the thinking, and the principle of the price support formula, of the CFA. They were more concerned with surplus production than with improved prices.

The *Act* guaranteed farmers 80 per cent of what we had been receiving.

The *Act* guaranteed farmers 80 per cent of what we were going broke on.

The *Act* guaranteed that, barring wars, crop failures, or famines, prices of farm products would inevitably trend downward.

The *Act* included supports for cattle, hogs, sheep, butter, cheese, eggs. It also included supports for wheat, oats, and barley — *but not what was sold by the Canadian Wheat Board.* The *Act* provided price supports for grain produced in Ontario and Quebec — *but not for western grains.*

The commodities that had triggered the demand for parity prices in western Canada were not covered by the Act.

The *Agricultural Prices Stabilization Act* was an elaborate fraud.

I was familiar with political newspeak: Clearly the government had no intention of enacting a parity price policy — if they meant what they said they would say what they mean — but they would harvest the farm votes by appearing to adopt what had been popularized by the MFU. The Conservatives had to be smoked out.

It all began so innocently.

Tory standard-bearer in the Dauphin riding was Elmer Forbes, a short, pleasant, middle-aged man with the notable facial feature of a bulbous, heavily veined nose. A successful farmer and *old-family* Conservative, he was a naïf in politics who believed he merely needed to spout *Diefenbakerisms.* He proved to be right.

To expose the government's intentions, I attended a Conservative election meeting at Sifton which was to be addressed by Northern Affairs Minister Alvin Hamilton. The hall was full. Hamilton did not come. Forbes delivered a disjointed address, parroting the party line. I waited for the question period: "Mr. Forbes, you stated that your party, if re-elected, will enact legislation to provide parity prices on farm products."

"Yes. We will."[4]

"Could you give us some written evidence of that."

"I have it here." He waved a copy of an election pamphlet.

"Mr. Forbes. That is your party election propaganda. I was referring to the *Act* itself. I have read the legislation and find no reference to parity prices except in the preamble."

"It's in the *Act.*"

"Sir, would you be good enough to show that to this audience."

"I would do so gladly, but I have mislaid my copy."

"Mr. Forbes, I just happen to have a copy right here in my jacket pocket. I will be happy to lend it to you."

I walked to the podium and handed him the document. He accepted it reluctantly, read the preamble and returned the paper to me.

"Mr. Forbes, I am sure this audience of some two hundred farmers and people whose income depends on the prosperity of farmers would be happy to give you time to read the balance of the document."

"No!"

"But Mr. Forbes, you are admitting then that what you said earlier is not true." Forbes replied with asperity: "These questions should be addressed to Mr. Harkness, the minister of agriculture, who is responsible for the legislation."

"But Mr. Harkness is not here and you are the person aspiring to be our MP so I want to know what you know about the *Act*."

"I have not read the *Act* but on my way here, on my car radio, I heard Mr. Diefenbaker say 'this is the greatest hope for farmers ever placed on our statute books' which will provide parity prices and help the small farmer, and I believe him."

The audience applauded wildly. If "the Chief" said it, it was gospel. An unbeliever did not have a chance.

The meeting was adjourned. The chairperson, an attractive, well-dressed, carefully groomed lady, well-known in co-operative, farm and women's organizations, came to me: "Herb, this was very impolite. We all know that you have studied this legislation thoroughly and that you know much more about it than poor Mr. Forbes. It was unforgivable of you to challenge him in this way and make a fool of him."

I had exposed the ignorance of their presumptive Member of Parliament, but I was the culprit! In fighting the Diefenbaker Conservatives, I could do nothing right: even when I was right.

By September, 1958, Trade Minister Churchill would state the government might place a ceiling on, not a floor under, farm prices. In November, Agriculture Minister Harkness warned farmers to reduce production or face reduced supports. In 1959 price supports were reduced for milk powder and turkeys, and terminated for hogs and eggs. But by then it was too late to protest.

A week after the Sifton meeting, on my way home from an MFU meeting in the Portage la Prairie area, the car radio announced Agriculture Minister Harkness would be speaking to an election meeting at Ste. Rose that evening. It was right on my way.

The hall was bursting with aggressive, fire-eyed Tories, and their offspring, who had been excluded from the decision-making councils since 1935 and saw Diefenbaker as their ticket back to the perks and prestige of government. Nothing would stop them. I was not welcome. Someone walked over to the minister, who had just mounted the platform to thunderous applause, whispered to him, and pointed to me.

The minister spoke at length, and then reached his peroration: "CCF'er Jake Schulz, who claims to represent the farmers, said in the house our legislation on cash advances, which has greatly benefited farmers, is 'stupid.'"

His dramatic pause was filled with wild applause for the minister and catcalls and hoots directed toward me.

The arrogance of the minister was palpable. His responses to what he deemed *unfriendly* questions were: "You are misrepresenting the facts"; "You are misrepresenting what I said"; "I do not believe you"; "You CCF'ers know nothing about democracy"; "You do not know what you are talking about"; "Ordinary people like you simply cannot understand this."

Then it was my turn: "Mr. Chairman, the honourable minister has stated his government will enact parity prices for farm goods and his Act has been proclaimed. Would he be good enough to show the reference to parity prices other than in the preamble."

The roof was almost lifted off the hall by shouts of derision. The chairman finally restored order. I was still standing: "Mr. Chairman, it seems anyone who dares speak here and does not agree with the minister risks being trampled underfoot by this herd of hand-clapping hooting ignoramuses...."

The noise was deafening: "Take off your red tie."

"Go back to Russia!"

It was a classical Jamesian *pragmatism*: truth is *expedient* — whatever one wants it to be.

"Mr. Chairman, the minister stated that Jake Schulz said in the House of Commons the legislation on cash advances is 'stupid.' I do not know to what statement the minister is referring, but since Jake Schulz did as much as any individual to promote the concept of cash advances, the minister's statement cannot be true."

The minister stood with arms folded across his chest in an attitude of belligerence while his adoring supporters replied: "Go home and suck your mother's tit!"

"Go to your own meetings, you idiot!"

"Mr. Chairman, this is clearly not the time to argue the point, but I understand the minister is speaking in my hometown of Grandview next Monday afternoon. I intend to be there. If the minister repeats what he said tonight about Schulz's statement on cash advances, I will expect him to prove it or to apologize."

I left quickly, passing through a gauntlet of swearing, fist-waving Tories, into the fresh air.

My neighbour, Stanley Puchalski, who had also attended the meetings at both Sifton and Ste. Rose, came to me next day: "These people must be exposed. But they will not allow it. If you attend that meeting on Monday they will never let you talk. Somehow you must arrange to be heard."

He referred to the last Manitoba Pool Elevator annual meeting: "A man in ordinary farm work clothes was sitting along the north wall of the hall. When the debate became really hot and personal he got up and suggested that we all cool down and get back to the issues we had come to discuss. And it worked."

"I remember the incident. Who was he?"

"Peter Bessaraba. He farms northeast of town. Why don't you call him and ask if he will come to the meeting and use his influence to calm things down again if necessary."

I phoned Bessaraba, introduced myself, and put the proposition.

"I will be there," he responded.

In the early afternoon of March 10, 1958, I should have been warned by the size of the crowd making its way toward the Parish Hall as though all roads led to Grandview, by the number of strangers in town, and by the four RCMP cars parked across the street from the hall. My eyes saw it all but my thoughts were elsewhere and it did not register in my mind.

The minister spoke to loud, incessant applause. And he repeated, with studied emphasis, the comment on which I had challenged him at Ste. Rose. Much of the crowd, as though earlier alerted, went wild. I assumed he had studied the relevant copy of *Hansard* since our earlier encounter and knew he was lying. So, this was a deliberate provocation just to show he could say what he pleased. And the bastard thought he could get away with it.

Then it was time for questions: "Mr. Chairman, last week in Ste. Rose the minister made a statement about Jake Schulz and I cautioned if he repeated it today I would demand he either prove it or apologize. He has repeated that statement. I have in my hand a copy of *Hansard*. It proves the minister has lied. I therefore ask him to apologize."

Lance-straight Colonel Douglas Harkness (retired), an esteemed company commander in World War II and now an esteemed MP for a Calgary riding, strode to the front of the four-foot-high stage, leaned slightly forward, and pointed at me: "I will not apologize to any damned CCF'er."

The applause, and catcalls, rolled across the hall in waves.

"Well, you are going to apologize to this one."

I began moving toward the platform. Men began moving to intercept me. The crowd began moving aimlessly.

"Mr. Chairman," a voice shouted loudly, "This man phoned me and asked me to come here and help him start a riot."

I looked back. It was Peter Bessaraba. He was pointing at me. The crowd was shouting, hooting, and stamping their feet.

I continued pushing my way through the crowd toward the stage.

The chairman, slight, soft-spoken William Abercrombie, was obviously prepared. He began reading a copy of the *Elections Act*, making it sound like the Riot Act by emphasizing "you must disperse" and "there are penalties if you do not."[5] At that instant I realized this had all been planned, but it was too late to stop. The adrenalin was pumping hard.

Goddammit! He thinks he can intimidate me with that piece of shit? The gratuitous insult made me more determined.

A young lady rushed to the piano and played *God Save the Queen*. The chairman declared the meeting closed. Few paid attention to either the anthem or to his declaration.

Forcing my way through the crush of bodies, I unexpectedly came face to face with John Lukie, a leader of the Ukrainian community which owned the Parish Hall: "John, can I rent the hall for another meeting?"

"Sure."

It proved a fateful exchange.

The hall was a blur of motion. As I approached the stage, four men from Dauphin grabbed me to hustle me out the side door. I did not want to go. They forced me to the floor. My supporters pulled them off me. I struggled to my feet....

Splat! Something hit me in the left eye. I wiped off the sticky mess with my hand. It was an egg. A second egg splattered on my beautiful, bright red, finely knitted, three-dollar tie.

I looked through egg yolk out into a jaundiced world. On the west side of the hall, halfway back, a woman was standing on a bench, a paper bag in her hand. And she was throwing eggs....

It was Peter Bessaraba's wife.

In the surreal scene before me, Walter Rutka from Pine River, six feet tall, seemingly four feet across the shoulders, and built like a Mac truck, moved toward Mrs. Bessaraba. The crowd parted for him like the Red Sea for Moses. He knocked the paper bag of eggs out of her hand.

But not before he caught her attention. An egg caught him dead centre on his massive chest and splashed out across his black leather jacket. It looked like a Japanese flag.

I reached the bottom of the short stairway leading up to the stage and pulled aside the curtain. Behind it, squatted on the stair, was an operative from the Dauphin radio station, adjusting a large tape recording machine. I never liked hidden recorders.

I put my boot through it.

Perhaps twenty men were milling about, bumping and pushing, on the stage. The minister had been hustled through the kitchen, out the back door, into a car taking him to Dauphin, out of harm's way.

Below me was pandemonium. The hall was a surging sea of motion: People crowding out through the doorways, clutches of frightened women huddling in groups surrounded by protective spouses, men running back and forth throughout the hall, or standing on benches waving and shouting, or facing each other in pugilistic stances.

Halfway back, on the east side of the hall, sat my wife. She was holding the large black briefcase which had developed a personality — and generated several attempts to steal it — because friend and foe alike knew it contained incendiary documents,[6] such as the *Hansard* I had drawn from it. She was clutching it tightly to her. Anyone wanting it would have had to tear off both her arms. In case anyone tried, on the bench directly behind her stood her father, a powerfully built man, with a look in his eye signalling he was ready to kill.

All was well. Nothing could touch me now. Holding my *Hansard* I moved to the a small table which served as a lectern, and the microphone beside it, still in place and open: "People, I'm taking over the hall and calling a new meeting...."

Ernie McGirr, a lawyer, former Conservative MLA, and committed, vociferous, foul-mouthed Tory from Dauphin, pulled my egg-stained tie behind my neck and was choking me with it. I laid my *Hansard* on the table and turned to strike. My neighbour, Fred Bohdanovich, grabbed my arm to keep me out of trouble. Another neighbour, Otto Young, pulled away my tormentor. I turned back to the lectern. My attention had been distracted for no more than five seconds....

My Hansard was gone!

The document I needed to prove the minister had deliberately misled the meeting, had disappeared. I was helpless....

I glanced around the stage. There was movement in every direction. Fifteen feet away I glimpsed a red cap, weaving its way through the crowd, moving fast, just as it disappeared through the stage exit door. I chased the running red cap through the crowd, off the stage, across the kitchen, out the doorway, into the snow. Under the red cap was Wilbert Molberg. I caught him. He had my *Hansard*. I took it back.

Armed with the document, I pushed my way back onto the stage: "Okay, folks, we will now have a meeting. I need a chairman."

Tall, lean, wind-burned Earl Meyers, referred to by his friends as "the big Indian guide" because of his love of hunting and fishing, chairman of the board of the local Manitoba Pool Elevator Association, loped up from the back of the hall and onto the stage. He was grinning like the Cheshire cat. He took charge: "Ladies and gentlemen. We are going to have another meeting. We will begin with *The Queen*." The crowd joined in.

"Folks. This is not a CCF meeting. The hall has been privately rented and we welcome contributions to pay the rent. This is going to be a meeting to clarify what is in this new agricultural act. It is going to be an orderly meeting. Anyone wishing to leave is free to do so. Those who want to stay are welcome. Mr. Schulz has made a serious charge. He will be given an opportunity to prove it. Then you can ask questions on anything he says."

There were about two hundred persons in the hall, perhaps half the original crowd, CCF'ers, Liberals, and politically unattached, but also some Conservatives intrigued by events. Most Conservatives had left the hall and were standing outside in the bitter cold, gnashing their teeth and plotting, appalled by the turn of events, passing back and forth through the doorways, shaking their fists at me and making rude noises.

I made my presentation, using *Hansard* for support. I explained the clauses of the *Agricultural Prices Stabilization Act* in detail, the nature of the altercation between myself and Harkness, and the hypocrisy of the government which boasted their *Act* included parity prices for farm products when it did not. I explained the intricacies of the operations of Parliament, the verbatim recording of debates by stenographers — whose job was so strenuous they were rotated every fifteen minutes — printed in *Hansard* every night and available to the MPs before next morning's session, so they could review the previous day's debates and change what they considered incorrectly transcribed.

My copy of *Hansard* showed that Jake Schulz had not called the cash advances legislation "stupid." He had referred to one particular clause as "disturbing."[7]

And my copy of *Hansard* also showed that Harkness had agreed in the House that the paragraph was indeed "disturbing" and had amended it to remove the flawed clause Jake Schulz, MP, had detected.

In the midst of my presentation the front door opened and the town constable, flanked by two RCMP officers, entered the hall. The RCMP stopped just inside the door. The constable continued slowly down the centre aisle toward the stage.

Mel Robb's five-foot ten-inch, 240-pound frame bulged in his natty, dark-blue uniform, resplendent with belt and braid. The Conservatives who had abandoned the hall had sent him in to reclaim it for them. He was patently terrified. He moved, ever more slowly, toward me. Partway up the aisle he removed his peaked cap with the police badge, the symbol of his authority, and held it in his trembling hands. He stood below me at the foot of the stage, looking up, waiting for me to acknowledge his presence: "Yes Mr. Robb. You wish to speak with me?"

"You are going to have to leave the hall." His voice sounded small for so large a man, and tremulous.

"Why?"

"The Conservative Party rented the hall."

"The Conservatives have adjourned their meeting and abandoned the hall. I've rented it and I'm having another meeting."

"You rented the hall?" Mel Robb's voice rose several decibels.

"I rented the hall." He did not believe me. He had me. His voice assumed a certain amount of self-assurance: "Who did you rent it from?" His voice rose.

"John Lukie."

"Is John Lukie in the hall?" His voice was now loud and authoritative. He put his officer's cap back on his head as though preparing to take an official action.

"Yes." Loudly, a voice from somewhere in the kitchen.

"Did Schulz rent the hall from you?"

"Yes." The disembodied voice was loud and positive.

The constable appeared to shrink. He took off his cap, held it a moment, looked up, his mouth working as though wanting to say something, put his cap back on, turned and, staring at the floor, shuffled down the aisle and out through the front door, flanked by the two RCMP officers waiting there for him to do his thing.

Then, away from the tumult and shouting of the dislodged Conservatives, we had a good, orderly, informative meeting.

"Herb. There are some very angry people out there. Perhaps we should leave by the back door." My neighbour, Andy Chornoby, shadowing me like a bodyguard, was solicitous of my welfare.

"No damn chance. These big-mouthed bastards from Dauphin and their minister who sneaked out the back door are not going to frighten us in our hometown. We came in the front door and we're going out the front door."

Throughout the evening, and for days afterward, every hour, the Dauphin radio station had lengthy reports on the *riot* at Grandview, and predicted I would be arrested and charged with *inciting to riot,* for which the penalty was *life imprisonment.*

CBC reported I had thrown the eggs and was arrested. I phoned: "Where did you get that report?"

"Why do you want to know?"

"It's not true. I didn't throw the eggs and I'm not arrested."

"Well then, you would be surprised where we got that report."

"No doubt."

"We got it from the town constable."

The newspaper headlines were lurid: "Political Meet Goes Wild: Tories to Lay Charges" (*Winnipeg Free Press,* March 11, 1958) "Eggs Thrown in Wild Political Skirmish" (*Winnipeg Tribune,* March 11, 1958). This was followed by an editorial entitled "Boomerang on the CCF" stating: "It will be surprising if the performance of Herb Schulz does not damage his father's candidature. Heckling within limits is expected … but [the CCF] is in trouble if rabble-rousers and bully-boys go out on the stump." There were no questions asked about why the Conservatives had brought and thrown the eggs, or about why the eggs were thrown, not at the speaker as is usually the case, but at me.

The *Dauphin Herald* editorial, headlined "A Black Week for Dauphin" stated: "It is only proper that … respect be accorded to those persons who hold highly responsible offices … there is evidence … that Mr. Schulz and other CCF supporters were prepared to *take over* any Conservative meetings in this constituency."

I had blindly walked into a baited trap. The CCF was to pay.

So I became an organizer and proselytizer for the CCF.

The *Grandview Exponent* had a report extolling the virtues of the minister and his *Agricultural Prices Stabilization Act,* and that: "One man told the meeting Mr. Schulz had phoned him on several occasions the day previous inviting him to join their crowd and take part in the disturbance." I asked the editor for space, at my expense, to correct his report. He refused. I wrote it out in black grease pencil and stuck it to the display window of the Co-op store for the world to read. It attracted considerable attention.

It was to be the only satisfaction I would get.

I did get my name in the papers, and two days after the event a panel truck drove into my farmyard. The driver introduced himself as Michael Mockry, organizer for the Manitoba Communist Party: "We have been reading about you in the newspapers. It seems to us our two parties have something in common in wanting to change Canadian society. We in the Communist Party have decided to vote Conservative in this election because we believe they will destroy the country faster than anyone else, and then we can take over. We suggest you CCF'ers consider doing the same thing."

We did not agree. My wife and I invited him in for lunch and we had a pleasant conversation. Then he got back into his panel truck and left. I did not see him again until twenty years later, when he was mayor of a pavilion at the annual Folklorama.

Four days after the egg-throwing event I purchased fifteen minutes of time on the Dauphin radio station and laid it on the line: "Obviously some people expected a riot and were prepared. *They* brought the police. *They* brought the eggs. *They* started the shouting. If the minister had told the truth, if the chairman had maintained order, if members of the audience had been less enthusiastic with their shouts of 'Sit Down!', 'Shut up!', 'Go back to Russia!', there would have been no disturbance."

"I challenge Mr. Harkness to come back and debate the remarks he made instead of insulting the intelligence of his audience and then running for a plane. If he returns and acts in the same imperious manner, I expect he will be run out of town again. I was taught to respect those in public positions, but it is sickening to see a supposedly responsible person wrap himself in the aura of his ministerial position to do with impunity what in others would be considered contemptible."

"I understand the Conservatives have announced plans to lay charges against me. I challenge them to do so. Presumably they will have the courage to do so before [election day] March 31."

It was a powerful challenge but I suspected this was a war we had lost. And my humiliation was not yet complete. My wife and I returned from Dauphin late in the night after my radio address. I turned on the radio and heard another report of my impending arrest for "inciting to riot" for which the penalty was *life imprisonment*. I fumed and cursed. My wife was philosophical: "Well, at least nothing much more can go wrong this week."

The phone rang. It was Sid Green. The judge had chosen this day to announce his decision on our suit against the MFAC over the way their convention delegates were chosen. We had lost!

Judge Maybank, who had been *elected* to city council in 1930, *elected* to the Manitoba Legislature in 1932, *elected* to the House of Commons in 1942, and subsequently *appointed* to the bench, resorted to practices in ancient Rome, Latin, and the dictionary, to determine *elect* does not mean *elect* as commonly understood: "Etymologically … the word comes from the Latin verb *elegere*, a compound of the prefix *e*, or *ex*, meaning 'out of' and *legere*, 'to choose'. The two words conjoined indicate a choice of some, of one, from among others. *Cassell's Dictionary* gives examples by Cicero to whom the word was used 'to choose one's friends' or 'to choose certain people out of the tribe.'"

He admitted *Webster's International Dictionary* defined the word *elect* as the Grandview Pool Elevator Association had, namely: "The act of choosing by ballot a person to fill an office … by ballot, uplifted hands, or *viva voce* … [but] the same dictionary defines the world *elect, to select*: to determine by choice; to decide upon; to choose."

In brief, it appeared that the word *elect* meant whatever one wanted it to mean at a given time. So the learned judge ruled: "There is nothing to prevent … delegates signifying they approve the seating of appointed delegates. The matter is one of internal management of the company and it is entirely within the control of that organization."

Mr. Justice Ralph Maybank concluded (a) it is not necessary for member bodies of the MFAC to choose delegates by popular vote, and (b) a shareholder has no right to sue his company over a management decision.[8] We had been demolished. It had all been such a waste of time, energy, and resources. Cyclops, like Diefenbaker, was inviolable.

The calendar beside the phone showed it was the Ides of March.

"That riot was great and so was your speech on the radio. I haven't enjoyed myself so much since the day the pigs ate my little brother." My neighbour, Milton Trembach, often expressed himself in colloquialisms, and he always made me laugh.

But we were doomed! The Tories' most effective piece of campaign literature was a large, white poster, blank except for a set of footprints crossing the page diagonally and the brief caption "Follow John." Millions did.

Diefenbaker's appeal swept across the political spectrum. The political crossover became a deluge. Old CCF'ers who had never voted for any other party, excused their conversion with "I want to vote for a winner for a change." People did not care what party he represented: he was "the Chief." He won the largest parliamentary majority in the history of Canada.[9] Social Credit was destroyed, the proud Liberal Party which had governed Canada for all but fifteen of the sixty-two years since Laurier won in 1896, was decimated. The CCF fell from its peak of twenty-five seats to eight.

Icons fell: Respected national CCF leader M. J. Coldwell, and Stanley Knowles who had inherited the seat of revered party founder J. S. Woodsworth in 1942, were among the casualties. Jake Schulz, who had seemed a permanent fixture in Parliament, was replaced by a man whose name no one seems able to remember. And Fred Zaplitny, the poet-philosopher MP, role model for non-Anglo-Saxons and admired by all who met him regardless of party affiliation — and my idol — was defeated by a nonentity.

"You must accept some responsibility for the defeat of both Fred and your father. That riot you were involved in did not help them." Montague Miller, old Saskatchewan CCF'er, general manager of the Grandview Consumers

Co-operative, and mayor of the town of Grandview, was uncharacteristically angry the following day.

"But Montie, I did not start the riot. They attacked me."

"Then you should have walked away."

"Listen, I am going to do what I believe to be right, and if people here don't like that I can always go back to my farm."

"That's your greatest problem. That damn farm. If you did not have that refuge to go back to you would learn how to deal with people without offending them or forcing them to attack you."

Until Election Day the attack on the *CCF goons* continued unmercifully. I had allowed myself, and the CCF, to be delivered into the hands of the enemy. It worked well for them.

The story unfolded slowly: my challenge to Harkness at Ste. Rose had apparently convinced some people that I must be disposed of. Peter Bessaraba's charge gave credence to the plot. I was amused when several friends took revenge by placing a handful of rotten eggs under the seat cushion of Bessaraba's car. When he sat on them the odour permeated the vehicle so completely he had to buy a new one. The rumour spread that a grateful Conservative Party had purchased it for him. If so, he got the last laugh.

12

Denouement

Things fall apart....
W. B. YEATS, *The Second Coming*

THERE WAS TO BE ONE MORE VICIOUS FIGHT. And one more defeat. For me, in more ways than one, it was *the terminal fight*.

In 1960, the provincial board of MPE decided to construct a new multimillion bushel grain terminal at Thunder Bay.

During the war, when transportation facilities were required for men and materiel, good crops resulted in local grain elevator associations throughout western Canada building more elevators, or adding jerry-built annexes to the elevators they had. The major terminals, where the grain was loaded for overseas shipments, were at Thunder Bay (supplemented by Vancouver and Prince Rupert). The result was that the greatest portion of the grain was stored inland, with slow and expensive access to saltwater ports. Grain shipped east went by rail to Thunder Bay, was transferred to ship to Georgian Bay ports, transferred back to rail to Montreal or Halifax, and then onto ships to Europe.[1] And that was in summer. In winter it was much worse: grain went by expensive rail from Manitoba all the way to east coast ports.

By the mid-fifties some began arguing for change. Since water transport was much cheaper than rail, why not get the grain as near as possible to seaboard during the summer when the lakes were open? Since almost all export grain went to Europe, why not add to inland terminals with oceanside facilities? Why build more storage space fifteen hundred miles from access to ocean shipping?

And there was the matter of price. University professors, economists, government members, and some farm leaders were telling us prices were decided by the market. So let us take them at their word: If surplus supply depressed the market, let us rid ourselves of the surplus. Let us put pressure on the system to sell rather than store our grain.

Furthermore, since storage charges contributed much of the revenue of the elevator companies, there was some concern they were more interested in storing grain than in having it sold. Our concern increased when the elevator companies asked the Board of Grain Commissioners for increased storage charges. When Max Hofford and I, the only MFU members left on the MFAC board after the slaughter of the previous June, moved a resolution that the MFAC oppose such increases, it was defeated by the *good MFAC'ers*. We were not impressed with the statement in the 1957 annual report of MPE that: "It is noted with concern that a 50 per cent reduction in storage earnings, resulting from freer movement of grain, could produce an overall deficit in [elevator] operations."

Our concern was increased further by MPE President Parker's reluctance to have grain shipped through Churchill. It meant a substantial saving to grain farmers, and the shipping lines had informed us that, if we got the grain into Churchill, they would get it out. Indeed, during the fifties, shipments of grain via the Bay route more than doubled — despite the elevator companies telling us every year that shipments through Churchill were at capacity and it could not handle another bushel.

Then, at an annual convention, during a debate on the merits of shipping grain via the Bay route, Parker clarified his position. He reminded the delegates they had a huge investment in terminals at Thunder Bay, and that much of the earnings that paid them dividends derived from these. It was a perfectly legitimate position, but it hardened the resolve of those of us already intent on reducing or relocating storage to force more sales.

The MPE executive decision outraged us. It appeared as another decision made because it was easy, not necessarily because it was best. The outrage increased when it was reported that Parker, when asked what would happen if some local associations objected, had stated they would be kicked out of MPE.

Several local MPE associations — Erickson, Bowsman, Ethelbert, Oakburn, Fork River, Dauphin, Gilbert Plains, *and* Grandview — decided to accept the challenge and stop what we saw as a terminal being built in the wrong place. However, the delegates to the annual convention had ratified the board's decision. Again, we were helpless.

And again, enter the *deus ex machina!*

Funding for the project, in the amount of $3.5 million, had been arranged with Prudential of New York. All was going swimmingly, except that each individual MPE association was an autonomous corporation that owned and controlled its facilities. Therefore, to obtain the necessary security for their prospective loan, Prudential required that each individual association executive approve the project and pledge their assets to guarantee the mortgage. We dissenters had a second chance.

By long practice, immediately following the annual convention, each local association held its annual membership meeting to hear the report of the delegate they had sent to the annual convention. The director who represented each district on the provincial board also attended these. The directors, having already agreed to build the terminal at Thunder Bay, insisted the associations in their district agree with their decision. The threat of associations being expelled from the MPE organization if they did not fall into line was powerful. The memberships of the local associations were persuaded. Over a period of several weeks following the annual convention, one by one the dissident associations capitulated. Of the total of 225 associations, 224 accepted and signed.

One refused. Grandview.

At our annual membership meeting, on November 15, 1961, the irresistible force met the immovable object. Our provincial director, Charles Hunt, was adamant: "We need approval by all associations before we can proceed."

"We are aware of that. That is precisely why you are not getting the approval of this association." I too was adamant.

"But do you realize all other associations have signed and you are going to be standing out like a black sheep?" Hunt asked.

"On the contrary, we are the one white sheep. In the crowd you represent it is not a bad thing to be different," I responded.

"Unless you accept, this association will suffer the opprobrium of the entire pool elevator organization in the province."

"This is not the first time that we in Grandview have been alone, and right."

"You know without your signature we cannot build the terminal?" Hunt's tone of voice was between a threat and a plea.

"We know and we're glad," someone in the audience responded.

"But if you don't agree to go along with the majority this association may be expelled from the MPE organization."

It was precisely what he should not have said. I took umbrage: "Mr. Hunt, you are not helping your case by adding insult to injury. It is MPE and not Grandview that is in trouble. This is our association and these are our assets. If you want us to mortgage them you *ask* our permission. You do not *tell* us you are going to do it and threaten us if we refuse to agree."

Hunt knew he was losing. We were about to take the vote, which would have overwhelmingly supported me, when he pulled his coup: "But the terminal is already partially built. We have already spent several million dollars on it. If we do not get the financing to complete it, what are we going to do with what we have already built?"

"Let it rot." My quick response was pure bravado and highly impolitic. I was stunned by the information. But this was not the time to surrender. It was 2:30 a.m. The three hundred farmers in the hall were becoming restive. I called for the vote on my resolution that we decline to sign the mortgage documents. I was almost too late.

My resolution carried by four votes. It was much less than I had expected, but I was exuberant. Hunt was frantic. The decision was made. There would be no loan and no terminal. We had won.

"Herb, you sure have guts," someone called encouragingly. I turned and smiled to acknowledge the kudos.

Hunt and I were good friends and I had been largely responsible for his election to the provincial executive of MPE by organizing the defeat of *Apollo*. But tonight our interests diverged. This was war, in which no quarter was asked or given. He snarled: "If Herb had some brains instead we wouldn't be in this mess."

Five days later I was on the tractor and stopped to adjust the snowplough. My neighbour, Milton Trembach, my personally chosen successor on the

Grandview MPE executive, drove up, parked his car, and walked to where I was. I knew by the way he dragged his feet and kept his eyes lowered that something was dreadfully wrong.

He gulped several times: "We had a special board meeting at noon today." "So?"

"Hunt attended. He persuaded the majority of the board to approve a resolution agreeing to have the terminal built and to sign the mortgage documents on behalf of Grandview. We salvaged what we could by insisting the board decision must be ratified by the membership. We have called another membership meeting for December 1. Barring something unforeseen, it's a done deal."

His eyes glistened. He was the bearer of very bad news and he regretted it deeply. I was not sympathetic: "Jesus Christ! Is there never an end to anything until the establishment gets their way no matter how wrong they are? Last week this was settled and now you've reopened this stinking can of worms. What a bunch of spineless assholes. I'm going to sell my farm and move into the city and live off you gutless bastards."

Two days later Ed Puchalski came to our home: "We cannot hold the line. You have given many people in this community courage and a sense of identity by demonstrating what can be done with a little willpower. But these are rational people. They are not going to cavalierly throw away several million dollars no matter how much they may agree the terminal should be built elsewhere. You are asking too much. At the last meeting you won by four votes when you should have won by forty. At the next meeting they will vote against you. You have earned the respect of these people but you cannot expect them to follow you blindly into unpredictable and expensive adventures."

"But I am more right on this one than I have ever been."

"Perhaps. But in politics being right is often not enough."

"So what else can one be?"

"One can be sensible."

It was a profundity I recalled often during the next forty years.

The anger ignited seven years earlier when Parker had skewered my resolution on cash advances by asking "what would you do with that money if you got it?" and was intensified by his refusal to support his own member's registered desire for parity prices at the CFA convention in Montreal, now burned at white heat over the issue of finding a more economical grain delivery system.

Must I concede or was there another way to win? Must the decision of the MPE executive to build the terminal be left to stand simply because it was made? And if that is the criterion for sustaining decisions, why should not our Grandview decision be equally valid simply because it was made? Could we come so close to victory and still lose? Must the establishment always be allowed to win? In mental anguish I turned to Puchalski: "Is there another way to handle this in a way that will allow the project to continue while preserving the decision-making integrity of our association? Oh, yes! And of saving a bit of self-respect for ourselves by denying Parker total victory?"

"Well, you have said several times in the past that Canada is borrowing too much foreign money. In this case, MPE is borrowing the money from New York. You might consider a diversionary tactic. You might propose a resolution approving the terminal if MPE borrows the money in Canada. It's a persuasive argument. If it is accepted by our membership Parker must either find the money in Canada or he will not get his terminal."

Ed Puchalski always had a back-up plan.

It made sense. But the board had already adopted a resolution to sign the necessary documents. That resolution would be presented to the special membership meeting, and it would take precedence. And Puchalski was right: if the board resolution was put to the meeting, it would receive majority support. I would never have an opportunity to move my proposal.

In the next eight days I lost ten pounds worrying and scheming. But I could find no way to crack the nut of the board resolution.

On Sunday afternoon, the day before the meeting, Puchalski came to visit. We sat in the kitchen and commiserated. We were trapped. There was no way out. We could propose that construction of the terminal be conditional upon obtaining funding in Canada. We could move it as a new resolution or as an amendment to the board resolution, but in either case the board resolution would take precedence. We had won by only four votes at the first meeting and now, with the sanction of the local board, we were certain to lose.

I could not allow the meeting to discuss the board resolution before hearing my proposal. But, how to get my resolution on the floor of the meeting for discussion before the board resolution?

"You can move it as a substitute resolution. That takes precedence and must be discussed and voted on first." My quiet, observant, ex-schoolteacher wife, who said little but thought deeply, had read *Robert's Rules of Order*.

She had cut the Gordian knot: my relief was as though I had been rescued after having been buried alive.

My wife was uneasy. She had shown me a tactic to win a cheap victory, but she was concerned with the larger picture: "Most of the people who will be at the meeting believe in you and they will follow you. But you must play fair with them. You cannot afford to be frivolous. This must be more than a transparent stalling tactic. In the event your resolution passes and MPE is paralysed, what will happen with the work already done on the terminal and the money spent?"

"That's Parker's problem. I don't give a shit what he does."

"I was not thinking of Parker. I was thinking of our friends and neighbours, and others who hardly know you but have supported you for a decade and have given you status in the community."

I made some inquiries and finally phoned the Saskatchewan Co-operative Credit Society, the central bank for the credit unions and co-operatives in Saskatchewan. I explained and asked if they would have money available in the event they were approached by MPE for a loan to substitute for that from Prudential.

"We would have several million dollars." I felt vindicated — and satisfied. I would now be able to simultaneously humiliate Parker and satisfy the concerns of the people of Grandview.

The following evening, before the meeting began, I took aside board President Earl Meyers, who would be chairing the meeting: "Earl. At the appropriate moment I am going to move a substitute resolution. Debate on that will take precedence over the board resolution. Charlie Hunt knows his rules of procedure so he knows that, but he also knows his only hope of defeating our position is to have the board resolution discussed first so he will fight to keep my substitute from being recognized by the Chair . Here is a copy of *Roberts Rules* with the page marked."

It went like a scripted movie. After the preliminaries I moved my substitute resolution: the Grandview MPE Association would agree to completion of the terminal at Thunder Bay *provided* financing was obtained in Canada. The relief among those who wanted to support me on principle but could not abide the waste of several million dollars, was palpable. Clearly the substitute resolution would pass.

Hunt was on his feet like a tiger: "Mr. Chairman. You must discuss and call for a vote on the board resolution first."

But Meyers replied without hesitation: "I believe a substitute resolution takes precedence."

"Mr. Chairman. I would have to question that," retorted Hunt.

"Well now, let's just see what this little red book has to say about that. This is our Bible tonight." Meyers reached behind the water jug where he had placed the book, out of sight, and held up the copy of *Robert's Rules of Order*.

Hunt was sitting two rows of seats directly in front of me. When he saw the book, his neck began to redden above his shirt collar. Then he appeared to deflate. He knew he was defeated. But he made one more desperate effort: "But that kind of long-term money is not available in Canada." I had informed Meyers of my call to Saskatoon and he told Hunt: "I am informed it is. Contact the Saskatchewan Credit Society."

My substitute resolution passed almost unanimously, to cheers.

Later I was informed the provincial board of MPE was apoplectic with fury and frustration when told of Grandview's recalcitrance. On December 7, 1961, the *Western Producer* reported: "MPE officials say the program will not be held up by the action. If Grandview didn't wish to go along with the majority it would be free to quit the MPE organization."

But we were not going anywhere and we knew the provincial organization would not invite the embarrassment of expelling the largest MPE association in Manitoba when we were merely asserting our right to disagree. Finally, we had them by the short hair. They had informed all and sundry they were borrowing the funds in New York because no money was available in Canada. They were on a hook of their own making. Let them twist in the wind.

But they wanted their terminal. So they built it. And the funds, previously not available, were now found in Canada: On February 15, 1962, the *Western Producer* reported: "The Saskatchewan Co-operative Credit Society has bought $3.5 million worth of Manitoba Pool Elevator debentures … at the rate of 6.25 per cent and is repayable over a twenty-year period."

The terms were identical to those earlier negotiated with Prudential. The difference was that funding would come from a Canadian source. And from a Co-op yet! It was the next best thing to having the terminal built at a saltwater port.

Later, when Hunt and I re-established our relationship, he informed me that, because of the decline of the Canadian dollar relative to the American, MPE had saved millions of dollars in interest and debt retirement charges by borrowing in Canada.

I was a hero!

But within MPE, the Co-operative Movement, and the general public, where few knew of the intense by-play that had led to this end, Cyclops got the credit for his business acumen.

I had lost again.

My few successes had been only delayed failures.

But it no longer mattered.

The words of my friend Montie Miller, the day after the 1958 federal election, had hurt. The accusation that, in attacking Harkness instead of walking away, I had helped defeat both my father and Fred Zaplitny, seemed so unfair. Yet, the more I reflected on it the more my mind admitted its essential truth. I was not some modern Cincinnatus called from my farm to defend the city: no one had asked for my services and few would weep if they were no longer offered. Old acquaintances were regarding me with some reserve — I was keeping the community in turmoil and, as Alexis de Tocqueville observed more than a century earlier, "people grow tired of confusion whose end is not in sight."

Despite the efforts of myself and others to expose the hollowness of the *Agricultural Prices Stabilization Act*, farmers had voted overwhelmingly Conservative. We had thrown ourselves on the rails, but the train had passed over us while crowds cheered. There was a magic about "Dief the Chief" and they identified with his cry that "Farmers need parity, not charity."

It proved a specious promise. Before the next election, we had the highest farm input costs in Canada's history and the lowest farm commodity prices since the Depression. The government had adopted the CFA philosophy of pegging supports at less than farmers were going broke on — and reducing the supports when market prices went down.

Five months after the election, Olaf Turnbull, a Saskatchewan farmer and a government-appointed member of the advisory committee to the Agricultural Prices Stabilization Board, reported: "The board refuses to accept available figures on production costs. The support policy is designed to move people off the farm.... Prices established by the board enable large operators to make a fortune but disregard the human factor in the agricultural industry.... Food production will become controlled by a few, like the *big four* in the auto industry. They will do to consumers what the auto manufacturers are doing now."[2]

In October, 1958, the government admitted the worthlessness of the *Act* to wheat growers by making a deficiency payment of one dollar per acre to a maximum of two hundred dollars per farm. Farmers' furious reaction led to an eleven-hundred-member march on Ottawa on March 10, 1959. They requested payments to compensate for the difference between prices and production costs (wheat–30 cents; barley–19 cents; oats–15 cents, per bushel) to a maximum of fifteen hundred dollars per farmer. The *Globe and Mail* advised the government to give farmers nothing and "put an end to the handouts."[3]

When the farmers stated they had come "to remind the prime minister of his election promises," they found iron discipline among the western MPs – forty-seven of forty-eight Conservative. And from "the Chief" whom many farmers had seen as a saviour a year earlier, they got the advice that "such payments would impede essential adjustments to changing conditions, technology and demand."[4]

The Diefenbaker government had swallowed the CFA position whole. But it was too late to protest.

And this was not all that was depressing.

On January 16, 1959, when the meeting of farm leaders was called to plan the farmers' march on Ottawa, I had attended as an observer. All morning W. J. Parker equivocated between agreeing to support the march if it went, but questioning if it should go. First to return after lunch, I was followed several minutes later by *Winnipeg Free Press* reporter Fred Cleverley. Still seething from the lacerating news reports about my role in the *riot* ten months earlier, and awaiting the return of the others, I initiated a discussion about media ethics and fairness: "Fred, I have read newspaper reports which I know to have been seriously slanted and incorrect. Some were about me. I may not have political or economic clout, but I am a citizen and taxpayer and have the right to fairness. I have attended meetings and witnessed incidents that no one present could honestly have seen as they were reported. It seems to me such unfair and untrue reports are politically motivated and are either the fault of the reporter or they are being distorted by the editors."

"Herb, we report facts. Different people see things differently but we write it the way we see it. And our editors do not change our stories nor has any editor ever asked me to change a story."

Just then the presidents returned, seated themselves, and the meeting was called to order. Immediately Parker, livid with anger and glaring at Cleverley, held up a copy of the early edition of the *Winnipeg Free Press* with the banner headline: "Parker Cool to March."[5]

"Mr. Chairman. I object to this report. I was *not* cool to the march. I want that understood by the farmers. Mr. Cleverly, I want a retraction and I want this story changed. I have already called your editor."

Cleverley jumped to his feet: "Yes, Mr. Parker. My editor has already contacted me. The story will be changed for the next edition."[6]

Cleverley sat down and turned to me: "But it's true. He *was* cool to the March. What was I to write?"

"Fred, we discussed this just a moment ago. You changed your story to please Parker. Would you have done the same for me?"

Cleverley turned in his chair to look at me directly: "Who are you?"

It was a question to which I had no answer. But, in any case, it was clear that Cyclops remained master of the cave.

The strenuous efforts by a cadre of activists, including myself, failed to redirect the dynamic of rural depopulation. In the dozen years we had been involved in farm organization activities, a subterranean revolution had been occurring, creating a result precisely opposite to what we sought. The community was emptying. Of the eight veterans who had settled along the nine-mile road between our home and the town after the war, only three remained.

Farmers or their wives were seeking jobs in the local stores, the hospital, or as school bus drivers, to supplement income, and it seemed that the larger their investment on the farm the more necessary it was to get off-farm jobs to pay the carrying costs of that investment. A dozen rural schools were about to be closed, and the children bussed to town, because there were too few left in the countryside to warrant keeping schools open. Farms were becoming larger but the cultural life of the community was dying, and the little rural towns that once supplied the farmers were becoming retirement communities.

And the pace was being deliberately accelerated. In late January, precisely while some 1,100 farmers were preparing to trek to Ottawa to demand better prices, the MFAC unveiled a policy of thinning out the farmers: "Parity living can only be achieved if the net agricultural income is divided among fewer farmers."[7]

The following day, the federal minister of agriculture accommodated them by assuring there would be fewer farmers. Harkness announced that, unless farmers voluntarily reduced their production, he would reduce their price supports.[8]

In the late sixties two high-powered studies gave their official stamp of approval to the prevailing philosophy: to get rid of the farm problem, get rid of the farmers.

In March, 1969, the Conservative government of Manitoba published their *Report of the Commission on Targets for Economic Development*. It reduced the *farm problem* to simple arithmetic: by 1980 aggregate net farm income would be $200 million, each farm should have a net income of $10,000, ergo by 1980 there should be 20,000 farms in Manitoba. But there was a problem: if nature were left to take its course, by 1980 Manitoba would have 30,000 farms — a surplus of 10,000 farms. Therefore government should develop policies to deliberately reduce the number of farms: "the decline should be faster than the natural rate of attrition and therefore farm people will have to seek new employment."⁹

This approach was confirmed, in December, 1969, by the *Report of the Federal Task Force on Agriculture: Canadian Agriculture in the Seventies*. It argued that "the surplus must be reduced by reducing production drastically," that "of the 430,000 farms only a third are large enough for long-term viability"¹⁰ and that "the only way to have family farms capable of a decent income is to have fewer of them."¹¹ To this end they proposed termination of the Cash Advance Program on farm-stored grain¹² and that: "Grain producers be provided under the Grain Price Stabilization Program with a minimum price support at a level equivalent to 80 per cent of the averages … for the preceding ten-year period."¹³ There was no explanation of how that related to the cost of production.

Governments, federations of agriculture and affiliates, editors of farmer-owned publications, opinion-makers in the media and the learned institutions, had become obsessed with *surpluses*. That problem could have been remedied, at least in part, by adoption of the Farmer's Union proposal for a "Two-price system with parity prices for domestically consumed farm products." That would have increased income for smaller farmers and given larger farmers a *cost-of-production* price for a basic amount of their production while leaving them free to take their chances on the world market if they wished to produce more. That would have ended the need for the farmer, like a dog chasing his tail, to increase production to compensate with volume for losses per unit of production. Surpluses would have dropped as farmers produced for an assured market price or changed their production pattern.

Essentially, this would have applied the marketing board concept, with voluntary participation, across the board on farm products. The federal *Task Force* discussed marketing boards as a rational form of marketing but did not recognize it as a mechanism for disposing of grain surpluses. It was easier to end the surplus of grain by ending the surplus of farmers.

A member of that blue-ribbon federal *Task Force* was the late Professor Clay Gilson. Ingeborg Boyens, in her recent acclaimed book about current conditions on Manitoba farms, wrote that in preparing her book she met with Dr. Gilson, "professor emeritus of agricultural economics at the University of Manitoba and long-time government advisor." He told her: "We should stop talking about exit strategies. Exit programs are a way of ignoring the plight of the farm. The challenge is to find ways to preserve the family farm in the face of the current structural crisis."[14]

A critical observer could argue the two government-commissioned studies offered little but "exit strategies." The policies of governments, the CFA, and the star-studded panels of *experts*, appeared to have all come to the same conclusion: save the family farm by getting rid of it. By the time they realized the fatal flaw in that argument, farmers were depending on rock concerts to publicize their plight and the *family farm*, like Margaret Mitchell's antebellum American South, was *Gone With the Wind*. And we had failed to communicate to the decision-makers, or even to most farmers, the totally predictable fact that if the family farm disappeared, so did the rural community.

The cadre of activists I had worked with strained mightily and believed our efforts had moved society and made the Welkin ring and that nothing would ever be the same again. We were to find that society is not that easily moved and that nothing would ever be the same, only for us. In the non-farm community, we were less than a ripple on the surface of the ocean. Manitoba's pre-eminent historian W. L. Morton, in his *Manitoba: A History*, published in 1957,[15] did not even mention the Manitoba Farmer's Union. Newspaper reporter and author, James H. Gray, was to write of what we saw as the hyperactivity of the decade that: "The [earlier] fires of agrarian revolt were doused forever ... there was not a farm leader on the horizon in the 1950s who could attract a big enough crowd of outraged agrarians to fill a woodshed."[16]

Not all was lost. The Manitoba Crop Insurance Program was established. Cash advances became enculturated in western Canada. A series of marketing boards came into being. The federal government later put in place a number of programs to underpin the agricultural industry. The cry for parity prices is still periodically heard when all other programs fail.

The strenuous efforts of the Manitoba Farmer's Union were to flower in another dimension when its activities brought forward a whole generation of new leaders who got their initial training in the MFU. In 1969, Edward Schreyer, Jake Schulz's son-in-law, became premier of Manitoba. MFU Director Sam Uskiw became minister of agriculture and determined that, while Ceres might fall from her high estate in the affairs of society, it would not be on his watch. MFU Director Peter Burtniak became minister of highways and minister for the revolutionary Manitoba Public Insurance Corporation. Rudy Usick and several other former MFU presidents worked with the Schreyer government on a number of projects. The Crop Insurance Board and the board of the Manitoba Agricultural Credit Corporation were filled with former MFU directors. Scores of others, men and women, who had been active in the MFU were appointed to a wide range of government boards and commissions, or were elected to civic positions.

I had matched myself against powerful opponents and won a few battles but, at thirty-five, was burned out by the all-consuming passions of the dissenter. I had fought the establishment gods and grasped the fire but failed to transfer it to the bellies of my fellows. I was seeing myself as more apostate than Promethean, running out of energy and out of patience. My earnest mediocrity could not retain my following nor win the battles for them as in earlier days. In a dozen years I had gone from enthusiasm to hope to determination to outrage to disillusionment to resignation.

By the spring of 1962 the farm which had given us pride of purpose and freedom of movement and action, no longer offered refuge to my mind, and:

> The mind is its own place, and in itself,
> Can make a Heaven of hell, a hell of Heaven.[17]

Our romance with farming was fading into stark reality. It was time for new perspectives, and for new challenges.

As the spring zephyrs blew gently over the land, and the snows melted and ran in tiny rivulets down along the furrows, we sold our farm and stored away its memories:

> A scarlet tulip nodding in the breeze,
> The dewy freshness of an April morn,
> A calf is born.
> The smell of earth fresh-turned beneath the plough,
> A misty rainbow arching through the sky …
> A butterfly.
> The gentle whisper of cascading leaves,
> A gang of puppies romping in the sun,
> The day's work done.[18]

We left the land we loved and the fields of crops "that clothe the wold and meet the sky," and the community that had nurtured us and given us root. We left the neighbours who, like the hill people of Texas described by President Lyndon Johnson, "care when you're sick and know when you die." We moved to the city, and into other adventures and areas of endeavour.

Notes

Chapter 1

1 *My Harp Is Turned To Mourning*, Winnipeg: Hyperion Press, 1985.

2 Albums show three successive generations of family in uniform. The first in Russian, the second (my father's generation) in Romanian, the third in German.

3 For the rest of his life, my father's eyes clouded whenever the horse was mentioned. It became tubercular and was destroyed. Seventy years later, I met a man, in Los Angeles, who was there and described the scene: "He stood with head high as though ready to gallop. When shot, he rolled into the grave with feet under him and head up, braced against the wall, as though ready to gallop."

4 Russian word for "German."

5 Edwin Markham, *The Man with the Hoe*.

6 Romanian currency.

7 The movie *Midnight Express* reminded the author of his father's description of villagers' treatment by the authorities.

8 Middle-class Russian farmers.

9 Pursuant to the secret clauses in the Hitler–Stalin Pact of 1939, in 1940 the Red Army occupied Bessarabia. The Germans were dispossessed and relocated to Poland and Czechoslovakia. Most died in the War or vanished in the Gulags of Novosibirsk or Kazakhstan when captured by the Red Army at the end of the war.

10 "How wonderful the time of youth; it will not come again."

11 "For the West, the end of the era (of confident speculation preceding the Depression) did not come in a single thunderclap like the Wall Street crash; disaster came slowly, imperceptibly, like a descending ice age fastening itself upon the land," James H. Gray, *The Winter Years*, Toronto: Macmillan, 1966, p. 106.

12 James H. Gray has written of a destitute southern Manitoba farmer he met in the relief office in Winnipeg: "The Bank sent a man from Brandon to get me to stay on the place cause they didn't want to foreclose on me. I figured if the mortgage company didn't want my farm, it was time to get off it." Ibid., p. 167.

13 German, "When one truly fears the tasks beyond one's might; Then, from somewhere strange, there comes a light."

14 I was assigned the task, at age ten, to saddle-break the horses – without a saddle. They threw me in great arcs. Once I fell on my head and could not utter a word for three days.

15 *Saskatchewan: A History*, Saskatoon: Western Producer Prairie Books, Saskatchewan Archives Board, 1980, p. 216.

16 In 1933 my future father-in-law, A.M. Alexander of Grandview, received a letter from the C.N.R. stating the price received for a cow shipped did not cover the freight and he owed sixty cents but he had lost enough so they were cancelling the bill.

17 They had only twenty-five dollars when they began to build the house. That bought the cement for the concrete footing but not for a basement wall, which was dug out and built years later.

18 Municipalities paid a bounty of one cent per gopher tail. That led to a great disappointment of my life. At age eight I carried an ocean of water to drown gophers out of holes, snaring them and cutting off their tails. One very hot day I accompanied my father to town on the wagon, carried my Eddy match box with twenty-five tails to the municipal office, and proudly placed it on the counter. The man gave me a shiny twenty-five-cent coin and broke my heart by taking the box of tails — which my imagination had embroidered into a significant contribution to the economy — holding his nose with one hand to shut out the putrid stench, while with the other carrying the box at arm's length to the back door and throwing it into the garbage barrel in the alley.

19 The relief camps were established by the Conservative government of R. B. Bennett and the single unemployed in them were paid twenty cents an hour plus tobacco (to a maximum of $1.45 a day) to build roads, drainage ditches, townsites such as the resort town of Clear Lake in the Riding Mountains and the highway to it. Most farmers perhaps paid less but provided better food and sleeping conditions, and something more satisfying than make work.

20 In late 1939 we hired a man at twenty dollars for each of the five winter months. In the spring he joined the army which removed his tonsils, repaired his teeth, gave him good clothing, and paid forty-nine dollars.

21 We had fields in several places. On one occasion my mother, wanting to serve the harvest crew a special treat, carried a basket of fresh sandwiches and a large container of chicken soup five miles. It broke her heart when the men skimmed off the fat.

22 My parents planted a half acre of berries, currants, and fruit trees. Just as they were ready to bear, during a winter of deep snow the rabbits came out of the bush and killed every plant.

23 Cure-alls were Watkins ointment, castor oil, and iodine, which was tested by pouring it on a wound. If the patient did not scream in pain, it was too old and needed to be replaced.

24 In 1937 several German neighbours with no radios drove to our home to hear the boxing match in which they fully expected Max Schmeling to pulverize Joe Louis. I helped the last one stable his team. By the time we got to the house the fight was over; Louis had flattened Schmeling in the first round.

25 James Gray, chronicler of the Depression, dates it from "The Wall Street crash October, 1929, to the invasion of Poland in September, 1939," *The Winter Years*, Toronto: Macmillan, 1966, p. 1.

26 Several German neighbours were warned by the RCMP to have less to say or they would be interned. My father had little sympathy: "They are in Canada and should behave like Canadians."

27 My father and I drove to the farm near Dauphin to pick up the Delco plant. The lady of the house took us to the barn, showed us a shiny, eight-hundred-pound cream separator complete with a thirty-two-volt motor, and asked if we wanted to buy it. My father commented that it was an excellent machine and indeed he would buy it, but "It's a Westphalia, a German make, and it might be impossible to get repair parts if it breaks down." The lady, whose son was flying bombing missions over Germany, looked shocked: "What, it's a German make! Take it. Get it out of here." We got a free machine.

28 Within less than twenty years after the end of the war almost all the country schools painstakingly built by the pioneers, where we learned our letters and were introduced to new horizons, where immigrants from a score of racial and linguistic groups were integrated into a new nation, where we bloodied each other's noses and chewed each other's gum, cursed each other's ancestors and married each other's sisters, were closed.

Chapter 2

1 New York: Dell, 1989, p. 144.

2 They were not as illiterate or naive as some thought. The theory of "sunspots" causing economic depressions by affecting weather patterns, crop yields and human energy levels, was legitimized in the 1890s by British economist Stanley Jevons.

3 A Social Credit MLA, Dr. Fox, was elected locally in 1935.

4 In a fireside chat FDR stated: "The money-changers have fled their seats in the temple of our civilization. We may now restore the temple to its ancient truths. [That] lies in applying social values more noble than monetary profit.... We now realize our interdependence on each other, that we cannot merely take but we must also give." Robert S. McElwanie, *The Great Depression in America*, Toronto: Fitzhenry & Whiteside, 1984, p. 140.

5 Like the Okies in John Steinbeck's 1939 classic, *The Grapes of Wrath*, the people of Saskatchewan's dust bowl moved out. Population dropped by more than 100,000 (to 832,000) between 1931 and 1951. In five of the ten years (1930–39) Saskatchewan's farm net income was reported in the *negative* and the ten-year average *total* net farm income was $12.4 million compared with $145 million in 1925–29 and $101 million in 1940–49. John H. Archer, *Saskatchewan: A History*, p. 317.

6 Seymour M. Lipsett, *Agrarian Socialism: The Co-operative Commonwealth Federation in Saskatchewan*, New York: Anchor Edition, Doubleday, 1968. First published as a PhD thesis by University of California Press, 1950.

7 Henry George, *An Inquiry into Causes of Industrial Depressions and Increase of Want with Increase of Wealth*, New York: Garden City Publishers, 1926. First published in 1879.

8 In March, 1994, an American publication named Saskatoon, Saskatchewan, as "the reading capital of North America."

9 Founded in 1923 when the dailies refused to support the farmers in establishment of the wheat pools.

10 A car from which the engine was removed because the owner could not afford gasoline, and for which horses supplied motive power.

11 Government grain marketing agency to remove speculation by pooling all sales and paying all producers the same price. Established on voluntary basis in 1935, made compulsory in 1943 and coarse grains added.

12 Established by the federal government in 1912, after farm protest, to police grain trade re grading, weighing, handling charges, dockage, transport, etc.

13 Edward Thomas, *The Dark Forest*.

14 Alexander Tvardovsky, *The Old Soldier*.

15 George Santayana — in full Jorge Agustín Nicolás de Santayana (1863–1952): Spanish-American philosopher, poet, and humanist.

16 Jim Connell (1852–1929) born in Kilskyre, County Meath, Eire. "The Red Flag" was written in 1889 on a train from Charing Cross (London) to New Cross after attending a lecture on socialism at a meeting of the Social Democratic Federation. It was inspired by the London dock strike, happening at that time, as well as activities of the Irish Land League, the Paris Commune, the Russian nihilists, and Chicago anarchists.

17 Being in the CCF in the 1940s had risks. In next door Gilbert Plains two of my father's wiry friends, Harvey Yuill and Alex Stoughton, would stand at the door of the polling venue to ensure known CCF'ers were not beaten up on the way to vote.

18 *Darkness at Noon*, London: Hutchinson, 1973.

19 *The New Class*, New York: Praeger, 1957.

20 Collection of articles by disillusioned ex-communists. Edited by Richard Crossman, New York: Harper and Row, 1949.

21 Georg Wilhelm Friedrich Hegel (1770–1831), German philosopher.

22 John Stuart Mill (1806–1873), English philosopher.

23 Julien Benda, *Treason of the Intellectuals*, New York: W.W. Norton, 1969. Written in France, 1928. A bitter denunciation of the intellectuals who converted spiritual values to serve the needs of the political state, and war.

24 *Second Treatise on Government*, 1690.

25 *American Declaration of Independence*, 1776.

Chapter 3

1 Her salary while on permit, teaching thirty students, was $85 monthly (minus $30 for board and room). As store clerk she received $55 monthly which, after board and room left nothing. After attending teacher's college she taught for two years (1947–49). With up to twenty-six students in nine grades, her salary was $125 a month (minus board and room).

2 A decade later the government of Duff Roblin realized few parents could leave their farm to their children. They set up the Manitoba Agricultural Credit Corporation from which children could borrow to buy the family farm and make payments to the government, while the parents had the cash and could relocate.

3 It was ever thus: "A hungry world, one drought from disaster is bidding up wheat and barley to record prices" (World Hunger for Grain, *Winnipeg Free Press*, September 1, 1995). A year later: "Western Canada's agricultural boom seems to have come to an end as world grain prices slide.... The price for wheat fell from $5.75 to about $4.25 [and] barley from $3.60 to about $1.98 per bushel.... The reason for the plunge is near-record crop yields" (Agri-Boom Stalls as Grain Prices Fall, ibid. December 17, 1996).

4 Robert Lacey, *Ford: The Men and the Machine*, Toronto: McClelland and Stewart, 1986, p. 347.

5 Using 2, 4D for spraying mustard was a joy after picking it stalk by stalk. I revelled in using it, mixing it with bare hands and sitting shirtless all day while the wind blew the spray on my body. Years later we discovered it could be carcinogenic.

6 Nothing has changed. "According to Statistics Canada, increased use of technology ... bigger machinery and more inputs has doubled the productivity of western Canadian farms over the past three decades. They are among the most efficient in the world ... [but] Prairie farmers will no sooner get this year's crop harvested than they will face a bin full of bills tied to the cost of growing it. For many, costs have grown from about fifty per cent of expected receipts to nearly ninety per cent in the past two decades." (High-Tech Farming Increases Output, *Winnipeg Free Press*, September 21, 1996). "A recent Stats-Can study shows input costs of farming 3.6% higher in the second quarter of 1996 than in the same period last year and 8.5% higher than 1994. (Farming Costs Go Sky

High, ibid. August 10, 1996). "Rising costs mean farmers must swallow another pay cut despite a second year of spectacular grain sales.... The squeeze on profits will encourage bigger farms and emptier small towns.... Prairie farmers will sell $10 billion worth of grain in 1996 — well above the ten-year average of $6.5 billion ... [but] for every loonie worth of grain sold, the farmer banks less than a dime" (ibid., November 8, 1996).

7 Archer, *Saskatchewan: A History*, pp. 269–70.

8 German, "Listening does not make one stupid."

9 Adam Smith (1723–1790), Scottish philosopher and economist.

10 Gray, *The Winter Years*, p.167.

11 As late as 1970 average net return on farm investment was about 5 per cent — less than the interest on gilt-edged bonds. Average net income for a farm family of four was $2,200 — less than they would receive on welfare. This was despite, in the previous ten years, farm borrowing having tripled to $4.5 billion to improve operations, average farm size in Saskatchewan having increased to nine hundred acres, the number of farmers in western Canada having been reduced by approximately a hundred thousand and the farm population by 40 per cent, from 12 per cent of total population to 7 per cent, and farm production efficiency having increased at twice the rate of industry.

Chapter 4

1 Motto of the Manitoba Farmer's Union.

2 German philosopher G.W.F. Hegel wrote in *The Philosophy of History* (1832): "Experience and history teach us that people and governments learn nothing from history or act on the principles deduced from it." In July, 1996, the Federally commissioned Western Grain Marketing Panel, studying the Canadian Wheat Board's monopoly in the sale of wheat and barley, recommended barley be returned to the open market. Complaints about the monopoly had come from American farmers who believe the CWB gives Canadian farmers a market advantage, from some wheat growers and southern Alberta who traditionally opposed government intervention in the market, and from a new generation of farmers captured by the myth of competition and who believe their laptop

computers give them more market information than available to the CWB and allows them to outsmart the world's grain traders, including the American grain oligopoly. The Winnipeg Commodity Exchange (which replaced the old Winnipeg Grain Exchange, 10 July 1996) salivated at the prospect. After an absence of sixty years, those profiting by buying low from farmers and selling high to consumers, momentarily seemed back in business ("Exchange Rejoices at Barley Proposal," *Winnipeg Free Press*, 10 July 1996). However, when the minister called an "either-in-or-out" referendum, the complainers protested "we do not want an either–or option, we want both." Of course: they want the "free-market" when it is good and CWB protection when it is bad).

3 In 1941, the FBI considered arresting Arthur Goldenberg, later a United States army officer, President Kennedy's secretary of labour, supreme court justice, and U.S. ambassador to the United Nations, because "J. Edgar Hoover was suspicious of his work with organized labour and organizer of a conference on constitutional liberties." *Los Angeles Times*, April 9, 1996.

4 *The Voice of the Farmer.*

5 *The Rise and Fall of Farm Organizations*, Winnipeg: Evans Printing, 1955.

6 In December, 1953, there were 923 registered delegates.

7 Joseph L. Phelps, born 1899 in Ontario, moved to Saskatchewan and was elected a Grain Growers director at age seventeen. He was a successful farmer at Wilkie and was active on the local school board and the Wheat Pool. Elected to the Legislature in 1938, he was minister of natural resources and began the Rural Electrification Program for the CCF government of T. C. Douglas who described him as "the most volatile and virile spokesman in Saskatchewan politics." Defeated in 1948, he was elected first president of the new Saskatchewan Farmer's Union and: "moved mountains, taking on national stature. Under Phelps' leadership membership rose rapidly, he revitalized all aspects of the union's work [and] the Women's Section under Bernice Norman took on new life and vigour" (Archer, *Saskatchewan: A History*, p. 282). Membership in the SFU was to reach a hundred thousand.

8 Henry Young was a successful farmer at Millet, Alberta, some forty miles southeast of Edmonton. He served as V.P. of the Rural Electrification Association, as executive member of the Alberta Association of Municipalities, as councillor for the Municipality of Wetaskiwin, and on the board of the Alberta Wheat Pool

and several other organizations. In 1950 he was elected President of the reorganized Farmer's Union of Alberta in which membership was to reach about fifty thousand.

9 In 1897 the CPR received a $3.4 million federal subsidy to build a line from Lethbridge, Alberta, through the Crowsnest Pass to the coalfields at Nelson, B.C. In return, the CPR was to move western grain to the Lakehead at statutory rates not related to the market. By the 1950s, the CPR was complaining this was "unfair" and found surprising sympathy in the farm community. In the 1990s the agreement was terminated and farmers had to pay the full cost of transportation, about five times the old rate. The CPR did not offer to return the telecommunications system, the airline, and the hotels (including that in Acapulco) they bought with profits from the railway built with taxpayer's money.

10 There were the usual verbal threats, but the only time I was frightened was when I found a letter in our mailbox, composed of words cut from a newspaper, which read: "One day your kids will not come home from school."

11 The lives of wives of farmers, especially those involved in politics, could be difficult. By the time I returned, my wife had given birth to a nine-pound baby girl. Her father had driven her ten miles to the hospital with horses and sleigh.

12 D. G. McKenzie, chair of the Board of Grain Commissioners since 1941, had been VP of United Grain Growers Grain Company.

13 MFU director, later a minister in the Schreyer government.

14 Gardiner came from Ontario as a school teacher in 1905, the year Saskatchewan became a province, won his BA in history and economics at Manitoba College, and established a farm. Elected to the Legislature in 1914, his name became synonymous with Saskatchewan politics for almost half a century. In World War II he chaired the Agricultural Supplies Board that expedited and controlled food production for the Empire. In 1958, after forty-four years of Federal political service he was defeated in the Diefenbaker sweep and retired to his farm to die in 1962.

15 In August, 1996, discovery of possible organic material in an ancient Martian meteorite in Antarctica again excited scientific minds to the possibility of other ambitious molecules.

16 A decade later the Rand Corporation in the United States reported that *only* sixty million Americans would die in a first strike by an enemy, so nuclear war could

be risked. Presumably, had they stated sixty million dogs would die, they might have had their testicles nailed to the tops of posts and then been pushed off backwards and left for the vultures to pick their eyes out. The policy of "balance of terror" would reign for thirty years.

17 William Wordsworth, *The Excursion*. American philosopher Noam Chomsky later wrote the obscenity of the sixties and seventies was not that the military, political, and economic elites believed in the insanity of nuclear war, but that millions of ordinary, sane persons were propagandized into contemplating it with equanimity.

18 Arguably, the true end of the Cold War, and symbolizing the triumph of human ingenuity, was the sight of the Russian space station *Mir* and the American space shuttle *Atlantis* joined and visible to the naked eye, in September 1996.

Chapter 5

1 Helen Sisson, *I Am Camp*.

2 When the Prairie Wheat Pools were organized in 1923, they established country elevators to buy the grain from the farmers and a Central Selling Agency to market it. The principle inherent in "pooling" was to buy the grain from the farmers at an initial price below what the market price was expected to be, sell it, deduct the costs of marketing, and return the balance to the farmers as a final payment. In 1929 the pools, failing to anticipate the market collapse, paid an initial payment of a dollar a bushel. When the market price dropped below that level, they were threatened with bankruptcy. They were bailed out (at the cost of terminating their Central Selling Agency) only when the Bennett government guaranteed the banks' loans to the pools (MPE's debt was not repaid until 1949). There was also the issue of taxing Co-operative revenue as income before being distributed as patronage dividends, which repeatedly raised it's head.

3 "Bill" Parker was on the MPE board from 1930 to 1968 and president after 1940. The bail-out loan of $2.1 million from the government in 1930 was paid off in 1949. By 1955 MPE had 212 associations representing some 35,000 farmers, with country elevator capacity of 19 million bushels and terminal capacity of 13 million bushels. It was built into an authentic conglomerate, handling (1955) over 50

per cent of all grain delivered in Manitoba, seed, pesticides, herbicides, life insurance, etc. MPE was involved in the community through sponsorships of seed clubs, crop improvement clubs, university extension service, grants to hospitals, etc. Parker was long-time VP of the CFA, helped negotiate the IWA in 1946, and attended meetings of FAO and IFAP. In *Service at Cost: History of Manitoba Pool Elevators* (Winnipeg: MPE, 1975) author F. W. Hamilton records that at the 1953 MPE convention, Trade Minister C. D. Howe called Parker "my good friend (whose) advice on national problems is sought in high places ... his sound judgement and sterling qualities are widely recognized" (p. 221). Hamilton adds: "Parker was a great farm spokesman who, as head of MPE, sought the most effective means of procuring for farmers a just share of the national wealth. Members of MPE owe [him] an incalculable debt" (p. 200). In 1974 he was elected to the Agriculture Hall of Fame. In 1969 he was retained as a director on the board of Manitoba Hydro — by Premier Schreyer, Jake Schulz's son-in-law.

4 After forty years the problem remains. In 1996 the CWB reported: "We are turning back orders now." Only two months into the new crop year, lack of rail cars caused loss of a 1.4 million tonne sale to Saudi Arabia. *Winnipeg Free Press*, October 1, 1996.

5 Convention delegates were elected a year in advance.

6 Minutes of Saskatoon meeting, August 14, 1956.

7 Minutes of Saskatoon meeting, September 8, 1956.

Chapter 6

1 Such salaries for corporate presidents are laughable now. However, in 1956, salaries of MPE local elevator agents, doing a very dirty job, averaged less than $3,600 annually. In 1956, my expenses for three days at the MPE annual convention totalled $22.30. (train fare 240 miles to Winnipeg –$7.40; taxi fare to the hotel – 60 cents; hotel one night – $2.50; one breakfast – 40 cents; four lunches – $7.20; two dinners – $4.20). As late as 1960, the Grandview MPE association paid staff (agents and helpers) for its four elevators a total of $18,675. Monarch Lumber was offering to build a 750 square-foot two-bedroom home with attic for $3,400. Women's dresses were advertised for $2.98. Comparative hourly

earnings were: coal mining – $2.79; construction – $2.79; railroads –$2.11; wholesale trade – $2.01; manufacturing – $1.98; telephone – $1.86; retail trade – $1.57; laundry – $1.05; farming – $0.70. In August 1958, the government of Canada was offering 4.5 per cent interest on twenty-five-year bonds. A new Ford half-ton pick-up truck was selling for $1,895, and a Mercury Meteor car, with a 25,000-mile warranty, for $2,391.

2 Minutes of Saskatoon meeting, March 1, 1957.

3 Graysville, Brunkild. Convention resolutions. October 1957.

4 All above newspaper statements quoted in *Western Producer*, official organ of the Saskatchewan Wheat Pool, November 7, 1957.

5 Reprinted, ibid.

Chapter 7

1 MPE later stopped contributions to both the MFAC and the MFU. The MFAC attempted, without success, to go to direct membership. In 1961, President Syd Ransom warned delegates at a conference that "financial support has been reduced and the survival of the organization is in doubt." (*Manitoba Co-operator*, January 26, 1961). Then, to find out what kind of organization farmers wanted, they asked the university instead of the farmers.

2 The MFAC later metamorphosed into the Keystone Agricultural Producers (KAP) and persuaded the government of Manitoba to legislate automatic, but voluntary, deductions from farm produce sales as KAP membership fees. In 1996 they hit the jackpot when the government legislated compulsory deductions of 1.5 per cent on gross sales of grain, to be collected by elevators and feed mills upon delivery. KAP general manager Craig Douglas explained this was necessitated by "a cash shortfall due to unstable funding ... [voluntarism] was not working.... KAP was collecting from fewer than 10 per cent of its members." One irate farmer demanded her money back: "If an organization is worth what they think they're worth they should be able to collect membership fees themselves." ("Lobby Harvests Anger," *Winnipeg Free Press*, September 7, 1996) However, KAP continues to be quoted regularly as a farm voice while the MFU is seldom heard of.

3 News release to *Grandview Exponent*, August 16, 1956.

4 After failure at the Amalgamation Convention the *Winnipeg Tribune* editorialized: "MFU zealots in the MFAC had a clear-cut lesson – there will be no farm unity on the basis of a political coup." (reprinted in *Grandview Exponent*, February 28, 1957).

5 Columbia Press, 1945.

6 Proverbs 29:18.

7 He died January 23, 1957.

8 Amelia Earhart, *Courage*.

Chapter 8

1 *Family Herald*, March 19, 1958.

2 *The Age of Reform*, New York: Random House, 1955, p. 23.

3 Farmers were not helped by those who lived off them. In 1961, devaluation of the Canadian dollar resulted in a five-cent-a-bushel increase in the price of wheat. Bakers increased bread prices one cent a loaf — the equivalent increase would have been one-eighth of 1 per cent — and consumers saw the farmer as culprit.

4 James A. Michener wrote of an incident on the South Pacific island of Espiritu Santo. Immediately after the war, when millions of dollars worth of "tractors, uncrated jeeps, earth moving equipment ... road graders, heavy trucks, ambulances, anything on wheels ... [and] warehouses of canned food, clothing, and tools, were dumped into the ocean rather than distributed to the local people when a dollar's worth of quinine could save a life. 'Million Dollar Point' they call it. Americans did much for Santo ... but we left one harrowing scar which will never be forgotten." *Return to Paradise*, Bantam, 1951, p. 189.

5 *Free Press* displayed the banner headline, "World's Food Production Must Double in Next Twenty Years — Expert." August 1, 1961.

6 In mid-1957, Prime Minister Diefenbaker stated: "I learned a lesson at the Commonwealth Conference in London. We must expand our agricultural production. With one quarter of the world's population going hungry, methods must be found to enable the distribution of our surpluses." *Western Producer*, August 8, 1957.

7 *Manitoba Co-operator*, January 18, 1962.

8 Someone defined "experts" as "those who avoid small errors as they sweep on to the grand fallacy."

9 *Manitoba Co-operator*, July 18, 1996.

10 Some non-farm subsidies in 1956–57: fisheries – $2 million; Labour Department – $67 million; gold, coal and iron – $18 million; shipping, railways, canals – $27 million.

11 *Hansard*, Ottawa: Queen's Printer, March 13, 1956.

12 Ibid.

13 *Western Producer*, November 8, 1956.

14 *Hansard*, March 13, 1956.

15 N. Ward and D. Smith, Toronto: University of Toronto Press, 1990, p. 331.

16 *Hansard*, 1956, p. 2673.

17 *Free Press Prairie Farmer*, February 2, 1955.

18 President's address to twentieth annual CFA convention.

19 *Western Producer*, November 29, 1956.

20 Hannam to Prime Minister Diefenbaker, August 1, 1957.

21 *Winnipeg Free Press*, April 17, 1956.

22 John E. Brownlee (1883–1961) had an illustrious career in law, farm organization, and politics. He was born in Ontario, took law at the University of Toronto, and moved to Calgary in 1912. He became solicitor for UGG (formed in 1916), and became involved with the Progressive Party which elected the second largest group of MPs in 1921, and in the United Farmers of Alberta which was elected government of Alberta the same year. He was appointed Attorney General and helped establish the Alberta Wheat Pool in 1923. He became premier of Alberta in 1925, negotiated the transfer of natural resources from Ottawa to Alberta, and became popular and powerful. In 1934 he resigned, a year before the UFA government was defeated by William Aberhart's Social Credit. He was a presence on the national scene, helping to establish the Bank of Canada and to negotiate the International Wheat Agreement to stabilize farm income. In 1948 he became president and GM of UGG, building it into Canada's second largest grain buyer with elevators in the West and a huge terminal at the Lakehead. He sat for many years on the board of the CFA (from Franklin Foster, *John Brownlee*, Lloydminster, Alberta: Foster Learning Inc., 1981).

23 The following year we removed Monkhouse as president of the MD&P co-op and sent him back to the farm to take "lower prices" and show us how to survive on "Seventy per cent of the cost of production."

24 John Milton (1608–1674), *Samson Agonistes*.

25 At the next MFAC board meeting in Winnipeg, I accused Monkhouse of failing to represent his member's wishes at the CFA. He replied: "Mr. Schulz says some of our Manitoba organizations passed resolutions on parity prices and we failed to present the policy in Ottawa. I must admit Mr. Schulz has a point. [But] the CFA is a melting pot. You go and promote your point of view to the best of your ability and go along with majority decisions." In fact he, Parker, and Brownlee had *refused* to "promote the point of view" of the members *before* the "majority decision" was made.

26 Arthur Clough, *Say Not the Struggle Naught Availeth*.

Chapter 9

1 The *Gold Mining Act*, 1948, based subsidies to that industry on a formula which divided total costs of production in a mine by the number of ounces produced. This was seen as the *average cost of production* and is defined as "cost of production of gold from the mine during any period means costs incurred by the operator of the mine in, and attributable to, production of gold from the mine during that period and includes mining, milling, transportation, and administrative costs so incurred and so attributable, and includes such amounts as depreciation, amortization of pre-production expenses, and costs of exploration and development of the mine, in accordance with the regulations."

2 The *Feed Freight Assistance Act* of 1941 subsidized the cost of moving western grain because Ottawa wanted to increase meat production in eastern Canada as part of the war effort. The *short term* expedient continued for more than forty years and became a subsidy of as much as $15 million a year to eastern livestock and poultry producers. It became a bone in the throat of many westerners because it reduced the comparative advantage of Prairie livestock producers and discouraged diversification.

3 Founded in 1908 to give farmers a voice when the dailies would not support the farmers fight against the Grain Exchange.

4 *Country Guide*, December, 1957.

5 Ibid., January, 1958.

6 Ibid., "Whither the Family Farm," September, 1958.

7 Ibid., "Farmers Deserve Responsible Leadership," November, 1958.

8 Ibid., "Changed Attitudes to Price Supports," December, 1959.

9 Ibid., Editorial, "Government Deficiencies," February, 1960.

10 *Manitoba Co-operator*, September 15, 1955.

11 Ibid., September 29, 1955.

12 Ibid., April 17, 1958.

13 Presentation to the prime minister of Canada and Cabinet by the Canadian Federation of Agriculture, February 5, 1958.

14 John Milton, *Paradise Lost*.

Chapter 10

1 Alfred Noyes, *Forty Singing Seamen*. Of Ulysses' encounter with Cyclops.

2 In fact, that day, Parker and the CFA board were making their annual presentation to the federal government.

3 The *Winnipeg Free Press*, under the headline "Schulz Attacks CFA Formula," gave the meeting two paragraphs reporting: "Mr. Schulz said 'we have some CFA Directors ... who go east and oppose the policies unanimously passed ... in Western Canada.' He did not elaborate." (February 6, 1958). That was after I had spent seventy-five minutes displaying documents and elaborating in detail.

4 "Pool to Help Organize Manitoba Feeder Groups" *Winnipeg Free Press*, June 17, 1959.

5 A decade later, MPE President Harold Sneath appealed to the NDP government to underwrite some of the "problematical [feeder] loans [because] the possibility of catastrophe to a number of herds is always on the minds of our bankers" (letter Sneath to Hofford, September 15, 1972). Manitoba Agricultural Credit Corporation Chairman Max Hofford replied: "You wish the MFAC to relieve the anxieties of your bankers by guaranteeing to use public funds to repay losses

they might suffer by lending to your organization money you will use to make loans to cattle feeders…. We are not in the business of underwriting bank loans."

6 *Free Press Weekly*, January 14, 1959.

7 *Winnipeg Free Press*, January 16, 1959, early edition.

8 The contrasting thinking of two Manitoba farm leaders was revealed in December, 1960, when Finance Minister Fleming brought down his budget. Parker responded: "It's shocking — the deficit, that is." MFU President Usick stated: "Every budget of this government has brought tariffs … that is opposite to what we need for wheat sales." Ibid. December 21, 1960.

9 MFAC board meeting minutes.

10 *Winnipeg Free Press*, February 10, 1958.

11 *Manitoba Co-operator*, January 8, 1959.

12 Forty-four years later, in an accidental encounter, one such delegate apologized to Hofford and admitted he had signed his own credential.

13 *Winnipeg Free Press*, June 26, 1957.

Chapter 11

1 Winnipeg CCF member of Parliament Alistair Stewart remarked: "The relationship between the prime minister and the cliché is not that of master and servant but of master and slave. He beats them, bruises them, dangles them before us, and having bludgeoned them with such violence, he buries them in the pages of *Hansard*."

2 Archer, *Saskatchewan: A History*, p. 296.

3 Speech by Agricultural Minister Douglas Harkness to CFA. convention, Montreal, January 29, 1958.

4 Forbes was not the only confused Conservative candidate. At a meeting in the Springfield riding, Val Yacula, Conservative candidate who was to defeat sitting MP Jake Schulz, when asked, "will this *Act* give farmers parity prices?" answered positively "Yes." *Winnipeg Free Press*, March 6, 1958.

5 At the time I believed he was quoting from the *Riot Act*.

6 One evening, at an MPE annual meeting at Grandview, I made some accusations. Challenged, I was forced to admit my proof was in my briefcase, which I had left

at my parent's home in Winnipeg the previous day, but my father had put it on the bus that would arrive at 12:15 A.M. If my challengers would remain another two hours I would be pleased to provide the proof. My critics went wild: "Ho, ho, ho; tell us another one; what a stupid joke." So I decided to keep the meeting going until the bus arrived. It was a wild evening. Shortly after midnight, my neighbour, Milton Trembach, entered the hall. He had come to the meeting from the harvest field, in his greasy bib overalls, well-worn denim jacket and dirty felt hat. In his right hand, almost dragging on the floor because of its weight, was my large, black briefcase. The crowd became deathly silent. I opened the briefcase and asked: "Now what was it you people wanted me to prove?" There was no sound. The meeting was adjourned. But after that several attempts were made to steal that briefcase.

7 *Hansard*, October 29, 1957, quotes MP Jake Schulz, speaking on the Bill on Cash Advances for farm stored grain, stating, "this legislation in its present form is not only inadequate but is stupid in some respects" (p. 517). Next morning *Hansard* quotes Schulz using his privilege to make a correction, stating he was misquoted: "In the top paragraph of the right-hand column the word 'stupid' appears.... I have checked my script and find I used the word "disturbing." (October 30, front page). The same day Harkness is shown amending his *Act* to comply with what Schulz had found "disturbing." (*Hansard*, October 30, p. 575). Next day Harkness is shown using his member's privilege to correct what he had said the previous day (*Hansard*, November 1, front page).

8 Queen's Bench Decision re: *The Grandview Co-Operative Elevator Association* (Plaintiff) *and the Manitoba Federation of Agriculture* (Defendant), March 14, 1958.

9 Before June 10, 1957, party standings in the 265-member House of Commons were: Liberals – 168; Conservatives – 50; CCF – 22; Social Credit – 15; Independents – 3; Vacant – 7. After March 31, 1958, standings were: Conservatives – 208; Liberals – 49; CCF – 8. On June 18, 1962, the Conservative majority was reduced to a plurality: Conservatives – 116; Liberals – 98; Creditistes – 31; CCF – 19. On April 18, 1963, Diefenbaker lost a vote of confidence when two of his own members (including Douglas Harkness) voted against his government, which was then defeated by Lester Pearson: Liberals – 128; Conservatives – 95 Creditistes – 24; CCF – 17. In 1967, opaque Robert Stanfield replaced messianic "Dief" as

Conservative Leader, but the magic held. Dief's constituents remained devoted and he died in 1979, still the MP for Prince Albert.

Chapter 12

1 Improved after 1965 by the St. Lawrence Seaway.

2 Reported in *Voice of the Farmer*, August, 1958.

3 March 9, 1959.

4 "Marchers Given Blunt Refusal," headline in *Winnipeg Tribune*, March 10, 1959.

5 January 16, 1959, early edition.

6 The news report in the final edition of the *Winnipeg Free Press*, January 16, 1959, was headed: "March on Ottawa" 'Well …'."

7 *Winnipeg Free Press*, January 23, 1959.

8 Ibid., January 24, 1959.

9 *Report of the Commission on Targets for Economic Development*, Queen's Printer, Winnipeg, March 1969, p. 59.

10 *Report of the Federal Task Force on Agriculture: Canadian Agriculture in the Seventies*, Queen's Printer, Ottawa, December, 1969, p. 129.

11 Ibid., p. 34.

12 Ibid., p. 127.

13 Ibid., p. 132.

14 Ingeborg Boyens, *Another Season's Promise: Hope and Despair in Canada's Farm Country*, Toronto: Penguin, 2001, p. 62.

15 Toronto: University of Toronto Press, 1957.

16 *Troublemaker*, Toronto: Macmillan, 1978, p. 249.

17 John Milton, *Paradise Lost*.

18 Barbara Hildreth, *Thanksgiving*.

Index

Z